T0302310

Cities and Economic Inequality in Latin America

This book examines trends and determinants of economic inequality in cities in Latin America, the world's most unequal region. It explores how the gap between the haves and the have nots manifests in every part of urban life – from housing to schooling to employment. It asks why some cities have higher inequality than others and what we can learn from these differences as we push back against inequality.

The book starts with reviewing the policies and forces that explain the rise and fall of inequality in Latin America since the 1990s and why progress in reducing inequality has stalled. It then focuses on Argentina's cities and applies a set of quantitative tools to identify inequality determinants. It finds that intra-urban inequality generally mirrors national-level trends, but local idiosyncrasies related to a city's labor market, informal employment, and social protection systems matter. The book discusses the pitfalls of privatizing public services that turned access to water in metropolitan Buenos Aires more unequal. It explores the promises and unintended consequences of slum upgrading initiatives in Buenos Aires' Villa 20.

The book presents lessons that can inform policies and practices in the region and beyond. Developing a strategy against inequality that incorporates local features and resists the temptation to rely on the "free market" for solutions to urban problems offers a powerful opportunity. Drawing from the field of economics and social and urban policy, this book shows that the battle against inequality is not only won and lost in cities but also requires a uniquely public and urban response. As such, it will be of interest to advanced students, researchers, and policymakers across development economics, urban studies, and Latin American studies.

Lena Simet is a scholar, writer, and researcher interested in cities, urban poverty, and intra-urban inequality. She is currently a senior researcher and advocate on poverty and inequality at Human Rights Watch. She received her PhD from The New School and lives in New York City.

Routledge Studies in Development Economics

For more information about this series, please visit: www.routledge.com/
series/SE0266

Cities and Economic Inequality in Latin America

Intra-Urban Inequality in Argentina

Lena Simet

Routledge
Taylor & Francis Group

LONDON AND NEW YORK

First published 2022
by Routledge
4 Park Square, Milton Park, Abingdon, Oxon OX14 4RN

and by Routledge
605 Third Avenue, New York, NY 10158

Routledge is an imprint of the Taylor & Francis Group, an informa business

© 2022 Lena Simet

The right of Lena Simet to be identified as author of this work has been asserted in accordance with sections 77 and 78 of the Copyright, Designs and Patents Act 1988.

Trademark notice: Product or corporate names may be trademarks or registered trademarks, and are used only for identification and explanation without intent to infringe.

British Library Cataloguing-in-Publication Data
A catalogue record for this book is available from the British Library

Library of Congress Cataloging-in-Publication Data
A catalog record has been requested for this book

ISBN: 978-1-032-06360-7 (hbk)
ISBN: 978-1-032-06359-1 (pbk)
ISBN: 978-1-003-20190-8 (ebk)

DOI: 10.4324/9781003201908

Typeset in Bembo
by KnowledgeWorks Global Ltd.

Contents

PART III
Closing the Gap   149

Illustrations

Figures

Tables

Box

Acknowledgments

This book would not have come to be without the vision, guidance, and wisdom of Michael A. Cohen, to whom I owe a lifetime of thanks. He first encouraged me to go to Argentina in 2012 and inspired my ambition to study inequality.

I also thank Alberto Minujin and David Howell for their thoughtful comments, suggestions, and encouragement for my PhD dissertation, which is the basis for this book. I am grateful to The New School for provoking critical thinking and installing in students the urge to fight for social justice.

I am also grateful to the acuity and brilliance of Margarita Gutman and the Buenos Aires team of the Observatory on Latin America for opening their door to me – a special thanks to Ileana Versace, Carolina Maglioni, Julia Nesprias, Matías Ruiz Díaz, and Martín Grómez.

Throughout my research, I counted on the support of several Argentine institutions. I am indebted to the indefatigable Adriana Clemente at the Centro de Estudios de Ciudad at the University of Buenos Aires and grateful for the support from Agustin Mario in shaping Chapter 6. I also appreciate the support of Marta Novick, director of CITRA at the UMET University, and their researchers and faculty, who answered my many questions.

Other friends and co-conspirators also helped refine and reconceive what I was trying to say in this book. I am grateful to Melissa De la Cruz for her careful reading and many comments on my manuscript and Belén Fodde for her thoughtful feedback on Chapter 8.

Tuca Vieira kindly provided permission to use his legendary image of inequality in Paraisópolis, São Paulo, Brazil (Figure 3.1). Johnny Miller, the founder of Unequal Scenes, granted permission to use his powerful photographs of inequality in Santa Fe, Mexico, and Rio de Janeiro, Brazil (Figures 3.2 and 3.3). Figure 3.9 is from Unsplash, taken by Rick Hippe. All other photographs and figures are my own.

The last and biggest thanks belong to my family. This book is ultimately the product of my parents as it is of my own. My family instilled in me the value of curiosity and non-conformism, essential ingredients for an explorative mind. Douglas has withstood my whims and recurring periods of stress for over a decade and always offered trust, love, and support.

I hope this research contributes to something that deeply unites us, the quest for a more equal and just society.

1   Why another book on inequality?

We live in a deeply unequal world, where the growing gap between the rich and the poor is one of the defining challenges of our time. The gains from modern economic growth and globalization have not been equally distributed, with some people not seeing any gain at all. Inequality has undermined the fight against poverty, damaged our economies and societies, contributed to mass migration, and harms ecological sustainability.

In its most extreme forms, inequality manifests in the contrasts between the hundreds of millions of people living in extreme poverty unable to afford drinking water or food and the ever-deepening pockets of those at the very top.

Some 736 million people lived on less than US$1.90 a day in 2015 – a daily allowance equivalent to two bus tickets in Sao Paulo (World Bank 2018a; Numbeo 2021). More than half of the world's population lives on just US$7.40 a day or less, no more than US$3,000 a year, which even in lower-income countries is not enough to live a decent life.

The COVID-19 pandemic has highlighted and exacerbated these inequalities like no other. While the virus could have infected anyone, people with low incomes and without savings were more exposed to the virus and likelier to catch it. They were also more prone to experience economic devastation and see their jobs and incomes disappear.

For hundreds of millions of workers, 2020 was one of the worst years in history. The International Labor Organization (ILO 2021) estimates that it costed workers about US$3.7 trillion in lost earnings. At the same time, an Oxfam report (Berkhout et al. 2021) calculates that the world's 2,200-plus billionaires saw their wealth grow by US$3.9 trillion. Job losses were concentrated in low-wage industries and disproportionately affected women and people of color. Hundreds of millions were pushed into poverty, experienced hunger, or faced risk of eviction. People who were already struggling with poverty before the pandemic sank even deeper into economic distress.

If one believes estimates by the American economist Jeffrey Sachs (2006), the growth in total billionaire wealth during the pandemic alone would be more than enough to end extreme poverty worldwide in 20 years (he suggests it takes about US$175 billion per year to do so).[1] And even if one believes

DOI: 10.4324/9781003201908-1

more is needed to tackle poverty, it can't be denied that without challenging the accumulation of wealth at the very top, the struggles at the bottom will continue.

In part due to the extreme and rising gap between the rich and the poor, inequality has become part of the public debate in the last decade. In 2013, former US president Barack Obama declared rising inequality as a national priority. In 2014, a survey by the Pew Research Center found that people in the United States perceived inequality as one of the "greatest dangers in the world." At the same time, this attention served as a magnet for non-profit and multilateral spending. Across the globe, the case against the super-rich is gaining support, stressing the adverse effects of wealth accumulation, tax avoidance, and abuse of power to corrupt political processes and policy-making, with some suggesting that "every billionaire is a policy failure" (Riffle 2019).

This book describes how inequality manifests in Latin American cities and discusses what cities can do to win the fight for more egalitarian societies. Cities are the places where most of humanity lives. In Latin America, one of the most urbanized regions of the world, more than eight in ten people live in cities. Cities are also the places where social tensions and economic inequality can be most clearly felt and seen, as they morph into sums of fragments, where quality urban living has become a commodity for those with money. Wealthy neighborhoods are often provided with all kinds of services, such as quality public and private schools, medical care, golf courses, tennis courts, and private police patrolling the area around the clock; this world is intertwined with informal settlements where water is scarce, no formal sanitation systems exist, electricity is pirated, the roads become mud streams when it rains, and where house sharing is the norm.

Just outside the central train station in Buenos Aires is no stranger to such fragmentation. On one side of the train tracks, one can find Retiro, Buenos Aires' wealthiest neighborhood home to large and beautiful houses, quiet streets, art galleries, and chic cafes. Luxurious five-star hotels like Four Seasons, Marriott, and Sheraton give their guests an aerial view of Plaza San Martin from their 40-floor bar. After crossing the train tracks in the other direction, a drastically different urban landscape appears when entering Barrio Mugica (also known as Villa 31), Buenos Aires' largest slum home to more than 40,000 people. Like most informal settlements in Argentina, Barrio Mugica is not connected to an official power grid, there are almost no paved roads, and there is no sewage system or piped water. Out of necessity, residents have developed a parallel economy, with housing, commerce, and many social services being handled informally.

These spatial divisions are a cardinal symptom of income and wealth inequality. Socioeconomic segregation in Latin American cities often comes with unequal access to municipal services and infrastructure, such as piped drinking water, formal and reliable electricity, or access to public transport. But these divisions did not happen by chance, nor were they the natural result of living preferences. They are the result of historical land use and urban development plans that disadvantaged those with fewer resources. They are the consequence of past and present municipal and political priorities, budgetary allocations, and public investment decisions, which respond more to the needs and demands of the wealthy than those of the poor.

In the early 2000s, New School Professor Michael A. Cohen and researcher Dario Debowicz (2004) examined the importance of place as a factor of urban poverty and inequality by reviewing spatial patterns of public investment in infrastructure and social services over six years. Their findings are striking: some districts received more than 130 times the level of public infrastructure investment per capita than others. People living in the wealthier parts of town were exponentially more likely to enjoy a high quality of life. Recoleta, one of the city's wealthiest neighborhoods, received 68 percent of all public investment in infrastructure, even though just 11.5 percent of the city's population lived there. In contrast, the lower-income neighborhoods in the south west and far west of the city, home to 67 percent of the city's population, received just about 25.3 percent of infrastructure investment. Investments in education and health care also favored wealthier parts of the city.

As these urban inequalities and the practices that reinforce them have become increasingly visible, cities also emerged as the places where people come together to demand for greater equality and social justice. Three years after the 2008 financial crisis, the Occupy Wall Street movement in New York City, which inspired rallies around the world, began as a protest against the concentrations of wealth in the hands of the top 1 percent. In Istanbul, the occupation of Gezi Park to prevent the construction of a shopping mall became a symbol of the fight against the privatization of public spaces. In Chile, a hike in the Santiago Metro's subway fare in 2019 grew into a widespread protest against the increased cost of living and the privatization of public services and the pension system. The eruption of unrest in Ferguson, Baltimore, and other US cities is the response to racialized policing and segregation. And the 2019 Berlin May Day protests were organized under the slogan of "the city of the rich," rallying against rising rents, displacement, and gentrification.

These collective struggles for justice call for the right to the city, a concept termed first by French philosopher Henri Lefebvre in 1968. It resurfaced again through British geographer David Harvey (2008), who described the right to the city as the fight for democratic control over the urban development process, which makes it a broader right than the individual freedom to access urban amenities. Foremost, it includes citizen participation in urban management via "the right to participate" and the "right to inhabit," which promotes inclusive cities through urban regulations. These struggles call for the urgent need for new knowledge, policies, and practices to move from a "planet of slums," as the American geographer Mike Davis (2007) illustrates, to a planet of inclusive cities.

The harms of inequality

Why is inequality so bad? There are so many ways in which inequality harms societies that it is hard to know where to start and how to give justice to inequality's many repercussions on our lives. Extreme and rising inequality is not only unjust but also negatively impacts economies, human rights, and political stability. It raises crime and corruption and undermines democracy. It has contributed to ever more fragmented cities where housing has become unaffordable for most and homeownership is becoming an ever more distant dream.

Inequality impedes the fight against poverty. Extreme and growing economic inequality undermines poverty reduction as the increasing power by the top 1 percent shifts the focus of governments to them and away from the majority of the population. For the rich, wealth begets power.[2] Extreme wealth "buys political power, it silences dissent, and serves primarily to perpetuate ever-greater wealth [...] (Manjoo 2019)." A 2018 Oxfam study (Cañete Alonso 2018) demonstrates the many ways Latin American politics continue to be captured by the super-rich, with substantial financial backing for many new populist and even racist leaders.

Early defenders of inequality argued that it is good for economic growth and that growth lifts all boats and eventually eradicates poverty. But decades of growth alongside poverty have proven these claims to be false. Bourguignon (2002) finds that poverty does not decrease automatically when average incomes rise, but it decreases when distribution patterns change. How else could we explain the hundreds of millions of people living in extreme poverty despite years of strong economic growth?

Take Honduras, a country that – before COVID-19 – experienced the second-highest economic growth rates in Central America, only behind Panama. Yet, almost half of its population lives in poverty, and inequality is among the highest in the region (World Bank 2021a). We see a similar situation in Chile, one of Latin America's fastest-growing economies in the last decades. Still, almost a third of the population is economically vulnerable, and the income gap has remained high. The social unrest in 2019 was in part a response to the high and persistent inequality, high unemployment, segregated labor markets, and the segmented service provision in education and health care (World Bank 2021b).

Not only does unequal growth hamper poverty reduction, but it also hurts long-term economic well-being. The Economic Commission on Latin America (ECLAC) describes "inequality as a development obstacle" (Bárcena et al. 2018, p. 115). Segal (2018) estimates that in Mexico, rising inequality since the 1970s has cost the average worker nearly 60 percent of their income. Evidence by the Organisation for Economic Co-operation and Development, short OECD, (Cingano 2014) shows that more equal countries grow faster and over a more extended period. This is because a broader consumer base, human capital, and the social stability that greater equality enables provide a stronger basis for sustained growth than concentrated wealth does. Even institutions like the World Bank (Brueckner and Lederman 2018) and the International Monetary Fund (IMF) (Ostry et al. 2017) have noted this.

Cities, in their very origin, were thought of as places of opportunity and socioeconomic mobility. However, the concentration of poverty can have a first-order impact on several policy-relevant outcomes. The British epidemiologists Richard Wilkinson and Kate Pickett (2009) studied inequality and societal well-being in several high-income countries and large metropolitan areas in the United States. They found that high inequality has detrimental effects on health outcomes (physical and mental health), educational levels, and crime. Countries and cities with high inequality perform worse in life expectancy, math and literacy, infant mortality, and social mobility. Crime and homicides are also higher in more unequal places.

In *Moving to Opportunity*, Chetty and Hendren (2015) look at the neighborhood effects on children in US cities. The study reviewed the results of an experiment initiated in 1994 by the Department of Housing and Urban Development, which randomly assigned public housing tenants in three groups. The first group received a housing voucher to move to a better neighborhood, the second group received a voucher to move anywhere they wanted, and the third group received no voucher. Chetty and Hendren find that children who moved to a better neighborhood before the age of 13 earned 31 percent more as adults than those who stayed.

In Latin America, intergenerational mobility appears even lower (Bárcena et al. 2018). Just 14 percent of children who do well at school come from homes with low educational achievements. The majority (about 60 percent) tend to match their parents' level of schooling. Returns to education can thus create an inherited meritocracy trap, given the inequalities of access and the barriers individuals face from less affluent households (Torche 2014).

These experiences are evidence that the concept of meritocracy, rewarding those who work hard while sustaining the notion that "we get what we deserve" only works for those with resources. Alan Krueger (2012), the Chairman of the Council of Economic Advisors, calls this the "Great Gatsby Curve," suggesting that social mobility is lower in countries with high inequality.

Reducing inequality helps not only people in poverty but also the majority of a society. Wilkinson and Pickett (2009, p. 213) even suggest that the rich too would benefit from narrowing the gap: "[m]ore equality also has notable advantages for people in higher-income groups, even for the richest quarter of a society, which even includes the super-rich" (p. 213). They write (p. 195), "in societies with higher inequality, people are more hierarchy focused, while in more equal societies, people favor empathy and inclusion."

Similarly, Côté et al. (2015) present evidence that inequality makes the rich less generous. Using nationally representative survey data of the United States, Côté et al. show when high-income individuals reside in an unequal area, it reduces their generosity and empathy for the "other." In a previously undocumented manner, their research shows that inequitable resource distribution undermines collective welfare. Sands (2017) uses experimental evidence to link the salience of inequality to antisocial behavior and reduced generosity. Perhaps most concerning is her finding that the exposure to inequality in an everyday setting negatively affects willingness to support a redistributive economic policy.

Inequality also threatens social stability and can undermine democracy. Studies by Acemoglu and Robinson (2006), Joe Stiglitz (2012), and others found that extreme inequality adversely affects political participation and the nature of political decision-making, undermining political processes. Besides, politicians are more responsive to views of the affluent than those of the middle class and people in poverty (Gilens and Page 2014). As a result, inequality has prompted voter disillusionment, distrust, perceptions of unfairness, and ultimately disenfranchisement. The erosion of trust and social ties can lead to psychological stresses such as anxiety, depression, aggression, and shame, which Wilkinson and Pickett found to result in violence, alcohol or drug abuse, or antisocial behavior.

In Honduras, many of the poorest and most excluded in society have turned to crime, while many more have left the country, seeking opportunity elsewhere. In Tegucigalpa, the capital of Honduras, crime has led to a rapid proliferation of gates throughout the city that communities construct to create "Safer Barrios," sanctioned by the city government. While these gates are a natural response to people's safety concerns, they barely scratch the roots of the problem: poverty and inequality (Handal and Irazábal 2019).

Economic inequality is also exacerbating disparities of race and gender. Women in Latin America, especially women of color, are often hit hardest by rising inequality. They find themselves in the lowest paying and most precarious jobs. Much of their work goes unrecognized or is unrewarded. They are still underrepresented in democratic institutions and are often excluded from economic, social, and political decision-making processes (Bando 2019). Gender and racial justice are thus indispensable for poverty reduction and crucial to reducing inequality.

The need for a multidimensional response

What exactly do we have in mind when talking about inequality? The answer probably depends on your own experiences and interests and could relate to several issues because inequality is a broad concept with numerous dimensions. When speaking about economic inequality, we mainly refer to income, capital, or wealth. But then there is inequality in political standing, gender, or race – dimensions deeply intertwined with and reinforced by economic disparities. Take the stubborn wage gap between men and women. Despite legislative advances in narrowing the pay differences, women worldwide make only 77 cents for every dollar earned by men (UN Women 2021). Over a lifetime, these pay differences result in women being more likely to retire into poverty than men. The gender pay gap in Latin America is even higher than the global average, with the widest gap recorded in Brazil. On average, women in Brazil make about a quarter less than men (ILO 2018).

Much of the seminal research on economic inequality focuses on the distribution of income. This is not surprising considering that income constitutes the principal means to access services and goods in capitalist societies. With the money we earn, we buy food, a ticket to the movie theater, or get a haircut. But even income prompts the need for further clarification since we receive income from a variety of sources.

Landlords, for example, gain most of their money by renting spaces they own as apartments or businesses. Carpenters earn hourly, weekly, or yearly wages in exchange for providing manual labor. Caring for an older person, a domestic worker receives hourly pay, and often their work is not formally registered. For a single mother, the money she receives in social assistance for a decent standard of living is her income. In all of these situations, people earn income in exchange for a service. It is not difficult to imagine that these sources of income relate very differently to inequality.

While some people get income from their labor – like the carpenter or the domestic worker – others – like the landlord – get income from their capital and wealth. Over the past decade, and especially following Thomas Piketty's (2014) book *Capital in the 21st Century*, there has been an explosion of research on wealth inequality with new estimates of long-run trends in wealth concentration. Wealth, which includes all the nonfinancial assets like land and buildings, and financial assets like equities, bonds, or pension funds, is substantially more concentrated than income. In most countries, the share of wealth owned by the bottom half of the population is close to zero. At the top end, by contrast, the wealthiest individuals own enormous fortunes compared to average wealth. It doesn't help that inheritance has become an increasingly important factor in perpetuating economic inequality of income and wealth and is the primary driver of top income shares (Alvaredo et al. 2018).

To further complicate this, the lines between earned and capital incomes are often blurred. The compensation of entrepreneurial income can have elements of both a salary and a return on capital investment. A senior executive with a very high income has a greater opportunity to accumulate capital than a factory worker. Wealth may provide access to high-paying employment due to family connections or membership in elite institutions.

Housing and land are among the biggest components in wealth portfolios and deserve special attention in inequality analyses. Housing is often celebrated as the pathway to the middle class and to create security and save. But with the rising cost of housing in cities across the world, this wealth creation tool has become a major barrier for people's enjoyment of an adequate standard of living. It has made it harder for those with lower incomes and even the middle class to become property owners and exacerbated inequality between them and the rich.

The opportunity to provide housing as a pathway for economic opportunity has been wasted in Latin America this last decade. While scholars and politicians alike have acknowledged the inequality in access to housing in cities and the affordability crisis, the response to the issue was a purely housing-based approach. It led to the phenomena that Cohen et al. (2019) describe as "gente sin casa and casas sin gente" (people without houses and houses without people) and "mucha vivienda pero poca ciudad" (lots of houses but little city).

The public and the private sector responded to the affordability crisis with a construction boom that catered to the speculators and investment markets instead of people's needs. Housing units were constructed without access to municipal services such as transport, water, sanitation, or electricity, or too far from work, school, or family. In 2010, Brazil reported some 6.1 million dwellings abandoned, and in Mexico, nearly 5 million new homes were uninhabited, which is equivalent to 14 percent of the total housing stock (ibid; Moreno and Blanco 2014).

These experiences show that the housing crisis can't be tackled by increasing the supply of housing units without thinking about the people in need of housing, their ability to pay, a city's labor market, infrastructure needs, and the environment. At the same time, narrowing the wage gap alone won't change inequality and segregation in cities. In a context of high and rising property prices and increasing socioeconomic segregation, an approach to redistributing incomes is undoubtedly essential but insufficient. The multifaceted and interconnected nature of inequality in cities requires redistributive tools beyond income-related instruments for governments to use.

Suppose we were to take the fight against inequality and for greater social justice seriously. In that case, we need a plurality of responses, or as the American political theorist Michael Walzer called it in 1983: answers for every "sphere of justice." Walzer argued for multiple distributive tools for each sphere of life, suggesting that societies are more unjust if one central principle to redistribute prevails, especially if this mechanism is income. A universal basic pension scheme can reduce poverty among older persons and reduce income inequality, but it does not necessarily tackle disparities in access to decent housing and health care. Said differently, each dimension of inequality, whether related to income, race, gender, transport, or housing, requires a different intervention and political response. Reversing the rising gap between the rich and the rest of us and responding to rising demands for the right to the city requires a more integrated and less siloed response to the problem at hand.

About this book

This is a book about inequality in cities. Throughout the book, I look at both income inequality and the other intra-urban inequality dimensions that determine people's ability to live a decent life. Because cities are not stagnant, and forces beyond a person's wage affect the cost of housing, food, or access to public services.

The book has three parts. Part I opens with a review of the evolution of inequality in Latin America since the 1970s. It situates Argentina within this broader trend before diving into the systems contributing to urban fragmentation in the 1990s and beyond. Part II provides new evidence on inequality in 30 Argentinian cities over two decades, tapping into uncharted waters of disaggregating inequality by income and city characteristics. Part III shifts to the challenges and opportunities of addressing disparities in cities. What kind of approaches are effective? What can cities do to create more equal and just societies? This part aims to provide the reader with informed insights about hyperlocal urban intervention projects and contrasts it with a broader view of what is needed.

Following this introduction, Chapter 2 reflects on economic, political, and policy variables associated with the waves of rising and falling inequality. I discuss the impact of neoliberalism and its contributions to making Latin America the most unequal region in the world. Chapter 3 focuses on cities, especially Argentinian cities. The chapter emphasizes new forms of intra-urban inequality that have become more striking after the 2001/02 economic crisis, which have a clear spatial footprint with the concentration of vulnerability on the one side and the concentration of wealth and power on the other side. Chapter 4 discusses water privatization in metropolitan Buenos Aires in the 1990s, describing its impact on unequal municipal service provision, reinforcing socioeconomic segregation with scars still visible today.

Chapter 5 starts Part II of the book with a detour to identify the possible drivers of intra-urban inequality in the literature. It does so by raising the question of how is economic inequality constructed? Where can we find the drivers of inequality? It answers these questions by proposing the Urban Inequality Matrix, a framework to assess intra-urban inequality that guides the following analytical chapters. This matrix recognizes not just one but multiple variables affecting inequality and the structural transformation required to address it.

In Chapters 6 and 7, I present new empirical findings of possible determinants of intra-urban inequality. In Chapter 6, I use Lerman and Yitzhaki's decomposition method to analyze the role of labor income, the wage gap between formal and informal employment, and the impact of social protection in shaping income inequality across cities and over time. Chapter 7 uses the Urban Inequality matrix to analyze two dozen determinants over 22 years (1996–2018) to shed light on why some cities have higher inequality than others. I discuss findings from a fixed-effects regression model that gives insight into the relationship between inequality and a city's economic growth and population, demographic factors, and the structure of the local labor market. With the findings, I piece together a picture of what drives inequality in Argentinian cities, which I present in a typology of cities: those with higher inequality and those with lower levels.

Chapter 8 kicks off Part III with a more local view and reflects on urban interventions that aim to integrate long-neglected neighborhoods into the rest of the city. I discuss the experiences in Villa 20, an informal settlement in Buenos Aires, and the opportunities and limitations to reduce socioeconomic disparities as part of an ongoing upgrading initiative by the city government. While Villa 20 residents may see their housing and access to basic services like water improve, many cannot afford the new financial obligations that come with upgrading and face risks of indebtedness. These experiences demonstrate that fighting urban poverty and inequality is incompatible with market solutions, and new community-based and people-focused approaches are utterly needed.

In the last chapter, Chapter 9, I review the book's main points, distilling its key lessons and making proposals essential for reducing inequalities in cities. I argue that the seemingly paradoxical decline in income inequality alongside an increase in urban segregation suggests that a new multifaceted urban social agenda is urgently needed. In a context of high and rising property prices and increasing socioeconomic segregation, an approach to redistributing incomes is undoubtedly essential but insufficient. The weak integration of housing policies in social and redistributive agendas shows that the subject of unequal access to the city has yet to reach all governments' attention. At the national level, policies to tackle inequality have generally focused on fiscal and social policies only. Without a clear territorial understanding of the problem at hand, this becomes especially evident in the distinct treatment of the formal and the informal. Local governments lack the administrative, financial, or legislative powers to implement core services, income, and redistributive land policies. I argue that these discrepancies between the local, the regional, and the national level ought to be addressed and propose a multifaceted approach that may do so.

I believe that this book can be read with equal appreciation and ease by specialists and members of the general public, whether well-informed on the subject matter or less well-informed.

I now offer the pleasure of taking the first step on the road to studying inequality in Latin America's cities by looking at some of the largest increases and declines ever recorded.

Notes

1 In his book, *The End of Poverty*, Jeffrey Sachs (2006) estimates that to end extreme poverty worldwide in 20 years, the total cost per year would be about US$175 billion.
2 An extensive political science literature stresses the role played by the wealthy in the political process. See Gilens and Page (2014) or Bertrand et al. (2018); for a critical survey of the evidence on the interplay between wealth and democracy, see Scheve and Stasavage (2017).

References

Acemoglu, Daron, and James A. Robinson. 2006. "Economic Backwardness in Political Perspective." *American Political Science Review* 100 (1): 115–31.
Alvaredo, Facundo, Lucas Chancel, Thomas Piketty, Emmanuel Saez, and Gabriel Zucman. 2018. World Inequality Report 2018. Paris: World Inequality Lab.

Bando, Rosangela. 2019. "Evidence-Based Gender Equality Policy and Pay in Latin America and the Caribbean: Progress and Challenges." *Latin American Economic Review* 28 (1): 1–23.

Bárcena, Alicia, Mario Cimoli, and United Nations, eds. 2018. *The Inefficiency of Inequality: 2018, Thirty-Seventh Session of ECLAC, Havana, 7–11 May.* Santiago, Chile: United Nations publication.

Berkhout, Esmé, Nick Galasso, Max Lawson, Pablo Andrés Rivero Morales, Anjela Taneja, and Diego AlejoVázquez Pimentel. 2021. "The Inequality Virus: Bringing together a world torn apart by coronavirus through a fair, just and sustainable economy." Oxford, UK: Oxfam GB for Oxfam International.

Bertrand, Marianne, Matilde Bombardini, Raymond Fisman, and Francesco Trebbi. 2018. *Tax-Exempt Lobbying: Corporate Philanthropy as a Tool for Political Influence.* National Bureau of Economic Research (NBER), Working Paper No. 24451.

Bourguignon, François. 2002. "The Growth Elasticity of Poverty Reduction: Explaining Heterogeneity across Countries and Time Periods." *DELTA Working Papers 2002-03, DELTA (Ecole normale supérieure).*

Brueckner, Markus, and Daniel Lederman. 2018. "Inequality and Economic Growth: The Role of Initial Income". *Policy Research Working Paper;* No. 8467. Washington, DC: World Bank.

Cañete Alonso, Rosa. 2018. *Democracias Capturadas: El Gobierno de Unos Pocos.* Oxfam International and CLACSO. Available at: https://policy-practice.oxfam.org/resources/democracias-capturadas-el-gobierno-de-unos-pocos-620600/, accessed November 28, 2021.

Chetty, Raj, and Nathaniel Hendren. 2015. *The Impacts of Neighborhoods on Intergenerational Mobility: Childhood Exposure Effects and County-Level Estimates. Harvard University and NBER: 1–144.*

Cingano, Federico. 2014. *Trends in Income Inequality and Its Impact on Economic Growth, OECD Social, Employment and Migration Working Papers;* No. 163. Paris: OECD Publishing.

Cohen, Michael A., and Dario Debowicz. 2004. "The Five Cities of Buenos Aires: An Inquiry into Poverty and Inequality in Urban Argentina." *The Encyclopedia of Sustainable Development, by Saskia Sassen.* Paris: UNESCO.

Cohen, Michael A., Maria Carrizosa, and Margarita Gutman. 2019. *Urban Policy in Latin America: Towards the Sustainable Development Goals?* Oxfordshire: Routledge.

Côté, Stéphane, Julian House, and Robb Willer. 2015. "High Economic Inequality Leads Higher-Income Individuals to Be Less Generous." *Proceedings of the National Academy of Science* 112 (December): 15838–43.

Davis, Mike. 2007. *Planet of Slums.* London, UK: Verso.

Gilens, Martin, and Benjamin I. Page. 2014. "Testing Theories of American Politics: Elites, Interest Groups, and Average Citizens." *Perspectives on Politics* 12 (3): 564–81.

Handal, Cristina, and Clara Irazábal. 2019. "Gating Tegucigalpa, Honduras: The Paradoxical Effects of "Safer Barrios"". *Journal of Urban Affairs* 1–23.

Harvey, David. 2008. "The Right to the City." *New Left Review* 53 (September – October). Online: https://newleftreview.org/issues/ii53/articles/david-harvey-the-right-to-the-city, accessed November 28, 2021.

International Labor Organization ILO. 2018. Global Wage Report 2018/19.

_____ ILO. 2021. *ILO Monitor: Covid-19 and the World of Work.* Seventh edition. Updated estimates and analysis. Briefing note. Geneva, Switzerland: ILO.

Krueger, Alan B. 2012. *The Rise and Consequences of Inequality in the United States.* Speech. Available at: https://obamawhitehouse.archives.gov/blog/2012/01/12/chairman-alan-krueger-discusses-rise-and-consequences-inequality-center-american-pro, accessed November 28, 2021.

Manjoo, Farhad. 2019. "Opinion | Abolish Billionaires." *The New York Times.* Available at: https://www.nytimes.com/2019/02/06/opinion/abolish-billionaires-tax.html, accessed September 6, 2021.

Moreno, Eduardo López, and Zeltia González Blanco. 2014. "Ghost Cities and Empty Houses: Wasted Prosperity." *American International Journal of Social Science* 3 (2): 10.

Numbeo. 2021. *Cost of Living in Sao Paulo.* Available at: https://www.numbeo.com/cost-of-living/in/Sao-Paulo, accessed September 6, 2021.

Obama, Barack. 2013. *Remarks by the President on Economic Mobility. The White House.* Available at: https://obamawhitehouse.archives.gov/the-press-office/2013/12/04/remarks-president-economic-mobility, accessed September 6, 2021.

Ostry, Jonathan D., Andrew Berg, and Charalambos G. Tsangarides, 2017. *Redistribution, Inequality, and Growth.* Washington, DC: IMF Staff Discussion Note.

Pew Research Center. 2014. *Greatest Dangers in the World.* Global Attitudes & Trends. Available at: https://www.pewresearch.org/global/2014/10/16/greatest-dangers-in-the-world/, accessed November 28, 2021.

Piketty, Thomas. 2014. *Capital in the Twenty-First Century.* Cambridge, MA: Harvard University Press.

Riffle, Dan. 2019. "Every Billionaire Is a Policy Failure." *Twitter.* https://twitter.com/danriffle

Sachs, Jeffrey D. 2006. *The End of Poverty: Economic Possibilities for Our Time.* London: Penguin.

Sands, Melissa. 2017. "Exposure to Inequality Affects Support for Redistribution." *Proceedings of the National Academy of Sciences of the United States of America* 114 (4): 663–68.

Scheve, Kenneth, and David Stasavage. 2017. "Wealth Inequality and Democracy." *Annual Review of Political Science* 20: 451–68.

Segal, Paul. 2018. *Inequality Represents a Wasted Opportunity for Poverty Reduction.* New York, NY: Institute of New Economic Thinking.

Stiglitz, Joseph E. 2012. *The Price of Inequality: How Today's Divided Society Endangers Our Future.* New York, NY: WW Norton & Company.

Torche, Florencia. 2014. "Intergenerational Mobility and Inequality: The Latin American Case." *Annual Review of Sociology* 40: 619–42.

UN Women. 2021. "Equal Pay for Work of Equal Value." https://www.unwomen.org/en/news/in-focus/csw61/equal-pay.

Walzer, Michael. 1983. *Spheres of Justice: A Defense of Pluralism and Equality.* New York, NY: Basic Books.

Wilkinson, Richard, and Kate Pickett. 2009. *The Spirit Level: Why Greater Equality Makes Societies Stronger.* Reprint. New York, NY: Bloomsbury Publishing.

World Bank. 2018. *Poverty and shared prosperity 2018: Piecing together the poverty puzzle.* DC: The World Bank.

————. 2021a. *The World Bank in Honduras.* Available at: https://www.worldbank.org/en/country/honduras/overview, accessed September 6, 2021.

————. 2021b. *The World Bank in Chile.* Available at: https://www.worldbank.org/en/country/chile/overview, accessed September 6, 2021.

2 From neoliberalism to the pink tide, and back

At the turn of the twenty-first century, Latin America showed the world how to push back against inequality. The region recorded strong economic growth coupled with substantial poverty reductions and declining economic inequality. The Latin American (LA) middle class expanded from 103 million people in 2003 to 152 million in 2009, a 50-percent increase and close to a third of the continent's population (Ferreira et al. 2013).

These achievements, however, were overshadowed by the realization that the region still has the world's highest inequality levels. Even more concerning is the seemingly short-lived nature of the success: inequality declines began to stall in 2013, and in some countries, including Argentina, inequality resurged.

This chapter describes how inequality in Latin America compares to other regions today, how it has evolved over time, and why it has evolved that way. The second part of the chapter situates Argentina within the LA experience.

Latin America within global inequality trends

Global economic inequality is extremely high. Credit Suisse (2021) reported that the world's richest 1 percent, those with more than US$1 million, owned 45.8 percent of global wealth at the end of 2020. In contrast, adults with less than US$10,000 who make up 55 percent of the world's population held less than 1.3 percent of global wealth.

Gaps in people's incomes are similarly extreme and largely depend on one's citizenship or place of birth. A person born in a rich country has, regardless of their work effort, a greater chance to make a higher income than a person born in a low-income country. This implies a lack of equal opportunity at the global scale and a potential trigger for migration.

Although today's level of global inequality is extreme, before the COVID-19 pandemic there were some indications of a narrowing or what some scholars call *convergence*. Branko Milanovic (2016) estimates that global income disparities were down for the first time since the beginning of the industrial revolution. For Milanovic, inequality was driven by today's high-income countries as they accumulated wealth, increasing the gaps between themselves and the rest of the world. Global inequality has been rising since the

DOI: 10.4324/9781003201908-3

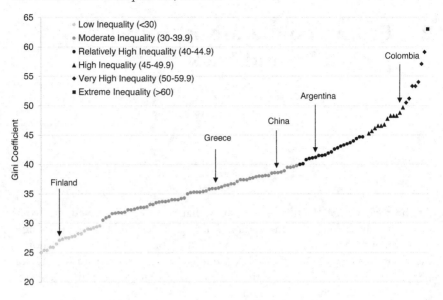

Figure 2.1 Income inequality across 125 countries (2018)

Data source: World Bank's World Development Indicators (WDI), 2018.

1850s then peaked in the 1970s and plateaued after that until the early 2000s when it started to drop.[1]

Milanovic argues that the decline was partly driven by a shift in income and globalization. While in Europe and the United States, middle and lower-middle-classes experienced stagnating wages, broad swaths of the population in emerging economies, especially in Asia, saw their incomes grow. It is the catchup by Asia's most populous countries China and India, but also Thailand, Vietnam, and Indonesia, that narrowed the global income divide.

Other estimates give less weight to the decline and stress the prevailing extreme levels. The 2018 World Inequality Report (Alvaredo et al. 2018) suggests that the decline after 2000 needs to be considered in light of the sharp rise in global inequality since the 1980s. One reason for the persistent extreme divide is that the global top 1 percent captured almost twice as much as the bottom half of the global population.

But both researchers at the World Inequality Lab and Milanovic agree that it was no longer the gap between countries, but within-country inequality that has driven global inequality before the COVID-19 pandemic.

Among 125 countries for which the World Bank has data on income inequality (measured with the Gini coefficient), 20 have low inequality with a Gini of less than 30; see Figure 2.1. Finland falls into this category (27.1). Sixty-three countries, including Greece, have moderate inequality. The remaining 42 countries distribute across relatively high inequality (21), high inequality (13), very high inequality (7), and extreme inequality (1, being South Africa).

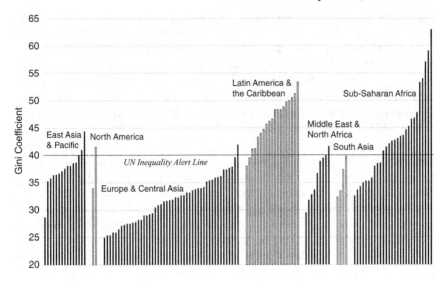

Figure 2.2 Latin America was the most unequal region in 2017

Data source: World Inequality Database and the World Bank's World Development Indicators (WDI).

UN-Habitat (2014) suggests that a Gini above 40 indicates inequalities to have particularly negative social, economic, and political consequences.

Figure 2.2 shows that LA income inequality is among the world's highest. All LA countries have a Gini above the world's average (37.8), and all except El Salvador and Uruguay exceed the UN's international alert line of 40.

In Chile, the richest 10 percent of income recipients earned 39.3 percent of national income in 2017, while the poorest 40 percent received just 13.1 percent. Hence, Chile's Gini of income inequality was very high, with 48.3. By comparison, in Denmark, these ratios were 24.18 for the top 10 percent and 22.4 percent for the bottom 40 percent, which gives a Gini of 29.4. On average, inequality is lowest in Europe and Central Asia, with a mean Gini of 32.

Inequality in Latin America is comparable only to Sub-Saharan Africa. South Africa, Namibia, and Zambia have Ginis above 57. Although five of the ten highest Gini coefficients belong to Southern African countries, the regional mean (43.3) is lower than in Latin America (46.2). In East Asia and the Pacific, the region's Gini is 37.5, it is 37.8 in North America (although the US Gini exceeds the alert line with 41.5), 36.1 in the Middle East and North Africa, and 35.8 in South Asia.

Colonialism, Latin America's unequal roots

The disparities in Latin America have persisted for decades and are likely connected to its long-run historical evolution and the legacy of colonialism. Despite the lack of robust series of comparable income inequality data before the 1950s', contemporary researchers emphasize the roots of present-day inequality in exclusionary and colonial institutions that formed in the late fifteenth to the early nineteenth century (Acemoglu et al. 2002; Engerman and Sokoloff 2005).

Ewout Frankema, Professor and Research Fellow at the UK Centre for Economic Policy Research, says that LA inequality is rooted firmly in the colonial past, especially when it comes to land inequality (2010). He attributes inequality in wealth, income, and assets to the pre-colonial institutions that shaped the colonial political economic context in which land was (re) distributed from natives to colonial settlers.

This unequal distribution of land formed the backbone of wealth inequality in colonial Latin America, shaping social and economic status and political voice. Complicated and often times corrupted bureaucracies to obtain land titles sustained the concentration of land ownership in the hands of a few (De Soto 2001). A subsequent social structure emerged with a privileged minority, excluding most people from access to land, education, and politics. Powerful elites were able to avoid paying taxes, thereby limiting the redistributive power of the state.

Engerman and Sokoloff (2005) argue that the concentration of power inherited from the colonial era led to the development of exclusionary and extractive institutions. They perpetuated the privileges of a small agrarian and commercial oligarchy well into the third quarter of the twentieth century, a period during which Latin America suffered from slow growth, frequent financial crisis, and rising income inequality.

Valuable commodities brought European settlers to the continent. From silver in Bolivia to oil in Venezuela, copper in Chile and Peru, and coffee in Brazil and Colombia. Latin America's endowments are thought by some to be the origins of the high inequality (ibid). While there is a shared colonial history across the region, factors such as location, climate, mineral endowments, and the presence or absence of indigenous populations created different possibilities for colonial settlers, affecting the nature and impact of their institutions.

The Andean, Central American, and Mexican regions were the center of colonial activity, as they were densely populated and rich in gold and silver. The coercive labor practices that ensured a steady supply of surplus labor were deeply embedded in a system of racial and ethnic discrimination. The institutionalization of inequality in colonial Latin America created a system that legitimized a social order in which a minority held exclusive economic and political privileges and where ethnicity formed a major determinant of social and economic class.

In contrast, what is today Argentina, Chile, southern Brazil, and Uruguay remained almost entirely untouched by the colonial era. They lacked sources of mineral wealth and high population density, which could sustain the colonial centers and their exploitative and extractive labor practices. At the time, Buenos Aires was a distant outpost of the Spanish American Empire. Argentina and Uruguay became immigration countries much later in the nineteenth century. The development, growth, and inequality records of countries like Argentina and Uruguay thus show a very different trajectory than countries that were at the core of colonialism, such as Mexico, Peru, and Brazil.

While colonialism shaped inequality of wealth and land at the time, its role in today's income disparities is disputed. The economist Jeffrey G. Williamson

(2015) contends that incomes in Latin America after colonialism and before industrialization (around 1870) were similar to Europe or the United States before their industrial revolution (the 1800s). He argues that inequality in Latin America grew significantly from 1870 to 1929, in part due to the impact of a secular commodity price boom that raised land rents relative to wages.

Despite the absence of robust historical data on income inequality, we know that the patterns of land ownership inherited from the colonial period shaped the trajectories during the nineteenth and twentieth centuries, when LA economies grew substantially but very unevenly. The high levels of volatility depended on the ever-changing global economic environment.

Neoliberalism, the Washington Consensus, and a rise in poverty and inequality

While others continue to grapple with the question of whether Latin America has always been unequal, this book's focus is on the more recent history, starting in the 1980s, a period frequently referred to as "the lost decade." This time was characterized by a much slower economic growth than earlier periods, fiscal crises, dramatically reduced public expenditures, inflation, and rising poverty and inequality.

The macroeconomic volatility experienced across the region between the 1960s to 1985 resulted in growing uncertainty, lower investment in trade, and a greater dependency on the global economy. Latin America became highly vulnerable to changes in energy prices, interest rates, and global market conditions. A cocktail of these circumstances brought about an unprecedented debt crisis in the 1980s. In 1983, LA countries owed US$209 billion to North American banks. To make things worse, interest rates skyrocketed, exacerbating debt levels. Argentina's case is illuminating. For its debt rescheduling, Argentina paid 219 percent more in 1982 than it did in 1981 (Cohen 2012).

It was in this context that many countries turned to the International Monetary Fund (IMF) and World Bank for financial support. Between 1980 and 1989, the IMF alone negotiated more than 100 loan programs in the region. Bailouts and loans often came with strings attached. To stabilize macroeconomic imbalances and reduce inflation, these institutions recommended (and imposed) a set of economic policy prescriptions known as the *Washington Consensus* or *structural adjustment*. This policy package started from the assumption that if countries could not pay their debts, they need to adjust their economic and fiscal structure to cut expenditure and balance budgets and avoid taking on additional debt. In specific terms, the reform package included the following:

- Fiscal reforms for balanced budgets and the rationalization and control of public spending to reduce the need for foreign and domestic borrowing
- Tax reforms
- Interest rate liberalization
- Trade liberalization (reduction of tariffs, ease of imports, elimination of subsidies to noncompetitive industries)

- Privatization of public services and public enterprises
- Deregulation
- Guarantees for property rights

These reforms reflected the growing distrust of the state's efficacy as an institutional actor, not just in the economy but also in society as a whole. This attitude gained strength and support during Margaret Thatcher and Ronald Reagan's ascendancy and conservative approach to governing. It gave the market a larger role, taking decisions for resource allocation away from governments and allowing them to be made by private companies and economic actors instead.

Pro-market reforms were hastily introduced across the region, often by authoritarian regimes. But the adjustments made did not bring the expected economic growth, and in hindsight, it is clear they failed to reach many of the goals they claimed to achieve.

Ricardo Ffrench Davis (2005), a Chilean economist, concludes that though the Washington Consensus appeared to lower inflation, balance budgets, and increase exports, at the aggregate level, macroeconomic growth was lower than before and stagnated for nearly every country in Latin America. And between 1999 and 2002, Argentina, Colombia, Ecuador, Paraguay, Uruguay, and Venezuela experienced severe economic crises. Nobel laureate Joseph Stiglitz explains in his 2002 bestseller *Globalization and its Discontents* that the structural adjustment policies driven by the IMF were made "on the basis of what seemed to be a curious blend of ideology and bad economics, dogma that sometimes seemed to be thinly veiling special interests."

These neoliberal reforms would cause further polarization of social classes, increase precarious employment, and push millions into unemployment. Public sector and formal employment declined, while a small group of entrepreneurs formed, alongside a sharp increase in informal jobs. The regressive nature of fiscal policies during the Washington Consensus also solidified poverty and inequality. In all countries in the region, except Colombia, Costa Rica, and Uruguay, inequality worsened and continued to do so throughout the 1990s (Cornia 2011). Poverty skyrocketed, with 32 percent of the population living in poverty in 1989. Older people and children were hit particularly hard by the wave of "new poverty" that struck the region. The labor market crisis and the increase in economic precarity strongly affected the living conditions of vast sectors of the middle class. In Argentina, infant mortality reached a devastating 26 percent, about 18,000 children younger than one died annually from malnutrition, diseases, and the inaccessibility to health care (Minujin 1996).

The achievements of the early 2000s

The early 2000s present a fundamental break with the 1980s and 1990s. Almost all countries in Latin America recorded strong reductions in poverty and inequality, especially countries in South America. Before the turn of the century, in 1999, nearly 15 percent of LAs, about 72.5 million people, lived

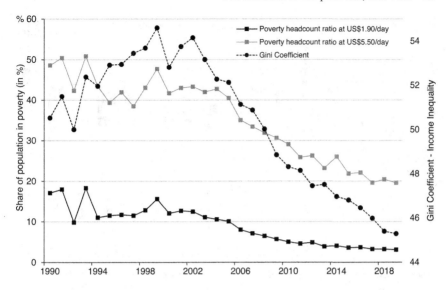

Figure 2.3 The rise and fall of poverty and inequality in Latin America (1990–2019)

Data sources: World Bank's World Development Indicators (WDI).

in extreme poverty on less than US$1.90 a day. By 2019, this share dropped to about 3 percent. According to the World Bank's poverty threshold for middle-income countries (US$5.50/day), a classification that fits for most countries in the region, almost half of LAs lived in poverty in 1999. In 2019, it was two out of ten people.[2]

Income inequality followed a similar trend; it increased in the late 1990s and declined significantly in the early 2000s in almost all of Latin America, along with what Cornia (2014, p.60) refers to "a Polanyian reversal of political, economic, and distributive trends." This Polanyian process signifies that several social and political forces countered globalization and the period of structural adjustment in the late twentieth century.

Figure 2.3 depicts the rise and fall of poverty and inequality in the region. Some countries exhibited a more equal distribution in the late 1990s (e.g., Brazil), while others began to do so only in the early 2000s (e.g., Argentina). By 2002, all countries had lower inequality than in the 1980s and 1990s. While these distributional changes were not necessarily substantial in all countries, they certainly stand in contrast to the trend from preceding decades.

Between 1999 and 2013, the average annual percentage decline in inequality was almost one. Ecuador, Argentina, and Bolivia experienced the most notable inequality reductions with yearly declines close or equal to 1.5; see Figure 2.4. Costa Rica was the only country in the region (for which comparable data was available) where inequality increased. After 2013, inequality decreased at a much lower rate in all countries except Uruguay and Panama, and even resurged in some, including Ecuador, Argentina, and Brazil.

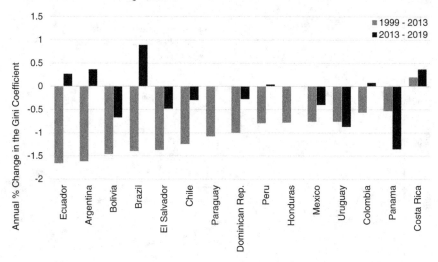

Figure 2.4 Annual changes in inequality in select countries

Data sources: Calculated from the World Inequality Database.

Note: The average change in the Gini for a country is calculated as the percentage change between the end year and the initial year divided by the number of years.

What explains these achievements in the early 2000s? While there is no silver bullet for fighting inequality, a mixture of macroeconomic policies, economic recovery, changes in the labor market, progressive fiscal policy and tax reforms, and the expansion of social protection measures pulled people out of poverty and created more equal societies.

Economists were quick to argue that the inequality decline was related to fortunate circumstances of improving economic conditions, with better terms of trade and rising remittances laying beneficial conditions for growth. Jose Antonio Ocampo (2012), a Colombian economist and former Under-Secretary-General for Economic and Social Affairs of the United Nations, referred to this period as "bonanza económica" with growth rates unexperienced since the 1970s.

Several economists (see Gasparini and Lustig 2011 or Cornia 2014) find that the region's commodity price boom facilitated this economic recovery. Latin America's commodity exporting countries experienced a significant boost in their terms of trade relative to others. A 2021 study by the IMF (Balakrishnan et al.) found that the largest gains in poverty and inequality were made in Bolivia and Ecuador, two countries highly dependent on commodity exports. Commodity exporters seemed to achieve larger gains in poverty reduction except for Chile and Honduras. For inequality, the picture is more mixed, with El Salvador and the Dominican Republic recording bigger reductions than commodity exporters (Chile, Colombia, Paraguay, and Honduras). This suggests once again that many factors drive inequality and social progress, of which commodity cycles is only one. In fact, in the absence of several policy changes, inequality would probably not have reduced.

At the time, the region experienced a return to democracy and a sudden shift toward center-left governments. In the mid-2000s, at the peak of the so-called *Pink Tide*, a phrase meant to suggest the surge of leftist, noncommunist governments, 11 LA countries were governed by left-wing parties (e.g., Nestor Kirchner in Argentina, Lula da Silva in Brazil). That is three-quarters of South America's population or about 350 million people. The growing support of left-leaning administrations was a growing frustration with high and rising unemployment, poverty, and large informal economies brought about by the Washington Consensus of the 1980s and 1990s (Panizza 2005).

The center-left governments had a very different approach to social, fiscal, and economic policy making. Cornia (2014) describes that their "redistribution with growth" paradigm was inspired by the European social-democratic model, leading to a new policy approach with the following components.

First, countries adopted a more progressive allocation of government spending and ramped up investment in public services, such as education, health care, and social protection (Inchauste et al. 2012). Between 2000 and 2012, overall social spending increased faster than GDP; the share of social spending in GDP rose between 14 and 19 percent in this period, to complement the previously spotty social protection coverage. Programs included cash transfers to reduce child poverty and ensure that children remain in school and have access to health services and proper nutrition (such as Brazil's famous Bolsa Familia). Argentina, Bolivia, Brazil, and Chile introduced a progressive noncontributory social pension to address old-age poverty.

In order to finance the increased investments in public services and social protection, LA countries focused on generating more revenue. They increased the tax revenue ratio to GDP more than any other region in the world, with an emphasis on progressive taxation, indirect taxes on luxuries, and reduced exemptions and excise duties (Mahon 2018). Colombia, for example, almost doubled its tax income over the past two decades. The most distinctively left-populist governments of the region – those of Venezuela, Ecuador, and Bolivia – have relied more on wealth from natural resource rents than taxing their citizens' consumption and incomes (Lustig et al. 2013).

The new policy approach also included significant changes in labor policy to address the problems inherited from previous decades. Most center-left governments launched programs to reduce the informal sector, expand social security to informal workers, and increased the minimum wage. Amarante and Prado (2017) estimate that in Argentina, the minimum wage accounted for 87 percent of lowering income inequality between 2003 and 2012; in Brazil, 72 percent between 2001 and 2012.

A shift toward more progressive macroeconomic policies sustained this new policy mix. Governments reduced vulnerability to external shocks by avoiding debt accumulation and payment deficits and reducing dependence on foreign finance.

2013 onwards – the end of a progressive decade?

Despite the successes in the early 2000s, several scholars have questioned the sustainability of policies and whether growth was truly inclusive and broadly shared. In a 2012 study, Gasparini et al. find that the economic growth came with an increase in the demand for low-skilled labor in service-intensive sectors tied to natural-resource-related production and almost entirely depended on a commodity boom. Instead of creating good jobs with social mobility, this type of growth reduced the education wage premium for those that expected returns on their advanced degrees. Rather than a sign of inclusive growth, he pointed to discouraging signs for training and education.

The bonanza económica ended with the 2008 global financial crisis when remittances, exports, and commodity prices plummeted, causing a 2-percent contraction of LA GDP in 2009, and a growth decline from 5 percent over 2002–8 to 3 percent over 2010–14 (ECLAC 2014). For a few years, inequality declined regardless, and the center-left governments continued to dominate the political scene.

However, in 2013, dissatisfaction with the economic situation and policy choices became stronger particularly in Argentina, Brazil, Venezuela, Paraguay, and El Salvador. Cornia (2014) describes that policy mistakes and the political choice to focus mainly on the poor during the years of slow growth and stagnating revenue may have alienated the support of the middle class. This conjecture is supported by data showing that in countries affected by political tensions, the inequality decline benefited low-income groups primarily. The lack of income and inequality gains by the middle class, which for several years had borne a heavy tax burden to finance redistribution without receiving in exchange adequate services and jobs, eroded support for the center-left regimes. In 2015, several countries experienced an electoral reversal. And after years of rapid inequality decline, inequality levels reduced at a much slower rate than after 2013. In Brazil, Ecuador, and Argentina, inequality even resurged.

These rising and falling inequality tides offer several lessons about the limits of success of the Pink Tide and suggest what else may be needed to win the battle for more egalitarian societies. One lesson relates to shortcomings of Latin America's economic growth paradigm, which remains foreign-financed, export-led, and highly dependent on the global economy. This economic model was pushed during the 1980s and 1990s and not sufficiently altered in the 2000s.

Another lesson relates to fiscal policy, which encompasses both revenue generation and public expenditure as a powerful tool to fight inequality. The revenue structure, meaning how public policies are funded and who contributes, and the distribution of spending, meaning whom these public policies favor, are good indicators of the level of commitment to equity and justice and the political will to address inequality. Raising the tax rate of consumption or indirect taxes is a policy choice to apply the tax collection effort relatively evenly across the population, rather than according to economic capacity. This can lead to greater inequality. On the other hand, taxes on luxury products or large fortunes demonstrate a clear commitment to redistribute income and wealth.

LA fiscal policy is substantially less progressive than in countries that form part of the Organization for Economic Co-operation and Development (OECD). Feierherd et al. (2021) find that in some LA countries, the net income of the poor and near-poor can be lower than it was before taxes and cash transfers. For the most part, political and economic elites of Latin America have shaped fiscal policies to have a minimal impact on reducing poverty and inequalities. While each country's specific circumstances are different, tax systems in the region as a whole have done little to reduce inequality. Hanni et al. (2015) estimate that the region's fiscal policies reduce the Gini by about nine percentage points, on average. To compare, in other middle and high-income countries, the inequality-reducing effect is much larger: in the OECD, fiscal policies reduce the Gini by 23 percentage points, in the EU by 26 percentage points.

For one, the region's tax collection is much lower than it could be. The lack of financial resources, resulting in part from the low tax collection, has high social costs when it becomes necessary to resort to foreign lending to comply with spending commitments or budget deficits. In such situations, experiences in the region have shown that lenders can impose conditions on access to funding, which has reduced countries' scope to define their social protection and economic development policies.

A bias toward indirect and consumption taxes like the value-added tax (VAT) dominates tax structures, whereas progressive taxation of personal income and property is weak. The Inter-American Development Bank (Corbacho et al. 2013) found that the VAT is the only tax whose average nominal rates have increased since 2000. In 2010, it accounted for 34.7 percent of tax revenues; it is 20.5 percent in OECD countries. This is problematic because the burden of indirect and consumption taxes falls more heavily on those with low incomes, making them regressive. Meanwhile, income taxes and taxes on utilities accounted for just 25.5 percent of tax collection (33.2 percent in the OECD). Besides, taxes on capital and other non-labor income are meager, and companies often pay a lower effective tax rate than employees, which suggests a tax bias against workers.

During the Pink Tide, center-left governments failed to address the vastly outsized accumulation of wealth of the very rich. Because the extreme concentration of wealth mainly was kept intact, the power of that group to organize a countermovement to the political left was not addressed. And when they succeeded, they could swiftly undo many progressive policies. The key lesson here is that wealth is a form of power.

Fighting inequality means being bold in ending the unjust concentration of wealth and power and addressing structural roots, which requires much more than addressing the consequences of inequality. Increasing the role of tax systems as instruments of the redistribution of income and wealth, reducing the current high levels of tax evasion, and fiscal systems that help address and reduce entrenched inequalities would go a far way to do that.

Despite the defeat of the Pink Tide, people continue to push back against structural inequality. In 2018, more than 80 percent of LAs said they perceive the income distribution in their country to be unfair (Latinobarómetro 2018).[3] The mass protests in Chile, Colombia, and Ecuador that erupted after 2015 reflect the discontent with the economic systems that leave the majority behind. These calls for change clearly indicate the shared outrage and expression of anger about unjust political and economic systems that continue to cater to the wealthy while neglecting the needs of the majority.

This situation has only worsened with the COVID-19 pandemic. In the immediate it has led to an unprecedented contraction in economic activity and a historic jobs loss. Employment in Brazil, Chile, Colombia, Peru, and Mexico fell by 30 percent between January and May 2020, the largest four-month contraction on record. The largest job losses were concentrated among low-income segments, most prominently informal workers in service sectors (Bottan et al. 2020).

In an expansive forward-looking microsimulation exercise on the impact of the crisis on poverty and inequality in Argentina, Brazil, Colombia, and Mexico, Lustig et al. (2020) estimate an increase of 4–9 percentage points in the poverty rate and an increase in the Gini of 2-4 points. But these estimates don't account for the governments' policy responses. Some governments have mitigated the economic fallouts with emergency government assistance. To sustain these initiatives, there is an important task of ring-fencing social safety nets from the looming risk of austerity.

Argentina: (A)typical for the region?

In many regards, Argentina is not typical for Latin America. Argentina experienced a reversal of fortune more dramatic than that of most other countries. Few countries see economic cycles fluctuate so widely, similarly high inflation rates, and capital flight as rampant. Argentine economist Claudio Katz estimates that in 2019, Argentine capital held abroad added up to 75–80 percent of GDP, equivalent to another Argentina abroad. Capital flight of that scale can impede growth, erode the tax base, and worsen income distribution.

These traits that characterize Argentina are partly the result of globalization. Between 1809 and 1929, Argentina's integration in the world economy "appeared to be a marriage made in heaven and blessed by the Invisible Hand (Donghi 2002, p. 22)." The country was relatively independent, economically speaking, exporting grains and beef, and experiencing a prosperous period of industrialization. Fast forward to the late 1990s, when the international value for grains and beef plunged, the country was forced to shift its economy toward supplying primary commodities like soy and minerals instead – items that are much lower on the global commodity chain. At the same time, international investments marched toward Asia's economic tigers putting Argentina's industries in an even tighter bind (Katz 2019).

Another aspect is that Argentina's level of politicization and political involvement is higher than in most countries: strong social movements and influential labor organizations set the country apart. Rarely a day goes by in Buenos Aires without a protest. In recent years, the women's movement have gained in strength – sparked by the battle for abortion rights – which brought millions to the streets. Unions and workers demand wage adjustments in response to the high rates of inflation, in addition to the reversal of massive layoffs of government workers. Since the democratic transition in 1983, there have been 40 general strikes, five of which took place during Macri's presidency (Katz 2019). France is perhaps the only country with comparable political involvement.

In a study on social movements, the Argentine sociologist Sebastián Pereyra (2016) finds that protestors' demands have changed since the 1980s. Pereyra assembled a database that captures a total of 10,679 protests between 1984 and 2007 across the country. He finds that over time, the share of protests organized by labor unions has decreased. In 1989, labor unions organized about 74 percent of all protests. By 2003, just about 16 percent. He attributes this shift to the deterioration of the formal labor market in the 1990s and the subsequent increase in informal and precarious jobs, which led to a decline in the political weight of labor unions. Whereas demands for improved labor conditions remain at the top of the list, calls for greater justice in access to urban land and housing have been increasingly on the agenda of social and protest movements.

Early inequality trajectories

Argentina's experience with inequality is somewhat distinct from the rest of the region as well. Despite recent increases, income inequality is relatively low and social and fiscal spending is progressive, at least compared to LA standards. Historians would argue that colonial experiences explain this difference. Argentina did not have large plantations and mining activities that employed forced labor, as was the case in Peru or Brazil. Like in North America, land was cheap and labor scarce, and fertile soil and good weather conditions attracted migrants. These conditions might have explained the success of Argentina up to 1913. Starting in the 1970s, however, Argentina's "European" income distribution with a large middle class and low inequality moved closer to the "Latin American" model, with vast disparities (Gasparini and Cruces 2013).

Argentina's commitment to equality and protection of the working class first gained steam with Juan Perón. Intending to promote industrialization, first as minister of labor in the military government from 1943 to 1945 and then as president from 1946 to 1955, he expanded the role of the public sector, grew the functions of each ministry, and took over public utilities. Unprecedented investment in social protection and public services followed suit, with the national budget for education alone rising from 6 to nearly 15 percent by the end of his term. He expanded the public pension system's coverage to address old age poverty. Argentina pioneered the LA version of the Bismarckian social security system.[4] Thanks to Perón's commitment to a strong welfare state, Argentina soon climbed the ranks in economic terms but also in improved living standards (Novick and Villafañe 2011).

Also notable was the rising labor movement at the time, which grew from half a million members in 1945 to two and a half in a matter of ten years (Collier and Collier 1991). Perón created pathways to integrate the labor movement into the government and provided a legal framework for their protection. The labor movement and unions continued to gain strength during the 18-year interregnum between the fall and restoration of Perón's administration. A network of hotels, hospitals, and health care centers for union members was created, financed by their contributions. Much of this network can still be admired today, although the suppression of the labor movement in later years left much of that infrastructure in shambles.

Perón also overhauled fiscal policy with a clear redistributive objective. He raised taxes on top incomes from 7 to 22 percent. Income tax collection grew, reaching 2.7 percent of GDP, compared to 0.7 percent in the previous decade. Despite these reforms, the government still had to tap into social security funds to cover the growing public expenditure. The increasing fiscal imbalances led to inflation, reaching nearly 10 percent of GDP in 1949. The economy sputtered to a halt, failing to achieve the promises of steady growth in the years to follow (ibid).

In the mid-1970s, Argentina's social welfare state suffered a severe setback with the start of a military regime. Jorge Videla's government was responsible for numerous human rights abuses during Argentina's "Dirty War," which resulted in the deaths of thousands of civilians. He eradicated the welfare state by privatizing public services, cutting social protection, and weakening labor movements and unions. With lower tax collection and rising inflation, the working class and people with fewer resources suffered enormously. In 1979, employers were no longer required to contribute to the national housing system (FONAVI), and the public housing program was dismantled. With this sharp turn in social and fiscal policy, inequality increased (Azpiazu and Basualdo 2004).

In the 1980s, democracy returned with the election of Raúl Alfonsin as president in 1983, and with that investment in social policy. Labor institutions and unions re-emerged, the minimum wage was reestablished, and collective bargaining gained strength once again. However, these changes were far from stable because the macroeconomic situation was on shaky grounds, and social spending was volatile to GDP growth and became pro-cyclical. Inequality remained relatively stable during this time (Gasparini and Cruces 2013).

The late 1980s were marked by a macroeconomic crisis with two hyperinflations, one in mid-1989 and one at the beginning of 1990. Economic output fell 11 percent between 1988 and 1990, and the annual inflation rates reached an unimaginable height with 343, 3080, and 2314 percent for 1988,

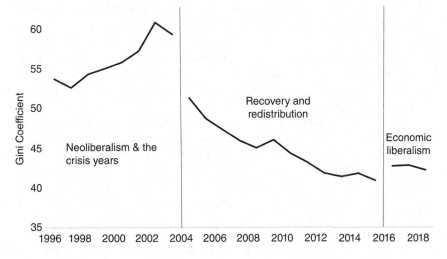

Figure 2.5 The rise and fall of inequality in Argentina (1996–2018)

Data sources: Calculated from the EPH household survey (INDEC).

Note: 1996 is chosen as the first year because that is when disaggregated and comparable data at the city level were first available.

1989, and 1990, with devastating effects on people's living standards. In just one year, between 1988 and 1989, poverty increased by 25 percentage points. Inequality had been rising steadily between the 1985 stabilization and the 1989 hyperinflation-induced jump (ibid).

Few long-term analyses about inequality exist before the 1990s due to the scarcity of microdata. One of the first studies was conducted by the United Nations Economic Commission for Latin America and the Caribbean (ECLAC), the Spanish acronym is CEPAL, in the 1970s. In the 1990s, data on socioeconomic conditions were more widely and consistently collected. More data-driven inequality studies would follow, likely also because of the drastic increase in poverty and inequality during that decade. Among others, the economists Oscar Altimir and Luis Beccaría (1999) and Leonardo Gasparini (1999) provided empirical evidence on the level, trends, and characteristics of inequality. Figure 2.5 depicts the evolution of income inequality in Argentina since 1996, when disaggregated and comparable data were first available at the city level.

Neoliberalism and the crisis years

Argentina embraced a drastic economic reform effort at the beginning of the 1990s to avoid a revival of the hyperinflation experienced in the late 1980s. In April 1991, the government adopted a fixed exchange rate pegging the peso at a one-to-one rate with the US dollar. A currency board was put into place to rule the exchange rate and monetary policies. The banking system became dollarized, and the exchange rate appreciated.

The government also adopted a series of deeply neoliberal policies to shrink the role of the state and reduce public spending. These reforms included massive privatization of public services, deep financial liberalization, the deregulation of domestic markets, and strict monetary policy. Argentina soon became known as the "poster child" of international financial institutions like the World Bank and the IMF, who had imposed many of these policies through lending programs (Cohen and Gutman 2002).

At first, deflation and fast economic recovery seemed to prove this policy cocktail of the Washington Consensus right. Yet, the early success of financial stabilization and economic expansion was short-lived, and a period of stagnation and increased financial fragility would soon follow, ultimately landing the country in a deep economic crisis (Frenkel 2002). Following the trails of economic crises in Southeast Asia in 1997 and Russia in early 1998, the economic recession fully unfolded in Argentina in 1998.

The accumulation of internal and external debt was yet another contributor to the financial predicament. Between 1976 and 2001, the country's debt multiplied nearly 20 times, augmenting from less than US$8 billion to almost US$160 billion. In the same period, Argentina reimbursed lenders by around US$200 billion or around 25 times what it owed in March 1976. Argentine sociologist Adriana Clemente (2002) estimates that in 2001, about 60 percent of the requested IMF loan would go to the next installment of the ongoing debt. The US$18 million that the state "earned" from privatization were used to shrink the fiscal deficit.

The trade reforms and changes in relative prices increased competition by imported goods and a strong upswing in the ratio between average wages and the cost of capital goods, leading to a drop in the demand of domestic labor. Even in the early expansionary period, demand increases could not offset the displacement of domestic production by imported goods. The privatization of state enterprises pushed more people out of the formal labor market into informality or unemployment. In the years between 1990 and 1998, the workforce in public enterprises was cut by 70 percent as offices closed or were handed to the private sector. Incomes dropped across the board, and unemployment more than doubled (Frenkel 2002). In 2000, average labor incomes were 11 percent lower than in 1994. The unemployment rate rose from 6.3 percent in 1991 to 14.7 percent by late 2000 (Beccaria and Maurizio 2003). Income inequality deepened.

Across the country, people voiced their anger with the economic and political situation in the streets. As the economic recession worsened, political demonstrations, police violence, and the death of 29 protestors brought President de la Rúa's administration to a dramatic end in December 2001, well before completing his constitutional term, which had begun at the end of 1999. In the two weeks that followed, the country had four different presidents. By Christmas of 2001, 15 million people, or upwards of 40 percent of the population, had fallen into poverty (Cohen and Gutman 2002).

This experience demonstrates that the proclaimed benefits of the neoliberal model don't materialize. Instead of economic prosperity and a better functioning state, the income distribution was at its worst in 2002 since data collection began in the 1970s. In Buenos Aires, the richest 10 percent of the population received 37.3 percent of total income, while the poorest 10 percent received only 1.3 percent. Unemployment reached nearly 24 percent. More than 3.7 million people fell into poverty, of which 80 percent came from the middle class.

The post-neoliberal period: strikes in fighting inequality

By January 2002, Argentina defaulted (the largest sovereign default in history) and devalued its currency by 300 percent. Poverty shot up to over 50 percent and inequality reached historic highs. Argentinians from different social and economic classes took to the streets and proclaimed that the time had arrived and, with one voice, demanded "everybody out" of the political elite (que se vayan todos), as public trust in the political system reached historically low levels (Cohen 2012).

The years following the crisis embody a profound rupture with the pro-market structural adjustment policies of the 1990s. Traumatized by the aftershocks of the crisis and the widespread social and economic turmoil it has caused, 2003 launched a series of new approaches meant to reactivate the economy with a clear redistributive objective (Catenazzi et al. 2020). The break with the Convertibility Plan (the currency board) and the peso's devaluation opened a new era in Argentina's economic history, which overlapped in political terms with the revival of Peronism with the election of Néstor Kirchner in May 2003. It marked the beginning of the so-called *Kirchnerismo*, a political movement based on populist ideas formed by Néstor Kirchner and his wife, Cristina Kirchner, who consecutively served as presidents until 2015.

Néstor Kirchner opened his inaugural ceremony with the promise to "turn a page in history," leaving behind the neoliberal model that led to "the consolidation of poverty and the condemnation of millions of Argentines to social exclusion, [to] national fragmentation, and an enormous and endless external debt (2003)."

Reducing a highly debilitating public debt – 140 percent of GDP – was high on Kirchner's agenda. To the surprise of financial analysts worldwide, Kirchner paid off the entire debt owed to the IMF in January 2006 (US$9.81 billion in one payment), well ahead of the 2008 deadline. One concern was that the IMF could continue to influence the country's financial planning unless the debt was paid. In a highly critical speech in 2005, Kirchner accused the IMF of having brought "exclusion, poverty, indigence, and the destruction of the productive apparatus" to Argentina and declared that the repayment of the debt represented a "transcendental step, which will... ... help us build a more just, inclusive and equitable future."

The break with the neoliberal period and the new macroeconomic approach accelerated economic and manufacturing growth, around 8 and 9 percent, respectively, with new companies mushrooming in the early years of Kirchner's presidency. According to the government's Observatory of Employment and

Business Dynamics (OEDE-MTEySS), the growth rate of new companies in the manufacturing sector increased by as much as 42 percent by 2007. People's incomes recovered, poverty declined, and unemployment dropped.

The Kirchner administration took a more proactive role in foreign trade policy, prioritizing relations with countries of similar development tending to protect local production sectors. They also re-prioritized the national scientific and technological sectors, increasing funding to institutions such as the CONICET, Argentina's National Scientific and Technical Research Council (Santarcángelo et al. 2018).

Cristina Kirchner assumed office in December 2007. Shortly into her first term, some macroeconomic, social, and even political tensions emerged, including the farm crisis that pitted the government and a proposed agricultural tax bill against the powerful agro-export sector. The government would lose the battle, but the conflict was a watershed moment and a moral victory for Kirchnerismo, giving birth to a political tale centered on the antagonism between "the people and the oligarchy (ibid)."

In 2008, the international financial crisis brought negative growth rates for the first time since 2003. To bolster the harmful effects of the crisis, the government implemented comprehensive policies to recover the industrial sector and, with it, the entire economy. Nestór's death in October 2010 injected an additional dose of mysticism into the Kirchner formula, bringing it into line with the overall tone of the Pink Tide.

One of the most important achievements during the Kirchner administrations was the decline in income inequality. Between 2003 and 2006, inequality declined more sharply in Argentina than in any other country in the region. Although the exact evolution of the Gini coefficient is disputable due to alterations in the national data collection process, a sharp decline in inequality is undeniable (Cornia 2009). Several factors contributed to this reduction in inequality.

First, the reactivation of the economy and the creation of upwards of four million jobs decreased unemployment dramatically. The share of people working in the informal sector also declined, but only marginally. In 1998, 41.6 percent of workers were informal; in 2013, that share dropped to 39.4 percent (Santarcángelo et al. 2018).

The beginning of Kirchnerismo also represented a turn toward a pro-labor and pro-poor government that strengthened labor and unions and supported collective bargaining efforts. These factors are crucial to smoothing unequal power dynamics between workers and employers and reducing inequality (Maurizio 2014). One of these changes included an overhaul of the minimum wage policy in 2003. Amarante and Prado (2017) estimate that about one-third of the decline in the Gini coefficient between 2003 and 2012 is attributable to changes in the minimum wage. Between 2008 and 2012 alone, the minimum wage increased by more than 200 percent (in real terms). Argentina had one of the region's highest minimum wages in 2012, equivalent to about half of median wages in the formal sector.

Another pillar in reducing inequality was the focus on social protection. One of the most effective policies was the Asignación Universal por Hijo

(AUH, universal child allowance). Upon its launch in 2009, it benefited about 1.65 million households, about 17 percent of the total population. Its most important feature is that it expanded family allowances to parts of the population previously excluded, such as families of unemployed workers, informal workers, domestic workers, and self-employed workers participating in the tax and contribution payment regime for small-scale contributors (monotributo) (Maurizio and Vázquez 2014).

The AUH provides benefits for children up to the age of 18 (no age limit for people with a disability), and up to five children per family, provided that beneficiaries fulfil certain health (such as vaccination) and educational (school attendance) requirements. Initially, it granted US$53 a month for each child. Studies suggest that the cash transfers helped increase real incomes of the poorest 40 percent of the population by 187 percent between 2002 and 2015, with huge effects on reducing poverty (Jiménez and Jiménez 2016).

The expansion of the social protection system also included an overhaul of the pension system, to cover individuals working in the informal sector and people with disabilities. Subsidies were introduced to keep tariffs on electricity and transportation low, and public investment in public services such as health and education multiplied. The Argentine economist Dario Rossignolo (2016) finds that in-kind transfers in education and health alone reduced the Gini by 24 percent from the market income Gini. When pensions and other transfers are added to the equation, the impact is even higher.

The rapid economic growth with rising employment, combined with a change in fiscal policy, an improvement in the distribution of human capital and social expenditures, and a reform of labor market policies all contributed to reducing inequality.

But some of the accomplishments slowed down in late 2011 when Argentina's economy stagnated. The balance of payments became negative, and the erratic management of the energy policy led to a loss of fuel self-sufficiency (Amico 2013). Plus, the international context became increasingly difficult, as Argentina's primary trading partner Brazil faced economic challenges, affecting the demand for Argentine products.

Economic liberalism: 2015–2018

In 2014, the reduction in inequality slowed down, and household survey data suggest that it has been increasing thereafter. Inequality and poverty appear to be resurging following the election of Mauricio Macri and the Cambiemos government in 2015, a conservative and market-oriented government promising lower inflation, stabilized monetary policy, and zero poverty. Actions, however, did not follow suit. Ill-suited policy decisions, such as deregulation and labor flexibilization, led to astronomic debt and resorting to foreign borrowing, which resembled the politics and economic decision-making practiced in the neoliberal nineties. Macri's government rolled back taxes on agricultural exports, primarily soy, which New School Professor Michael A. Cohen (2019) calls "one of the most critical decisions in the downward spiral." The resulting drop in public revenue (about US$2 billion per year) created a huge federal deficit.

Macri however did not privatize assets nationalized under the previous government (e.g., Aerolíneas Argentinas, YPF) and maintained sector-level collective bargaining. He also refrained from cutting social programs like the AUH or the noncontributory pensions. Instead, Macri tapped international credit markets to bridge the fiscal gap. Macri's pro-market discourse turned him into an emerging market darling. In his first two years in office, Argentina borrowed US$85 billion (ibid).

In 2015, debt repayment stood at 40 percent of GDP. In 2019, the level of public debt reached 100 percent of GDP (Katz 2019). According to Katz (2019), the massive debt accumulation spurred capital flight. The use of debt issuance to finance fiscal accounts, combined with a continuing depreciation of the exchange rate, caused investors to doubt the country's ability to cover upcoming maturities. This insecurity in the financial market triggered a run on the currency. As Katz states, "[w]hat happens is the state takes on debt, it sells bonds on the market, and Argentine capitalists take out dollars and relocate their money abroad. Argentina is exceptional in terms of the amount of wealth held abroad, and this phenomenon has accelerated dramatically under President Macri. Using debt to finance capital flight is a recipe for a nationwide collapse."

In September 2018, Macri's government took on the "biggest loan in the history of the IMF" to shoring up the country's weak finances: US$57.1bn, equivalent to 12 percent of GDP, to be disbursed over the next three years (Goñi 2018). The IMF package came with a set of demands for a strict reduction of public spending, trade liberalization, a slashing of labor regulations, and cuts in retirement benefits.

Instead of achieving zero poverty as the government had promised, rising inflation increased the cost of public services such as water, electricity, gas, transport, and food. Between 2015 and 2018, the cost of food alone increased by 106 percent (CEC 2018). The cost of water increased by 680 percent, and of electricity by 1,317 percent between 2015 and 2019 (Davis 2019). What followed is a déjà vu of the early 2000s: inflation rates climbed further reaching 50 percent, 40 small businesses closed daily, 70 percent interest rates suffocated the already fragile industrial sector, and wages plummeted to their lowest level in decades. In 2019, 35 percent of Argentines lived in poverty. In metropolitan Buenos Aires, 60 percent of the population reduced their food consumption (Cohen 2019). Children were among the most affected. Data from Indec suggest that in 2019, 52.6 percent of children under the age of 15 lived in poverty, and houselessness involving children rose from 8 to 13 percent.

The election of Alberto Fernandez as president (and Cristina Kirchner as vice president) in October 2019 represents a return to a Peronist government and a rejection of Macri's economic and social policies. With the new government, rising expectations on social justice, poverty, and inequality returned to the center of the government's attention. As part of his proposal for government, Fernandez introduced the plan "Argentina contra el hambre" (Argentina against hunger), proposing a set of policies and programs to reduce inequality and poverty.

In November 2020, Fernández reaffirmed his commitment to repeat the successes of Néstor Kirchner's presidency, bringing economic growth and social justice back to Argentina. However, the days of the commodity boom of the early 2000s are long gone. The value of Argentine exports fell by 40 percent between their peak in 2011 and October 2020, and the COVID-19 pandemic and ongoing pressure from the IMF cast a menacing shadow over Argentina's prospects of economic recovery and lower inequality. The regional and national context has also changed dramatically, which further complicates Fernández's task.

Conclusion

Over the past decades, economic inequality has risen in countries across the world, becoming one of the key global challenges. Throughout the twentieth century and still today, Latin America has some of the world's highest inequality.

This chapter describes the evolution of inequality in Latin America, with a focus on Argentina. It first compares Latin America to other parts of the world and identifies factors contributing to the dynamics that make it so unequal. While some forms of economic inequality, especially land and asset ownership, are deeply rooted in the region's colonial past, the chapter is mainly concerned with the more recent history, starting in the late twentieth century.

Especially the 1980s have been influential in deepening poverty and inequality. This period, frequently referred to as "the lost decade," was characterized by low economic growth, fiscal crises, deep cuts to public services, and inflation. The macroeconomic volatility at the time opened the door for structural adjustment, a set of neoliberal policy reforms including massive privatization, deregulation, and trade liberalization, a toxic cocktail that pushed millions into poverty and widened the gap between the haves and the have nots.

Yet something remarkable happened in the first decade and a half of the twenty-first century, when Latin America became one of the world's examples of how governments can tackle inequality. Inequality scholar and activist Ben Phillips (2020) suggests that these achievements in reducing poverty and inequality were driven by social movements demanding change, which led to the election of center-left governments, referred to as the Pink Tide. To address inequality, they used a mix of policies including new approaches to macroeconomic policy, economic recovery and growth, labor protections, the introduction of progressive fiscal policy and tax reforms, and the expansion of social protection measures.

In some ways, Argentina is not a typical representation of the region, as inequality is lower and social and fiscal spending is more progressive. But the large swings of rising and falling inequality experienced in Latin America after the 1970s are very much a reflection of trends in Argentina. Political mismanagement led to economic crises, hyperinflation, deteriorating living standards, and impoverishment of broad swaths of the population in the 1980s. In the first half of the twenty-first century, Argentina recorded some of the largest gains in reducing inequality. But unfavorable terms of trade and a sub-siding commodity boom hit the country hard after 2012 and reversed some of the earlier gains. The progress in tackling inequality did not get everything right and has suffered a swing back both in political terms and in inequality but provides many important lessons on what ought to change for more lasting impact.

Years before the COVID-19 pandemic, poverty and inequality gains had already slowed in the region and in some countries reversed. Part of the setbacks across the region can be attributed to inadequate targeting of government and social spending, and systems of collecting taxes which remain regressive and have done little to improve inequality. The COVID-19 shock, which is still playing out, has already worsened short-term poverty and inequality dynam-ics. It requires governments committed to economic and social justice to use the pandemic to rethink policies and practices that can address structural ine-qualities, rather than reinforce pre-existing disparities.

Notes

1 Milanovic estimates that the global Gini coefficient, the most commonly used indi-cator to measure income inequality, fell from 72.2 in 1988 to 67 in 2011.
2 While the US$5.50 per day poverty threshold is more adequate than the US$1.90 cutoff, it still only yields an annual income of a bit more than US$2,000, which could hardly be considered livable. Several scholars have critiqued the World Bank's poverty thresholds and advocated for measures that more adequately cap-ture people's needs (see Alston 2020).
3 Latinobarómetro is a Santiago de Chile based non-governmental organization conducting annual surveys on Latin American public opinion.
4 Otto von Bismarck, the first Chancellor of the German Empire in 1871, is consid-ered the creator of the first modern welfare state. It should be noted that Bismarck had different motives than Perón, given that he created the welfare system to pre-vent a radical socialist takeover rather than in the interest of bettering people's living standards.

References

Acemoglu, Daron, Simon Johnson, and James A. Robinson. 2002. "Reversal of Fortune: Geography and Institutions in the Making of the Modern World Income Distribution." *The Quarterly Journal of Economics* 117 (4): 1231–94.
Alston, Philip. 2020. "Report on the Parlous State of Poverty Eradication." *United Nations Office of the High Commissioner.* A/HRC/44/40.
Amico, Fabián. 2013. "Crecimiento, distribución y restricción externa en Argentina." *Circus, Revista Argentina de Economía* 5: 31–80.
Altimir, Oscar, and Luis Alberto Beccaría. 1999. "Distribución del ingreso en la Argentina." Serie Reformas Económicas. Santiago, Chile: CEPAL.
Alvaredo, Facundo, Lucas Chancel, Thomas Piketty, Emmanuel Saez, and Gabriel Zucman. 2018. World Inequality Report 2018. Paris: World Inequality Lab.

Amarante, Verónica, and Antonio Prado. 2017. "Inequality in Latin America: ECLAC's Perspective." In Bértola L., Williamson J. (eds). *Has Latin American Inequality Changed Direction?*, 285–315. Cham: Springer.

Azpiazu, Daniel, and Eduardo Basualdo. 2004. "Las privatizaciones en la Argentina. Génesis, desarrollo y principales impactos estructurales." In *Las privatizaciones y la desnacionalización de América*. Latina, Buenos Aires: Ediciones Prometeo.

Balakrishnan, Ravi, Sandra Lizarazo, Marika Santoro, Frederik Toscani, and Mauricio Vargas. 2021. *Commodity Cycles, Inequality, and Poverty in Latin America*. Washington, DC: International Monetary Fund.

Beccaria, Luis, and Roxana Maurizio. 2003. *Movilidad ocupacional en Argentina*. Zapopan: Instituto de Ciencias, Universidad Nacional de General Sarmiento.

Bottan, Nicolas, Bridget Hoffmann, and Diego Vera-Cossio. 2020. "The Unequal Impact of the Coronavirus Pandemic: Evidence from Seventeen Developing Countries." *PloS One* 15 (10): e0239797.

Catenazzi, Andrea, Eduardo Reese, and Agustin Manuel Mango. 2020. "Argentina: 20 Years of Habitat II: The Pending Subjects." In *Urban Policy in Latin America: Towards the Sustainable Development Goals?* New York, NY: Routledge.

CEC. 2018. "Informe de Coyuntura n° 16 – Restricción de la asistencia alimentaria en tiempos de hambre." *Centro de studio de Ciudad*. Available at: http://cec.sociales.uba. ar/?p=1294, accessed November 28, 2021.

Clemente, Andrea. 2002. "The Crisis and the Social Question in Argentina: Notes for the Debate." In *Argentina in Collapse: The Americas Debate*, edited by M. Cohen and Margarita Gutman. New York, NY: The New School.

Cohen, Michael A. 2012. *Argentina's Economic Growth and Recovery: The Economy in a Time of Default*. Oxfordshire: Routledge.

_____. 2019. "Assessing the Macri Legacy." In *Public Seminar (Blog)*. September 17. http://www.publicseminar.org/essays/assessing-the-macri-legacy-2/

Cohen, Michael A., and Margarita Gutman. 2002. "Argentina in Collapse." In *The Americas Debate*. New York, NY: The New School.

Collier, Ruth B., and David Collier. 1991. "Critical Junctures and Historical Legacies." In *Shaping the Political Arena: Critical Junctures, The Labor Movement, and Regime Dynamics in Latin America*. Princeton, NJ: Princeton University Press.

Corbacho, Ana, Vicente Fretes, and Eduardo Lora. 2013. *Recaudar no basta: los impuestos como instrumento de desarrollo*. Washington, DC: *Banco Interamericano de Desarrollo*.

Cornia, Giovanni Andrea. 2009. "Income Distribution under Latin America's New Left Regime." *Journal of Human Development and Capabilities* 11 (1): 85–114.

_____. 2011. "Economic Integration, Inequality and Growth: Latin America vs. the European Economies in Transition." United Nations Department of Economics and Social Affairs Working Paper No. 101. New York: UNDESA.

_____. 2014. *Falling Inequality in Latin America: Policy Changes and Lessons. WIDER Studies in Development Economics*. Oxford, New York, NY: Oxford University Press.

Credit Suisse. 2021. *Global Wealth Report 2021*. Zurich:Credit Suisse Research Institute.

Davis, Julian White. 2019. "Government Approves Price Increases in Electricity, Gas, Transportation in 2019." *The Bubble*.

De Soto, Hernando. 2001. "The Mystery of Capital." *Finance & Development, IMF*. March 2001, Volume 38, Number 1. Available at: https://www.imf.org/external/pubs/ft/fandd/2001/03/desoto.htm, accessed November 28, 2021.

Donghi, Tulio Halperin. 2002. "Why Did Argentina Adopt a Neoliberal Model?" In *Argentina in Collapse: The America*, edited by M. Coehn and Margarita Gutman. New York, NY: The New School.

Economic Commission for Latin America and the Caribbean (ECLAC). 2014. *Economic Survey of Latin America and the Caribbean*, 2014 (LC/G.2619-P), Santiago, Chile: United Nations Publication.

Engerman, S. L. and Sokoloff, K. L. 2005. "Colonialism, Inequality, and Long-Run Paths of Development." In *Working Paper 11057*. Cambridge, MA: National Bureau of Economic Research.

Feierherd, Germán, Patricio Larroulet, Wei Long, and Nora Lustig. 2021. "The Pink Tide and Inequality in Latin America." In *CEQ Working Paper 105, Commitment to Equity Institute*. Louisiana, LA: Tulane University.

Ferreira, Francisco HG, Julian Messina, Jamele Rigolini, Luis-Felipe López-Calva, Maria Ana Lugo, Renos Vakis, and Luis Felipe Ló. 2013. *Economic Mobility and the Rise of the Latin American Middle Class*. Washington, DC: World Bank Publications.

Ffrench-Davis, Ricardo. 2005. "Reforming Latin America's Economies." *After Market Fundamentalism*. Basingstoke, New York, NY: Palgrave.

Frankema, Ewout. 2010. "The Colonial Roots of Land Inequality: Geography, Factor Endowments, or Institutions?" *The Economic History Review* 63 (2): 418–51.

Frenkel, Roberto. 2002. "Argentina: A Decade of the Convertibility Regime." *Challenge* 45 (4): 41–59.

Gasparini, Leonardo. 1999. "Desigualdad en la distribución del ingreso y bienestar. Estimaciones para la Argentina." In *La distribución del ingreso en la Argentina*, 35–83. Buenos Aires, Argentina: Fundación de Investigaciones Económicas Latinoamericanas.

Gasparini, Leonardo, and Guillermo Cruces. 2013. "Poverty and Inequality in Latin America: A Story of Two Decades." *Journal of International Affairs*, vol. 66, no. 2, Journal of International Affairs Editorial Board: pp.51–63.

Gasparini, Leonardo, and Nora Lustig. 2011. "The Rise and Fall of Income Inequality in Latin America." In *The Oxford Handbook of Latin American Economics, Edited by: José Antonio Ocampo and Jaime Ros. Oxford, England: Oxford University Press.*

Goñi, Uki. 2018. "Argentina Gets Biggest Loan in IMF's History at $57bn." *The Guardian*, 26 September 2018. https://www.theguardian.com/world/2018/sep/26/argentina-imf-biggest-loan

Hanni, Michael Stephen, Ricardo Martner, and Andrea Podesta. 2015. "The Redistributive Potential of Taxation in Latin America."*Cepal Review* 116. Santiago, Chile: United Nations publication.

Inchauste, Gabriela, João Pedro Azevedo, Sergio Olivieri, Jaime Saavedra, and Hernan Winkler. 2012. *When Job Earnings Are Behind Poverty Reduction. No. 17067*. Washington, DC: The World Bank.

Indec. 2020. *Bases de Datos*. Argentina: INDEC.

Jiménez, Maribel, and Mónica Jiménez. 2016. "Efectos del programa Asignación Universal por Hijo en la deserción escolar adolescente." *Cuadernos de Economía* 35(69): 709–752.

Katz, Claudio. 2019. "Argentina in Its Labyrinth." *Jacobin*, June 2019. https://jacobinmag.com/2019/06/argentina-macri-imf-austerity-kirchner

Kirchner, Néstor. 2003. "Discurso de asunción del Presidente Néstor Kirchner." *Cristina Fernández de Kirchner*, May 25, 2003, https://www.cfkargentina.com/discurso-de-asuncion-del-presidente-nestor-kirchner-a-la-asamblea-legislativa-el-25-de-mayo-del-2003/

Kirchner, Néstor. 2005. "Palabras del Presidente de la Nación, Néstor Kirchner, en el Acto de anuncio del Plan de Desendeudamiento con el Fondo Monetario Internacional." *Casa Rosada*, 15 December 2005, https://www.casarosada.gob.ar/informacion/archivo/24862-blank-41184041

Latinobarómetro. 2018. "Datos." Available at: https://www.latinobarometro.org/latContents.jsp, accessed November 28, 2021.

Lustig, Nora, Carola Pessino, and John Scott. 2013. "The Impact of Taxes and Social Spending on Inequality and Poverty in Argentina, Bolivia, Brazil, Mexico, Peru and Uruguay: An Overview," Working Papers 1313, Tulane University, Department of Economics.

Lustig, Nora, Valentina Martinez Pabon, Federico Sanz, and Stephen D. Younger. 2020. "The Impact of COVID-19 Lockdowns and Expanded Social Assistance on Inequality, Poverty and Mobility in Argentina, Brazil, Colombia and Mexico." In *Working Paper No. 558*. Polma de Mallorca: ECINEQ, Society for the Study of Economic Inequality.

Mahon, James E. 2018. "Taxation, Redistribution, and Models of Fiscal Politics in Latin America." *Japanese Journal of Political Science* 19 (3): 353–75.

Maurizio, Roxana. 2014. *Labor Formalization and Declining Inequality in Argentina and Brazil in the 2000s: A Dynamic Approach.* Geneva: International Labor Office.

Maurizio, Roxana, and Gustavo Vázquez. 2014. "Argentina: efectos del programa Asignación Universal por Hijo en el comportamiento laboral de los adultos." In *Revista Cepal* 113. Santiago, Chile: United Nations publication.

Milanovic, Branko. 2016. *Global Inequality: A New Approach for the Age of Globalization.* Cambridge, MA: Harvard University Press.

Minujin, Alberto. 1996. *Desigualdad y Exclusion.* Buenos Aires: UNICEF.

Novick, Marta, and Soledad Villafañe. 2011. *Distribución del ingreso: enfoques y políticas públicas desde el Sur.* Buenos Aires, Argentina: UNDP Argentina, Ministerio de Trabajo, Empleo y Seguridad Social, Presidencia de la Nación.

Ocampo, José Antonio. 2012. *The Development Implications of External Integration in Latin America.* WIDER Working Paper 2012/048 Helsinki: UNU-WIDER.

Panizza, Francisco. 2005. "Unarmed Utopia Revisited: The Resurgence of Left-of-centre Politics in Latin America." *Political Studies* 53 (4): 716–34.

Pereyra, Sebastian. 2016. "La estructura social y la movilizacion. Conflictos politicos y demandas sociales." In *La Sociedad argentina hoy: radiografia de una nueva estructura, by Gabriel Kessler.* Buenos Aires, Argentina: Siglo Veintiuno Editores.

Phillips, Ben. 2020. *How to Fight Inequality: (and Why That Fight Needs You).* Oxford: Polity Press.

Rossignolo, Darío. 2016. "Taxes, Expenditures, Poverty and Income Distribution in Argentina." In *CEQ Working Paper 30.* New Orleans, LA: Tulane University.

Santarcángelo, Juan E., Daniel Schteingart, and Fernando Porta. 2018. "Industrial Policy in Argentina, Brazil, Chile and Mexico: A Comparative Approach." *Revue Interventions économiques. Papers in Political Economy* 59. Available at: https://journals.openedition.org/interventionseconomiques/3852#quotation, accessed November 28, 2021.

Stiglitz, Joseph E. 2002. *Globalization and Its Discontents.* New York, NY: W. W. Norton & Company.

UN-Habitat. 2014. *Construction of More Equitable Cities.* Nairobi, Kenya: United Nations Human Settlements Programme, CAF, and Avina.

Williamson, Jeffrey G. 2015. "Latin American Inequality: Colonial Origins, Commodity Booms or a Missed Twentieth-Century Leveling?." *Journal of Human Development and Capabilities* 16.3: 324–341.

World Bank. 2021. *World Development Indicators.* DataBank. The World Bank Group. Available at: https://databank.worldbank.org/source/world-development-indicators

World Inequality Database. 2021. *WID.World.* Available at: https://wid.world/data/

3 Old and new forms of intra-urban inequality

More people than ever before live in cities. In 2020, 56.2 percent of the world population resided in urban areas, a steep increase from just 46 percent about 20 years before (World Bank 2021). UN figures (2018) suggest that the share of people living in cities will increase further, reaching close to 70 percent by 2050. This rapid urbanization process adds three million people to cities every week. In other words, more than 400,000 people – about the size of Lisbon – are moving to cities every single day. Cities have also become the drivers of national economic growth, contributing to over 80 percent of global GDP. In Organisation for Economic Co-operation and Development (OECD) member countries, cities have contributed 60 percent of total employment creation in the past 15 years (OECD 2021).

However, cities' economic growth is often not distributed equitably and has fed into intra-urban divides and social exclusion. Despite the increasing wealth found in and generated by cities, we have been moving toward a "planet of slums," as Mike Davis first described in 2007. Informal housing and employment have become the blueprint of twenty-first-century urban development. Rapid urbanization has led to infrastructure stresses, and the construction boom in cities has a significant ecological impact, challenging climate goals to keep global temperature rise below 1.5°C.

This chapter reviews a set of diverse manifestations of inequalities in cities. The focus is on cities in Latin America, where informality in land, housing, and employment is high and has shaped the urbanization process. Using a global dataset of 775 cities, the chapter presents new evidence on income inequality in Latin American cities and compares it with other regions. The chapter also describes and discusses intra-urban inequality in Argentina and places trends within the country's system of cities, its political dynamics, and within the increasingly conflicted context of income and housing.

Fragmented cities and the new geography of poverty

In Europe during the Middle Ages, most people lived under manorial rule, quasi-enslavement, where the landlord of a manor owned not only the land but also the people who lived on it. For some people, the manor rule meant paying fees similar to taxes for living on the land, but others lived in conditions of

DOI: 10.4324/9781003201908-4

servitude, working without pay and with their civil rights violated. As towns and cities started to emerge and grow in the eleventh century, people began leaving the manors searching for freedom and better living conditions in cities. Many never came back, and landlords merely lost track. In an effort to turn cities into gateways to freedom, the following legal custom arose in many places: a landlord could no longer reclaim someone after the person lived "a year and a day" in a city (BR 2016). Cities turned into territories outside the feudal system and offered one of the few ways to gain freedom, self-governance, and economic autonomy. This legal custom turned into a German expression that is still commonly used today: "city air makes you free (Stadtluft macht frei)."

Fast forward to the twenty-first century. Cities continue to function as safe havens for people with different lifestyles and beliefs and offer various economic opportunities. This makes urban populations more heterogeneous in terms of ethnicity, preferences, and socioeconomic positions than rural areas. However, economic opportunities and access to infrastructure and urban amenities tend to be increasingly unevenly distributed, leading German scholars (Emunds et al. 2018) to amend that medieval expression to say that "city air makes you either rich or poor."

And while urban populations are heterogeneous, these diverse groups of people often congregate in specific neighborhoods, forming patterns of segregation. Some happen organically and are to the people's benefit. For instance, immigrants may prefer neighborhoods with a high share of immigrants due to their proximity to people of the same national, ethnic, or linguistic group, allowing for an exchange in knowledge and a foothold into a new city (Massey 1990). The presence of Chinese neighborhoods, so-called "Chinatowns," in almost every large city globally is one example. The largest and most well-known Chinatowns are in New York City, Melbourne, and Bangkok. Buenos Aires' Chinatown or Barrio chino is much smaller in size, consisting of just about five blocks in the neighborhood of Belgrano. Despite its comparatively small size, it is the core center of the Chinese community in Argentina.

However, segregation by housing conditions or employment status is rarely the result of a person's preference and instead reflects patterns of poverty and inequality. There is growing evidence that since the 1950s, territorial inequalities in cities have worsened in tandem with unemployment, social deprivation, homelessness, and health problems. A UN-Habitat (2014) study estimates that three-quarters of the world's cities had higher levels of income inequality in 2016 than two decades prior, with inequalities becoming increasingly visible.

Never before have cities appeared so starkly as they do today as nodes of economic, social, cultural, and political links within self-contained if ever-expanding spaces. Never before have so many people been attracted to these concentrations of wealth and productive capacity than today – nor these resources been so inequitably distributed that "the urban divide" between rich and poor has never looked so wide (p. 76).

The geographical concentration of households with similar income levels manifests itself also in access to basic services and infrastructure like electricity and water and sanitation, and access to quality education and health care. People living in poverty or with low incomes have little to no choice on where to live as they depend on the most affordable options. Such spatial concentrations of disadvantage can be lifelong obstacles to opportunities available for those who grow up in these spaces.

In cities in developing countries, spatial and socioeconomic marginalization is often equated with the symbolic term "slum," which, in some Spanish-speaking countries, is translated *villa miseria*, *bidonville* in French, *favela* in Brazilian Portuguese, and *shantytown* in English. Yet, behind these etymologies lies the same reality.

The contemporary city – be it planned or not, and whether well or inadequately managed – develops at the price of contradictions: though a shelter and home to families and individuals, and while serving as center for economic, cultural, and educational opportunities, the city is an arena for antagonistic struggles between individual interests and the common good, public and private, and rich and poor.

One of the most iconic photographs of the territorial manifestation of intra-urban inequality was taken by the Brazilian photojournalist Tuca Vieira in 2004. The photo portrays the boundary between the favela of Paraisópolis and the wealthy district Morumbi in São Paulo, a slum bordering a luxury high-rise apartment block, with balcony swimming pools on every floor. While the image happens to be taken in Brazil, it is symbolic of the physical, economic, and cultural divides in cities worldwide (Figure 3.1).

Figure 3.1 São Paulo, Brazil, 2005. The Paraisópolis favela borders the affluent district of Morumbi

Credit: Tuca Vieira.

"Unequal Scenes," a project by photographer Johnny Miller, who is based in South Africa and the USA, depicts the roads, canals, and fences that separate the rich and poor in cities across the world. Similar to Vieira's images of Brazil, Miller shows the powerful spatial divisions in cities, which are both the outcomes and processes of unjust local, national, and international policies and practices (Figure 3.2).

According to the United Nations (UN-Habitat 2016), one billion individuals live in slums. Five hundred and sixty million have no access to sanitation. In sub-Saharan Africa (SSA), where deprivations in terms of living conditions are the most severe, slum dwellers represent more than half – about 56 percent – of the urban population (ibid). The share is about 25 percent in Latin America, where more than 160 million people live in slums (IDB 2015).

Informality is a persistent characteristic of the current urbanization process in many low- and middle-income countries and its enduring nature raises concerns. New School Professor Michael A. Cohen (2019) refers to this as "the new geography of vulnerability." Slums are often densely populated with inadequate water, sanitation, and housing, little or no waste management, overcrowded public transport, and limited access to formal health care facilities. This explosive mix of high demand and low supply of essential services makes them particularly prone to climate change, natural disasters, new epidemics and diseases, and acute water shortages. These vulnerabilities have become highly visible during the COVID-19 pandemic. Even the most basic prevention measures, such as hand washing, social distancing, and working from home, are not possible for slum residents.

Figure 3.2 Santa Fe, Mexico. 2018. An upscale "new downtown" in the foothills of the mountains above the smog-choked center

A study by Cities Alliance (Cohen et al. 2019a) found that as many as 70 percent of people in cities in Africa, Asia, and Latin America rely on informal arrangements to procure core services. The lack of a public option means that individuals and businesses spend more time or face higher costs to treat or manage waste or rely on generators for energy, which can be prohibitively expensive. It also means that those who can least afford it pay higher rates for services.

In Cebu, the second-largest city in the Philippines, public water pipes are hard to find in low-income neighborhoods, and almost none reach slum settlements. People living in those areas, who are disproportionately low income, have to rely on the private market to purchase water, which means they pay comparatively higher water rates than middle- and high-income households. Cohen et al. (2019a) find that they in Cebu privately purchased water costs about 18 times that of the public sector.

Those who cannot afford to buy water fetch it elsewhere. This may lead to health-related consequences. Achilles Kallergis (2018) estimates that low-income households in sub-Saharan African cities spend one-third of their income on treating water-related illnesses. While nineteenth-century epidemics affected entire cities, today, waterborne-related diseases are concentrated in specific neighborhoods, predominantly affecting those with few resources.

The inequality in access to services is troubling from a human rights perspective because the lack of piped water and sanitation in low-income neighborhoods is a violation of people's rights, presenting the failure of governments to guarantee an adequate standard of living for everyone. It is also troubling from an economic view since the absence of core services harms people's economic prospects and traps them in poverty. Aside from the individual loss of productivity, it slanders the economy of an entire city.

Informality is also ubiquitous in the economy of cities. The street vendor offering water and freshly cut mangos in New York City, the driver of the okada motorcycle taxi in Lagos, the domestic worker taking care of an older person in Manila, and the informal recycler in Rio de Janeiro (see Figure 3.3) – all these workers operate in the so-called informal economy. As one can tell, the informal economy is highly diverse with the common feature that informal work is not regulated or protected by the state. Some give the unfair and inappropriate characterization that informal work is illegal. The vast majority of informal workers are trying to make an honest living against great odds, and for many, it is the only option to put food on the table and keep a roof over their heads.

Instead of an exception, informal work appears to be the norm. Worldwide, more people earn their livelihoods in the informal economy than in the formal. The first-ever global assessment of the size of informal employment in cities, published jointly by the International Labour Office (ILO) and the global network Women in Informal Employment: Globalizing and Organizing (WIEGO) in 2018, found that 50–80 percent of all workers in Asia, Africa, and Latin America operate in the "informal economy." In SSA, the informal economy comprises over three-quarters of urban employment, over half in Asia and the Pacific, and just under half in Latin America and the Caribbean.

Figure 3.3 Rio de Janeiro, Brazil. An informal recycler carrying aluminum cans on Copacabana Beach

Credit: Johnny Miller / Unequal Scenes

In the post-war fervor, the Nobel Prize winning economist W. Arthur Lewis (1954) predicted that economic development in developing countries would, in the long term, generate enough jobs to absorb surplus labor from the informal economy. But the theory that the informal economy would peter as countries grow economically has yet to happen. On the contrary, the informal economy has persisted and is increasing in many parts of the world.

In China, where the rates of economic growth and poverty reduction have been remarkable in the past two decades (before the COVID-19 pandemic), the informal economy remains large. While public data on informal urban employment are lacking, the historian Philip C.C. Huang estimates that in 2009, the informal economy in China accounted for 168 million of the 283 million workers, about 60 percent of total employment. Informal employment has also been found to expand in times of economic crises. We are currently witnessing the economic impacts of the COVID-19 pandemic as businesses downsized or shut down and workers were laid-off or unable to find alternative formal employment. This is particularly true of those who cannot afford to be unemployed, more so in countries with tattered or inexistent social safety nets.

It is almost impossible to imagine a situation where the formal economy functions without its informal counterpart. There is hardly a global supply chain that does not depend on informal workers. Few informal businesses, except perhaps some survival activities, operate in isolation. Most formally registered companies source raw materials or goods from informal businesses, either directly or through intermediaries. Take the case of the garment sector. Some workers produce for the open market selling clothes and fabric directly to individual customers, but most sell to large formal firms. The majority of the global fashion brands heavily rely on informal garment workers, which allows them to keep prices low. The contribution of the urban informal economy to national economies should thus not be underestimated. In some African countries, the urban informal economy is responsible for as much as 50–80 percent of GDP (ILO and WIEGO 2018). Mumbai's largest slum Dharavi, where one million people work and live, is said to have an estimated annual economic output of about US$600 million to US$1 billion (Yardley 2011).

Despite their invaluable contributions to local and national economies, informal workers earn less for comparable activities than formal workers. They generally have no employment security, receive few or no benefits, lack membership in formal trade unions, and are usually unprotected by labor laws. The lack of protection makes informal workers particularly prone to exploitation, precarity, and poverty. Supporting and safeguarding the rights of informal workers is thus a pathway to reducing poverty and inequality. It is also an opportunity to fight gender inequality. Women are more likely to work in the informal sector, and they tend to have more precarious and low-paid forms of employment, such as domestic or care work (Chen 2012).

The heterogeneity of informal work and living defies the ability to draw broad conclusions from the experiences of one low-income neighborhood or one type of job in isolation. Instead, we ought to consider the relationship of individual communities to the broader urban system. For example, a slum might be located in the city center, close to employment, transport, and education. Another slum might be on the periphery of the city, far from all of those opportunities, with residents who cannot afford the costs of urban transport, limiting them to lower-paying gigs in their neighborhood. A similarly distant location might be the site of a middle-class neighborhood, but its residents can afford transportation to allow access to various opportunities.

People's relationships with the prospects of the city are highly asymmetrical. Inequalities in cities are thus not just about differences in income and capital, but asymmetries in a wider contextual and social sense, such as differential access to spaces, services, opportunities, resources, and information. These asymmetries can take specific material forms, such as in the linkages between a community and the city as a whole, for example, in whether a bus line equitably services different communities. These linkages are inherently integrative because they help connect neighborhoods, households, and individuals to broader contexts, potentially overcoming social and economic exclusion (Cohen and Simet 2018).

The large presence and persistence of informality raises questions. How did we invest so many human and financial resources to better manage cities and their future without having eliminated (or at least greatly reduced) the thousand and one material and social forms of inequality and poverty?

Cities and inequality in Latin America

Latin America is the region with the highest inequality in the world. It is also the most urbanized region, with 85 percent of Latin America's population living in cities (UN 2018). Most of Latin America's urbanization occurred in the twentieth century, at an incredible speed. In just two generations – between 1950 and 2010 – the share of people living in cities grew from 30 percent to more than 80 percent. No other part of the world has urbanized more rapidly. The United Nations projects that this trend will continue and that by 2050, 90 percent of Latin Americans will be living in cities. Latin America is also home to some of the largest metropolitan areas and counts more than 55 cities with one million people or more (BBVA 2017). More than 20 million people call São Paulo their home, the region's largest metro area alongside Mexico City. Buenos Aires ranks third with 13.7 million people, followed by Rio de Janeiro, Lima, Bogotá, and Santiago.

Since the urbanization process began in the 1950s, the nature of urban growth has changed. More people moved to large and capital cities early on, but since the 1990s, mid-sized cities rather than megacities have been growing the fastest. And whereas in the twentieth century, a move from rural to urban areas characterized urbanization, today, people are frequently moving between cities of different sizes and economic compositions. The Argentine sociologist Gabriel Kessler (2016) suggests that this change has shifted the demographic nature of migration and people's financial standing. While rural-to-urban migrants are generally lower-income, urban-to-urban migrants often have similar means to those already living in cities.

Urbanization has delivered a host of social and economic benefits (see Brookings Institution 2018). But cities have struggled to manage the growth to provide an adequate quality of life for everyone. Instead, inequality has increased. Between 2005 and 2012, Argentina, Brazil, Colombia, and Peru have more than doubled their per capita GDP. Still, the Gini has not improved accordingly, and the accumulation of income at the top has skyrocketed. A 2018 report by ECLAC finds that the total income share of the wealthiest quintile ranges from 40 percent in Montevideo, La Paz, and Caracas to close to 60 percent in Santiago, Brasilia, and Santo Domingo.

Despite the vital role of cities in Latin American economies and societal structures, most available statistics on inequality and economic well-being are national aggregates. Quantitative information on how inequality has evolved in the cities is surprisingly hard to come by, especially statistics comparable to other regions. One explanation can be traced to the misleading assumption that redistributive policies are the exclusive responsibility of national governments.

To fill that void, I analyzed data from the Oxford Economics Global Cities Database of 775 cities from across the globe from 2000 to 2016. Grouping

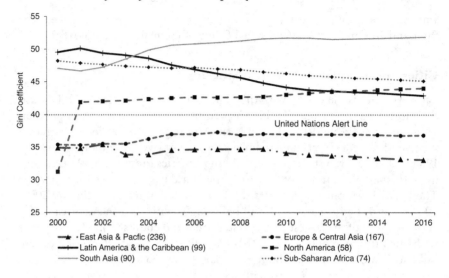

Figure 3.4 Income inequality in 775 cities by region, over time (2000–2016)

Data source: Calculated from the Oxford Economics Global Cities Database. Cities were clustered by regions, using World Bank classifications.

them by regions, I find that in cities in East Asia and the Pacific (236 cities), the Middle East and North Africa (51), and SSA (74), inequality has declined slightly since 2000, while in Europe and Central Asia and North America, inequality has increased marginally. Cities in South Asia (90) and Latin America and the Caribbean (99) indicate the most substantial changes. In South Asian cities, the Gini increased from 47 in 2000 to 52.5 in 2016. Reflecting national level trends described in Chapter 2, the average Gini for cities in Latin America has dropped from about 50 in 2000 to 43 in 2016, albeit they generally remain above the UN's alert line (Figure 3.4).

Between 2000 and 2016, inequality dropped in about two-thirds of the 99 LA cities in the sample and increased in about one-third. This trend confirms a 2014 study by UN-Habitat, which analyzed income inequality in 284 LA cities in 2010. Of the LA cities in the Oxford database, close to 30 percent had "high" to "very high inequality" in 2016 (see Table 3.1). The bulk of the cities – 46.6. percent – had "relatively high inequality" with Gini coefficients above the international alert line (40); 24.2 percent had "moderate

Table 3.1 Latin American cities clustered by inequality levels (2016)

	Low inequality (29 and below)	Moderate inequality (30–39.9)	Relatively high inequality (40–44.9)	High inequality (45–49.9)	Very high inequality (50–59.9)	Extreme inequality (60 and above)
% of cities	0.0%	24.2%	46.6%	21.2%	8.1%	0%

Data source: Calculated from the Oxford Economics Global Cities Database, clustered in inequality categories by the United Nations.

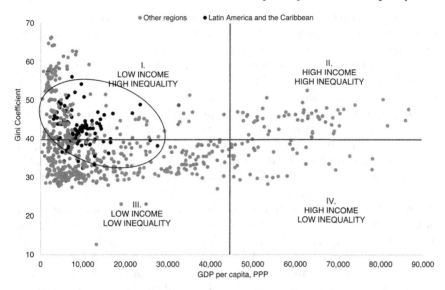

Figure 3.5 Inequality by region and GDP per capita (PPP) in 775 cities (2016)

Data source: Calculated from the Oxford Economics Global Cities Database.

Note: PPP (Purchasing power parity) is a method of accounting for differences in the cost of living when comparing national economies.

inequality," and no city had a Gini below 29, which would be considered "low inequality." [1]

Figure 3.5 groups the 775 cities by income and inequality. Although to a lesser extent than in SSA, inequality levels in Latin America are considerably dispersed, and so are income levels. Cities have GDP per capita (PPP) thresholds ranging between US$1,735 (Port-au-Prince, Haiti) and US$3,084 (Cochabamba, Bolivia) on the lower end and US$32,507 (Panama City, Panama) and US$27,567 in San Juan (Costa Rica) on the higher end. The Ginis range from 32 in the Chilean cities Valparaiso and Concepción to 54.1 in Bogotá (Colombia) 57.5 in Port-au-Prince (Haiti).

But LA cities almost exclusively fall into Quadrant I – low income and high inequality – with a few also in Quadrant II – low income and low inequality. While the statistical relationship between the Gini and income is not clear-cut, no city with a GDP per capita larger than US$20,000 has very high inequality.[2] The data indicate that efforts to reduce inequality do not necessarily affect growth, and the distribution of incomes does not automatically affect the average level of income. This finding rejects Nobel laureate Robert Lucas' (2004) claim that "inequality is necessary for growth." Instead, it confirms that we have a choice as a society to decide what kind of growth we seek and the level of inequality we consider acceptable.

Rapid urbanization in Latin America not only shaped the distribution of incomes, but it also affected people's access to public services and the physical configuration of cities. Shlomo Angel et al. (2012) at the New York University's Marron Institute and director of the team that created the Atlas of Urban Expansion found that most cities' footprint has increased faster than their populations, reducing urban density. A decline in density may become a significant problem, as sprawling cities are more likely to suffer from low physical and social connectivity and high fragmentation.

Low population density increases the per capita costs of trunk infrastructure, electricity, transport, and road networks, especially for people living in the periphery. As the price of servicing land increases with sprawl, so does the cost of real estate, exacerbating the disequilibrium of affordable housing supply and demand. High housing cost further encourages sprawl, as peripheral areas remain the only parts affordable to those with low incomes. Since many people cannot afford to connect to public services, new low-income settlements remain "informal," lacking water, sanitation, and electricity. The Inter-American Development Bank (IDB 2015) found that three-quarters of all new housing in the region are informal. The low-density urban expansion pattern has thus encouraged urban segregation as the wealthiest choose to self-isolate, and the poorest are driven to the edge of the city.

Sprawl may also have negative economic effects. A study by Muzzini et al. (2016) finds that this is the case in Argentina, where due to sprawl firms lose out on productivity and positive externalities associated with economic density.

Urban sprawl and the expansion of informal settlements primarily result from inadequate urban planning and housing policies. To address the growth of slums and the shortage of affordable housing, governments across the region increased housing budgets and financially encouraged the construction of low-cost housing. But government subsidies essentially functioned as gifts to developers without addressing the root of the problem. The lack of regulations allowed private developers to build housing on cheap land, often in peripheral areas that lack urban amenities, far away from employment. Many families that moved from inner-city slums to these new housing complexes as part of public programs returned shortly after because their new housing lacked economic opportunities. What they had received was housing, but no city.

The massive numbers of abandoned subsidized houses depict the gravity of the policy failure more than words can describe. Upwards of one million subsidized housing units are unoccupied in Chile, five million in Mexico, and six million in Brazil. The New School's Observatory on Latin America assessed the failure and disconnect of urban and housing policy in six countries in the region, concluding that "...housing policy has not only neglected urban policy but has run against its primary intention: to promote sustainable territorial development and to improve the living conditions of the population (Cohen et al. 2019b, p. 352)." Instead of building more inclusive cities, government policy exacerbated inequalities.

The idiosyncrasies of Argentina's cities

With 92 percent of its population living cities, Argentina is one of the most urbanized countries in the world (World Bank 2021). Argentina is also one of the few countries in the region – together with Uruguay, Chile, and Cuba – with high levels of urbanization from the beginning of the twentieth century. Already in 1914, more people lived in cities than rural areas. According to Velásquez (2015) and the Ministry of Planning's population censuses (MPF 2011), urban growth has continued ever since (1914: 53% urbanized; 1947: 62%, 1960: 72%, 1980: 83%, 1990: 86%, 2000: 90%, and 2008: 92%).

A central characteristic of urban Argentina is the political and economic weight of metropolitan Buenos Aires. It is home to nearly 16 million people, or about 36 percent of the national population, and accounts for nearly half its GDP (Muzzini et al. 2016). This feature, also referred to as urban primacy, is prevalent across Latin America, where megacities and large metropolitan areas mark the urban landscape (Prévôt-Schapira and Velut 2016). Social and urban scientists consider urban primacy as harmful to the balanced development of a country. For one, these urban centers often receive more political attention, at the expense of other secondary and tertiary cities. In addition, rapid growth paired with inadequate urban planning can leave large metropolitan areas overburdened and unable to meet the increasing demand for adequate, affordable housing and essential basic services (Figure 3.6).

Figure 3.6 Buenos Aires from above, 2017

Credit: Lena Simet

Another distinctive feature of urban Argentina is the heterogeneity of local governments. There are approximately 13,500 localities (*localidades*) across the country's 24 provinces and 5 regions (Pampas, Patagonia, Cuyo, the Northeast, and the Northwest), ranging from Buenos Aires to the tiny settlements in the argentine Antarctic. To be classified as a locality, a municipality needs to have more than 2,000 inhabitants. This threshold, established in 1914, is relatively low compared to other countries. In India, the threshold is 5,000 inhabitants – with the qualification that half of the male population work in non-agricultural activities. In Germany, population density rather than a population threshold establishes what is considered a city (Schmidt-Kallert 2016).

According to the Ministry of Federal Planning (MPF 2011), there are 862 cities of more than 2,000 inhabitants, which can be divided into four categories: first, there is Greater Buenos Aires, which is of international relevance. This is followed by four large urban agglomerations of national relevance – Córdoba, Rosario, Mendoza, and San Miguel de Tucumán (about 13 percent of the urban population). These are followed by cross-regional cities (18, with an average population of 280,000, representing 16 percent of the urban population), followed by sub-regional nodes (82 cities with at least 52,000 inhabitants, representing 13 percent of the total urban population). Three additional categories of smaller-sized cities, which are active mainly at the regional level, can be added to this list.

To address the wide range in population size, Indec, Argentina's national statistics office, introduced the *urban agglomerations* category, for cities with more than 100,000 people. The built-up of these agglomerates often extends across localities and jurisdictional boundaries. If that is the case, they are identified as "greater X" (gran X), such as Greater Rosario or Greater Buenos Aires. Greater Rosario, for example, consists of the municipality of Rosario, plus nine adjacent municipalities. Indec regularly examines city borders to accommodate the continued growth and expansion of urban areas. It also provides the most granular data source at the city level via the Encuesta Permanente de Hogares (EPH), Argentina's permanent household survey. The EPH covers 32 urban agglomerates, representing around 64.6 percent of the country's total population. Throughout this book, I generally refer to an urban agglomerate as a city.

Regional distribution of cities

Across Argentina's five regions, the Pampeana region (or Pampas) has the highest concentration of cities. Some 22 million people live just between Buenos Aires and Córdoba, that's nearly half the country's population (Catenazzi et al. 2020). The stretch between the two cities is the most densely populated part of the country. It encompasses Greater Buenos Aires, Greater Rosario, Greater Córdoba, and some smaller cities like San Nicolas, Zarate, Campana. The three large cities were planned as industrialized metropolitan areas with a strong tertiary sector and benefitted from a development model that invested mainly in human capital and innovative production processes.

Today, Rosario plays a vital role as an intermediary in the processing and exporting of grains. Córdoba has multiple functions as a provincial capital, supporting agricultural production for the region, and as a connector to other medium-sized cities. Although the growth of the three cities took place at the expense of smaller settlements, some northern cities benefitted from the uptake in demand for regional products such as soy. The increase in production had positive spillover effects for cities specializing in commercial activities and secondary industries, for instance, those concentrating on machinery maintenance (Reboratti 2010). The southern parts of the region are less densely populated and include Bahia Blanca and the port city Mar del Plata.

Several migration processes shaped this. During the final decades of the nineteenth century and the first decades of the twentieth century, migrants from abroad, mainly Spaniards and Italians, remained close to the ports where they disembarked. By 1910, more than 50 percent of the working class in Buenos Aires and Rosario had been born abroad. Another flow of migrants from the less developed interior of the country to the growing agglomerations in the Pampas began in the final years of the nineteenth century. This "periphery-center" migration was due to the increasing economic deterioration of the interior because of foreign competition (Rofman 1985).

In the three regions Cuyo, the Northeast, and the Northwest, the provincial capital cities dominate and capture most of the economic activity, with the public sector being a significant source of employment. In the city of Resistencia, nearly 30 percent of residents work in the public sector (Indec 2020). However strong the political capitals are, they are supported by networks of small cities, many of which focus on agricultural and mining activities and increasingly tourism. Puerto Iguazu, for instance, serves as the gateway to the Iguazú Waterfalls, or Humahuaca and Purmamarca provide accommodation near the mountain valley Quebrada de Humahuaca with its dramatic rock formations – a UNESCO World Heritage Site.

The urbanization rate in the north is generally much lower than in other regions. In the Northeast, just 76 percent live in cities, compared to the national average of 92 percent. In Cuyo, the city that receives the most attention is Mendoza due to its wineries that attract international and regional tourism (the province generates 70 percent of Argentina's wine production) (Prévôt-Schapira and Velut 2016).

In Patagonia, there are no large cities, and the few that exist are medium-sized. The northern parts of Patagonia, which include Rio Negro, focus on tourism and a growing presence of the scientific community. The southern cities are much smaller, with economies based on agriculture, fisheries, tourism, and mining.

Oil is a defining feature as well. Many of Patagonia's oil cities benefitted from the reactivation and renationalization of the sector after the 2001–02 crisis. The cities Neuquén and Comodoro Rivadavia are Argentina's centers of oil exploitation and developed into YPF (Yacimientos Petrolíferos Fiscales, English: "Fiscal Oilfields") company-towns that were profoundly affected by the privatization of YPF in 1999. The cities, however, did not cease to function as centers for oil extraction. Neuquén has experienced robust growth associated with the discovery of the world's second-largest shale gas reserves and the fourth-largest shale oil reserves in 2010, situated in the Vaca Muerta formation (Fontevecchia 2019). These discoveries attracted workers from across the country, pushing the demand for housing while jumpstarting new construction of gated communities along the Limay river, residential towers in the city center, and large shopping centers. At the same time, informal settlements expanded and formed on the city's outskirts (Prévôt-Schapira and Velut 2016).

Argentina's ten largest cities, which are ranked in Table 3.2 by population size, amount to a bit more than half of the country's total population. Buenos Aires dominates, with a population nearly ten times larger than the second-largest city Córdoba. The method of comparing the population sizes of a country's two largest cities is referred to as the Two City Index and gives insight in the level of urban primacy (Cohen 2004). According to this method, urban primacy exists if the index' value exceeds two – which is clearly the case in Argentina. Another helpful index is the Four City Index, which constitutes the ratio of the largest city to the sum of the second-, third-, and fourth-largest cities. In the case of Argentina, the ratio of Buenos Aires to the following four largest cities is close to three. In international literature, a value larger than one is considered extreme primacy.

Buenos Aires's urban primacy can be traced back to the eighteenth century and Argentina's position as an agricultural exporter. It gained further importance as industrial and commercial activities gained steam in 1937, with Europe on the brink of the war. But in the 1970s, the import-substitution model, which led to the spread of Buenos Aires' metropolitan area and the development of Rosario and Córdoba, was challenged by the political changes imposed by the military dictatorship. As the Argentine architect and urban planner Luis Ainstein (2012) explains, Argentina's urban expansion has

Table 3.2 Population trends in Argentina's ten largest cities (2001–2019)

City	2001	2010	2019	Growth (annual) – 2001–10	Growth (annual) – 2010–19
Gran Buenos Aires	12,050,912	13,588,171	15,172,700	1.34%	1.23%
Córdoba	1,232,827	1,373,973	1,612,100	1.21%	1.79%
Rosario	1,118,905	1,161,188	1,339,500	0.41%	1.60%
Mendoza	773,113	848,732	1,053,500	1.04%	2.43%
San Miguel de Tucumán	623,916	740,601	902,200	1.92%	2.22%
La Plata	642,802	694,253	852,800	0.86%	2.31%
Salta	378,340	478,083	644,400	2.63%	3.37%
Mar del Plata	512,989	541,951	626,300	0.61%	1.62%
Santa Fe	407,293	454,238	540,200	1.22%	1.94%
San Juan	354,760	421,640	512,000	1.94%	2.18%

Data source: Calculated from citypopulation.de.

since been marked by the waning primacy of Buenos Aires and several other large Argentine cities. While urban primacy remains, Greater Buenos Aires shifted from being the home to half of the country's urban population in 1970 to hold 37.2 percent in 2002. The result has been a population increase in intermediary and small cities.

Post-2000 EPH data suggest that this trend has continued. Between 2001 and 2010, some intermediate cities with populations between 50,000 and 500,000 had annual growth rates exceeding two percent, far greater than Gran Buenos Aires' annual growth of 1.34 percent. For example, Salta's population increased at 2.63 percent per year, from 378,340 in 2001 to 478,083 in 2010. This even accelerated between 2010 and 2019, when Salta's annual growth rate jumped to 3.37 percent, lifting its population to 644,400 in 2019.

It is also poorer cities and neighborhoods that experienced the most rapid population increases. In Metropolitan Buenos Aires, the municipality La Matanza, where poverty is high, had the most substantial population gains, increasing from 1.2 in 2001 to 1.7 million in 2010, translating to close to 4 percent annual growth. Within Buenos Aires city, the population grew by 114,000 inhabitants between 2010 and 2019. Most new arrivals moved to the southern districts, which have the city's highest poverty and precarious living conditions.

As urban populations multiplied, cities' territories grew even more rapidly. Just as across Latin America, urban density has been declining in Argentina as urban expansion outstripped population growth in the last three decades. Most of the expansion of Argentine agglomerations has happened by extension, that is, outward development in areas adjacent to the urban area. Cities have been expanding into low–density, fragmented, and spatially segregated forms that are characterized by isolated gated communities and low–income settlements marginalized to the periphery.

Between 1990 and 2010, Neuquén, the largest city in Patagonia, expanded its territory by 69 percent, whereas its population increased by 42 percent. In San Miguel de Tucumán, in the northwest, population density declined from 68 to 45 inhabitants per hectare. And in Posadas, the capital city of the province Misiones in the far north-east on the left bank of the Paraná River, opposite Paraguay, population density declined from 93 to 54 inhabitants per hectare. One of the most worrying challenges faced with this decline in density is the increased cost of delivering public services such as water, sanitation, and electricity. Besides, the lack of access to public transport in expansion areas has contributed to increased motorization, with substantial implications on air quality and pollution (Prévôt-Schapira and Velut 2016).

Despite Argentina's high rate of urbanization, most political powers lie with the national government and the provinces, not the cities. Cities are also considered weak, institutionally and financially speaking. An analysis by World Bank researchers (Muzzini et al. 2016) finds that only 10 out of 24 provinces have decentralized some type of tax authority to their municipalities, and only 7 have decentralized the urban property tax. Municipalities that lack the power to raise taxes have limited ability to raise revenues and rely on subsidy transfers from provincial and national governments and a broad range of fees, which have high efficiency costs. A substantial portion of subsidies alone– almost half – of local budgets is allocated to administration, meaning the mere functioning of the municipal bureaucracy. The allocation formula for transfers is problematic, with low weight given to local needs and redistributive criteria. Differences in subsidy transfers from city to city are large. In Mendoza, the capital of the same-named province located in the center-west, the percentage of transfers in total resources amounts to 65 percent. This share is just 31 percent in Buenos Aires.

The financial and political weakness explains why cities are not responsible for providing, maintaining, and regulating many public services, such as water, sanitation, transport, education, and health. In the words of Rémy Prud'homme et al. (2004), "it seems fair to say that municipalities do much less in Argentina than in many or most other countries." However, since cities have complete discretion on how to use funds, including subsidy transfers, they are increasingly involved in providing their residents with health care, education, and social protection – often under the pressure of their electorate.

Old and new forms of inequality: income, housing, and conflicted urban territories

Urbanization in Argentina has taken place in a context of economic inequality and spatial divides in access to land, housing, and public services, and environmental pollution. If one was to establish regional characteristics pertaining to income inequality, one would find that the most unequal cities are situated in the Pampas region. In Patagonia and Cuyo, cities appear to be slightly less unequal. In the two northern regions, both ends of the spectrum are represented: some cities reach very high inequality (e.g., Salta), others have much lower inequality (e.g., Resistencia).

Among the 32 cities covered in the 2018 EPH household survey, the Gini coefficient spanned from 35 in the cities Ushuaia, Comodoro Rivadavia, and San Luis, to 43 in Paraná and Cordoba. Notwithstanding the surge in inequality in 2015, 2018 levels remain significantly below 1996 levels, as is summarized in Table 3.3 and dissected by select cities in Figure 3.7.

Table 3.3 Argentinian cities clustered by inequality levels (1996 and 2018)

	Low inequality (29 and below)	Moderate inequality (30–39.9)	Relatively high inequality (40–44.9)	High Inequality (45–49.9)	Very high inequality (50–59.9)	Extreme inequality (60 and above)
2018	0.0%	62.5%	37.5%	0%	0%	0%
1996	0%	0%	6.9%	51.7%	41.4%	0%

Data source: Calculated from the EPH Household survey (INDEC), clustered in inequality categories by the United Nations.

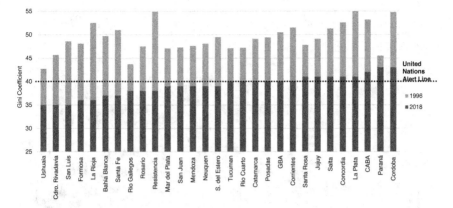

Figure 3.7 Income inequality in 29 cities in Argentina (1996 and 2018)

Data sources: Calculated from the EPH Household survey (INDEC).

The massive privatization of public services in the 1990s, the cuts to social spending, the undermining of labor organizing, and the crisis in industrial sectors worsened poverty and inequality in all cities. In 1996, more than half of the cities had high inequality, 41.4 percent even had very high inequality. In 2018, this picture was drastically different, with no cities falling into the high or very high inequality bracket. In the city La Plata the Gini dropped the most, from 58 in 1996 to 41 in 2018. However, despite these achievements, close to half of the cities were at or exceeded the UN's alert line in 2018.

After 2014, 19 of 29 cities saw inequality worsen. The most significant increases were noted in Jujuy (+5.6 Gini points), Paraná (+4.9), Buenos Aires city (+3.7), and La Plata (+3.5). Ushuaia (−3.8) and Posadas (−2.5) recorded the largest decline in 2014–18 (Figure 3.7).

Income inequality is a primary concern for cities like Buenos Aires, whose Gini of 42 is one of the highest in the country. The Buenos Aires-based Center for Metropolitan Studies (CEM 2020) found that in 2019, average household income was 140 percent higher in the northern parts of the city compared to the city's south – a sharp increase from 125 percent difference in 2017. The largest difference exists between district 14 (Palermo) and district 8 (Villa Soldati, Villa Riachuelo y Villa Lugano).

Income inequality is reflected in living conditions and well-being generally—neighborhoods in the south of Buenos Aires fare considerably worse in terms of health, employment, and housing. In 2019, unemployment was 134 percent greater, overcrowding 77 percent more prevalent, and infant mortality 50 percent higher than in the rest of the city (Gutman 2019).

Even the architecture and streets reflect disparities (see Figures 3.8 and 3.9). Neighborhoods in the north of Buenos Aires resemble a European city with adorned buildings from the late nineteenth century, complemented by modern high-rise buildings. While in the south, buildings around district 8 tend to be low-rise, self-built, and crushed between unpaved roads with little

Figure 3.8 Views from the street in Buenos Aires City: the south (Barrio 21/24)

Credit: Lena Simet

access to formal services. These intra-urban divides persist across the country, despite the notable achievements in income inequality after the early 2000s. In 2018, an estimated 30 percent of the country's population resided in inadequate housing, 15 percent had no access to potable water, and 45 percent lacked access to the sewage system (Lanfranchi and Yañez 2018).

This fragmentation is the result of a largely unplanned urbanization process and weak urban management. Cities have few financial resources and are not responsible for the delivery of most urban public services. This presents a challenge for local administrations, who know the territorial realities like no other, such as areas of unmet demand for services like water and electricity. Limiting local governments' ability in providing these services has led to inefficiencies and an inadequate provision and allocation of services. The challenges are most complex in large metropolitan areas where institutional fragmentation obstructs decision-making, as urban problems have extended beyond the traditional boundaries of the city. In most cases, land use regulations, when they exist and are implemented, govern specific jurisdictions, but not at the metropolitan scale. These inefficiencies have also opened the door for private developers and market forces to shape the spatial development of cities, be it residential, industrial, or commercial.

Housing is at the heart of the inequality challenge in urban Argentina. An intensifying mismatch between the demand and supply of urban land and housing has driven up their cost, making housing the primary obstacle to fighting intra-urban inequality, especially as people's incomes have not risen in line with housing cost. Following David Harvey's (1973, p. 121)

Figure 3.9 Views from the street in Buenos Aires City: the north

Credit: Rick Hippe

hypothesis, the market has limited the housing possibilities of different social actors. As the late Manuel Castells suggested (1989, p. 37), this mismatch process "can only be corrected through a public housing policy that goes beyond the pure and simple acceptance of market trends." But urban and housing policies in Argentina have reproduced and intensified residential segregation rather than created more inclusive cities.

Real estate was always a source of great value and capital investment in Argentina. The financial uncertainties that resulted from the internal 2001–02 crisis and the international financial crisis in 2009 turned the real estate market into a safe haven for investment. It has since become even more lucrative as the value of land increased with public infrastructure investments. Upper and upper-middle-income households cashed in and invested in real estate in the post-crisis years. They did not have to rely on mortgage financing to the same extent as lower-income households do, with mortgage finance being in minimal supply in Argentina (Catenazzi et al. 2020). Low-income families generally cannot save for a down payment or are often ineligible for a mort-gage because of the informal nature of their income.

Real estate investment first took off in Buenos Aires city, where local investment demand combined with a reactivation of the business sector. The megaproject Puerto Madero demonstrates the beginning of the construction of new and tall buildings, as well as private cultural spaces (Museo Fortabat and Usina del Arte) and luxury hotels (such as the Hilton and Faena) (Prévôt-Schapira and Velut 2016). Investment appeared with the rehabilitation of old residential units and the construction of "torres," multi-story buildings with exclusive amenities such as a gym or a pool. Perhaps the most emblematic case is the neighborhood Palermo, where new tall buildings with security walls that remind of vertical gated communities replaced the so-called "casas chorizo," colonial-style houses built in the late nineteenth and early twenti-eth century (Figures 3.10 and 3.11).

The unfolding urban transformation implies a continuous increase in the cost of land and housing – a trend notable all over the country. Tables 3.4 and 3.5 list the changes in real terms in the cost of renting (in Argentine pesos) and buying (in US$) for seven large cities. Across the seven cities, the price of buying a home has risen between 16 and 96 percent from 2009 to 2019. The steepest increase was recorded in Buenos Aires city, in the neighborhood Palermo.

As buying a home has become increasingly unattainable for those with lower incomes, the rental market expanded. Between 2001 and 2010, some 840,000 households started renting, with tenants holding almost 16 percent of all units across the country. The rental market in Argentina is not regulated

Figure 3.10 Highrise buildings in Puerto Madero

Credit: Lena Simet

Figure 3.11 Shiny and empty: office space in Puerto Madero

Credit: Lena Simet

and mainly depends on short-term supply and demand. The government does not control price increases, nor does it monitor or inspect the quality of the units offered, which explains the large number of abuses reported (Catenazzi et al. 2020).

Across the seven cities, rental prices have increased at an even faster pace than the purchasing prices. Between 2009 and 2018, rents multiplied by five. In

Table 3.4 Cost of m² for two- and three-bedroom apartments (used), in dollar

	Sale prices (m², US$)			
	2009	*2014*	*2018*	*2009–2019*
Córdoba	1,140	1,097	1,320	16%
Mar del Plata	1,245	1,495	1,635	31%
Neuquén	1,220	1,200	1,910	57%
Rosario	1,175	1,120	1,870	59%
Salta	1,010	1,090	1,500	49%
Santa Fe	1,020	1,065	1,350	32%
City of Buenos Aires				
Barracas	1,370	1,670	2,220	62%
Palermo	1,670	2,190	3,280	96%
Villa Urquiza	2,115	2,350	3,380	60%
Barrio Norte	1,505	1,770	2,440	62%

Data source: Calculated from Reporte Inmobiliario.

Table 3.5 Cost of rental units (two-bedroom units in selected cities)

	Cost of rent (ARS, monthly)			
	2009	2014	2018	2009–2018
Córdoba	1,320	2,715	8,790	566%
Mar del Plata	1,760	3,045	10,890	519%
Neuquén	1,490	2,700	15,500	940%
Rosario	1,070	2,680	8,320	678%
Salta	1,430	2,575	9,999	599%
Santa Fe	1,010	2,870	9,998	890%
City of Buenos Aires				
Barracas	1,600	3,650	14,030	777%
Palermo	1,875	4,300	21,500	1047%
Villa Urquiza	2,110	4,275	17,910	749%
Barrio Norte	1,530	3,705	14,844	870%

Data source: Calculated from Reporte Inmobiliario.

Rosario, where 20 percent of the population rents their home, the average rent increased by 678 percent in this period, equivalent to an annual rent increase of about 25.6 percent. The greatest increase was again recorded in the neighborhood Palermo, with a yearly price hike of more than 31.1 percent.

Informal settlements are often the only affordable option for low-income families. Argentina has two categories of informal settlements (see Cravino 2008). The first category are *villas* (or villas miseria), which have an irregular urban structure located generally in the consolidated part of the formal city and often built on public land. Villas tend to have high population density, with populations establishing temporary accommodations in abandoned structures, which become permanent. Villa 21-24 for example, see Figure 3.12, is situated between the neighborhoods Barracas, Nueva Pompeya, the Riachuelo river in the south and the Belgrano railway in the north, in Comuna 4 in the south of Buenos Aires city. It is a highly built-up neighborhood and one of the most densely populated in the country, home to about 45,285 residents, on about 0.66 km^2)

The second category refers to precarious settlements called *asentamientos*, generally built on privately owned poor-quality land, with planned urban structures in place. Asentamientos tend to be located in the peripheries of the cities and have a lower density. Figure 3.13 depicts an asentamiento in the Reconquista river basin in metropolitan Buenos Aires. It is located on contaminated soil, on the riverbanks, with many houses in highly precarious conditions.

While exact numbers are difficult to come by, it is estimated that between 14 and 18 percent of Argentina's total population resides in informal settlements. This share has increased since 2001, with the most dramatic surge in Buenos Aires city, where informality increased by 69 percent; close to 54,700 more families lived in slums than in 2001 (Goytia and Dorna 2016).

Figure 3.12 Villa 21-24 in Buenos Aires city

Credit: Lena Simet

Figure 3.13 Asentamiento in Greater Buenos Aires (Reconquista, Merlo)

Credit: Lena Simet

The challenges of informal housing are particularly severe in metropolitan Buenos Aires, considering the sheer size of the slum population. Across 25 municipalities, there are about 819 informal settlements. Of those, 23 are in Buenos Aires city, 473 in the first ring of the metropolitan area – which comprises higher-density municipalities – and 323 in the second ring, made up of less densely populated municipalities, some of which still have rural areas. Although they house a little more than one million people, such informal settlements are high density and account for only about 2.3 percent of occupied land territory. While many informal settlements have existed for more than 50 years, most growth has occurred during the past 30 years.

Without diving into an in-depth analysis of housing policies (for this, see Andrea Catenazzi and Eduardo Reese 2016), it is clear that housing and land do not cease to be among the most pressing issues when addressing inequality in urban Argentina. Gated communities, slums, and precarious living situations symbolize the tension between the rising cost of urban land and housing and the stagnant and low incomes.

Notably, there is an inherently different government response in housing needs for the wealthy versus the poor. As Cantenazzi et al. write (2020, p. 204), "on the one hand, it is assumed that the problems of the formal city are solved by the public agencies responsible for urban planning and, on the other hand the problems of the informal city are subject to social policies in general, and low-income housing policies in particular."

Policies have failed to provide an equal footing in cities. Instead, they have segregated income classes by design under the veneer of helping the poor, perpetuating inequalities, and caving to the private motives driving urban development. While governments invested in affordable housing, units were often built in locations undesirable for private developers, in the peripheries of cities where land is cheap, driving low-income populations out of the city proper.

The "Mi Casa Mi Vida" (MCMV) – "My House My Life" – the largest affordable housing program (2003–09) in the Province Córdoba – is exemplary for policy-driven segregation. Backed up by a US$95 million loan by the Inter-American Development Bank, the provincial government hired private companies to build nearly 9,000 housing units for families living in inner-city slums. But the units were constructed on isolated and ill-serviced areas in the city's outskirts, far from jobs. No public transport connected the new units to the city, which prompted people to look for new economic opportunities, of which there were few in the remote location.

Marengo and Monayar (2020) find that many people felt they had no choice but participate in MCMV, because their old homes in the city center had been bulldozed to make room for new and shiny development projects for higher-income classes. While the MCMV proclaimed to support people living in precarious conditions by providing them with adequate housing, it reinforced segregation by income, moving poor residents from the inner city where land values are high to cheap grounds on the city's outskirts. In the words of Smolka (2013), the "solution became part of the problem."

Following a similarly flawed logic, in 2009 the municipality San Isidro in metropolitan Buenos Aires built a wall spanning 16 blocks and measuring 3 meters in height to separate the wealthy neighborhood La Horqueta from San Fernando, which is largely low-income, with the pretext to reduce insecurity and crime (Gobbi 2009).

To achieve more equal cities, access to affordable urban land and housing should be a priority for all levels of government. As Marcela Nicastro of the Rosario-based research center Igualdad Argentina states, "we believe that more egalitarian public policies of land and habitat should be proposed for the most vulnerable sectors, but also for the middle sectors that today do not find a response either from the state or from the market. It is necessary to deepen a social project of more equitable use of the territory that reaffirms the social function of the city and property" (translated from Igualdad Argentina 2016).

A handful of cities have actively fought inequality, turning themselves into laboratories for new initiatives against territorial fragmentation. In 2010, Rosario introduced the law "Ya Basta" (Ordenanza 6492), which prohibits the construction of new gated communities as a response to the increased division between slums and enclaves of the rich (Zysman 2010). At this point in time, gated communities covered nine percent of Rosario.

While other cities can learn from such achievements, not all have the same capacity. The dynamism of local governments is conditioned by their financial autonomy, which leads them to prioritize problems derived from the national and provincial agendas on which their access to resources depends (Clemente 2014). Besides, the lack of institutional instruments for metropolitan management is a constraint for scaling up local initiatives.

Whether due to budgetary or technical constraints, or situations in which isolated decision-making is inadequate, local governments cannot face the challenges of urban development alone. Instead, integrated national strategies for urbanization are needed to foster social, economic, and territorial inclusion. A new model of urban governance is necessary, which grants cities and local governments a role that corresponds to their development contributions and vulnerabilities and where urban leadership has a legitimate and valuable place. Urban planning needs to be a collectively negotiated and agreed upon development process. If national policies aim to develop solutions to local problems without actively involving the local community, their effectiveness tends to be radically diminished.

Latin America, the world's most unequal and most urbanized region, has achieved remarkable successes in reducing income inequality in the early 2000s. But early gains have slowed, and in some cities, inequalities have worsened again. And while incomes became more equally distributed on average, urban territories turned more divided, a sum of fragments where the rich separate themselves from the poor through walls or policies that move the poor to the city's fringes.

With close to a fifth of Argentina's population now living in informal settlements, 15 percent without potable water, and 45 percent without access to adequate sanitation, a new approach to urban policy is urgently needed. Municipal land-use practices and housing policies have fostered exclusionary and profit-driven urban development patterns for too long. It is time to work across disciplines to tackle inequality by taking a cross-sectoral approach to urban policy and planning.

Notes

1   UN-Habitat categorization: "very high inequality" (Gini between 0.5 and 0.599), "high inequality" (Gini between 0.45 and 0.499), "relatively high inequality" (Gini between 0.400 and 0.449), "moderate inequality" (Gini between 0.3 and 0.399), "extreme inequality," Gini > 0.6. Low inequality 0.299 and below, moderate inequality 0.3–0.399.
2   I should note that conclusions from global inequality analyses should be considered with a great deal of caution. While the Gini coefficient is estimated based on income in LA cities, it is based on consumption expenditure per capita in most cities in Asia and SSA.

References

Ainstein Luis. 2012. "Urbanización, medio ambiente y sustentabilidad en Argentina." *Cuaderno urbano* 12 (12): 173–89.

Angel, Shlomo, Alejandro M. Blei, Daniel L. Civco, and Jason Parent. 2012. *Atlas of Urban Expansion.* Cambridge, MA: Lincoln Institute of Land Policy.

Economic Commission for Latin America and the Caribbean (ECLAC). 2018. *The Inefficiency of Inequality* (LC/SES.37/3-P). Santiago, Chile: United Nations.

BBVA. 2017. *Urbanization in Latin America.* BBVA Research. Online, available at: https://www.bbvaresearch.com/wp-content/uploads/2017/07/Urbanization-in-Latin-America-BBVA-Research.pdf, accessed November 28, 2021.

BR. 2016. "Stadtluft macht frei" – die Stadt als Chance." *Bayern 2*, October 27, 2016. https://www.br.de/radio/bayern2/sendungen/radiowissen/soziale-politische-bildung/stadtgeschichte-urbanisierung-stadt-als-chance-100.html

Brookings Institution. 2018. "Urban Growth and Access to Opportunities in Latin America." February 8, 2018. https://www.brookings.edu/events/urban-growth-and-access-to-opportunities-in-latin-america/

Catenazzi, Andrea, and Eduardo Reese. 2016. "Argentina: a 20 años de Hábitat II, las asignaturas pendientes." *Hábitat en deuda*, edited by M. Cohen et al., Buenos Aires, Argentina: Café de las ciudades.

Catenazzi, Andrea, Eduardo Reese, and Agustin Manuel Mango. 2020. "Argentina: 20 Years of Habitat II: The Pending Subjects." In *Urban Policy in Latin America: Towards the Sustainable Development Goals?, edited by Cohen et al.* New York, NY: Routledge.

Castells, Manuel. 1989. *The Informational City: Information Technology, Economic Restructuring, and the Urban-Regional Process.* Oxford: Blackwell.

CEM (Centro de Estudios Metropolitanos). 2020. "Las Desigualdades en la Ciudad de Buenos Aires." In *Radiografías Metropolitanas N°7.* Available at: http://estudiosmetro politanos.com.ar/2020/04/29/radiografia-desigualdades-caba/, accessed November 28, 2021.

Chen, Martha Alter. 2012. "The Informal Economy: Definitions, Theories and Policies." *WIEGO Working Paper No 1*. Cambridge, Massachusetts: Women in Informal Employment: Globalizing and Organizing.

Clemente, Adriana. 2014. *Territorios urbanos y pobreza persistente*. Buenos Aires: Espacio Editorial.

Cohen, Barney. 2004. "Urban Growth in Developing Countries: A Review of Current Trends and a Caution Regarding Existing Forecasts." *World Development* 32 (1): 23–51.

Cohen, Michael A. 2019. "The Two Faces of Informality: Informal Settlements and Informal Employment." *Unpublished draft*. New York, NY: Observatory on Latin America (OLA).

Cohen, Michael A., and Lena Simet. 2018. "Macroeconomy and Urban Productivity." In *Urban Planet: Knowledge Towards Sustainable Cities*, edited by Thomas Elmqvist et al. Cambridge: Cambridge University Press.

Cohen, Michael A., Maria Carrizosa, and Margarita Gutman. 2019b. *Urban Policy in Latin America: Towards the Sustainable Development Goals?* Oxfordshire: Routledge.

Cohen, Michael A., Mitch Cook, Achilles Kallergis, and Lena Simet. 2019a. "Pathways to Pricing Municipal Services in the Global South." In *JWP Equitable Economic Growth in Cities*. Brussels: Cities Alliance.

Cravino, Maria Cristina. 2008. Los mil barrios (in)formales. Aportes para la construccion de un observatorio del habitat popular del area Metropolitana de Buenos Aires. Buenos Aires: Universidad Nacional de General Sarmiento Press.

Davis, Mike. 2007. *Planet of Slums*. London, UK: Verso.

Emunds, Bernhard, Claudia Czingon, and Michael Wolff. 2018. *Stadtluft macht reich/arm: Stadtentwicklung, soziale Ungleichheit und Raumgerechtigkeit*. Morburg: Metropolis-Verlag.

Fontevecchia, Agustino. 2019. "Argentina's Vaca Muerta Could Lead to a Shale Boom to Rival the United States." *Forbes*, December 9, 2019. https://www.forbes.com/sites/afontevecchia/2019/12/09/argentinas-vaca-muerta-could-lead-to-a-shale-boom-to-rival-the-united-states/?sh=3e41d66a211a

Gobbi, Jorge. 2009. "Argentina: A Wall Separating Two Neighborhoods in Buenos Aires." *Global Voices*, April 12, 2009. https://globalvoices.org/2009/04/12/argentina-a-wall-separating-two-neighborhoods-in-buenos-aires/

Goytia, Cynthia, and Guadalupe Dorna. 2016. *What Is the Role of Urban Growth on Inequality, and Segregation? The Case of Urban Argentina's Urban Agglomerations*. Working Paper N° 2016/12. Buenos Aires: CAF.

Gutman, Margarita. 2019. "Stormy Times in Argentina: A View from Buenos Aires." In *Public Seminar. Blog*. http://www.publicseminar.org/essays/stormy-times-in-argentina/

Harvey, David. 1973. *Social Justice and the City*. Athens, GA: University of Georgia Press.

Huang, Philip CC. 2009. "China's Neglected Informal Economy: Reality and Theory." *Modern China* 35 (4): 405–38.

IDB. 2015. "The Experience of Latin America and the Caribbean in Urbanization." *Discussion Paper*, IDB-DP-395.

ILO and WIEGO. 2018. *Women and Men in the Informal Economy: A Statistical Picture*. Geneva: International Labour Office.

Indec. 2020. *Bases de Datos*. Argentina: INDEC.

_____. 2018. *Encuesta Permanente de Hogares*. Argentina: INDEC.

Kallergis, Achilles. 2018. "Addressing the Need for Local Data: A Systematic Low-Cost Way for Monitoring Living Conditions in Informal Settlements." PhD Dissertation. New York, NY: The New School.

Kessler, Gabriel. 2016. *La Sociedad Argentina Hoy: Radiografía de Una Nueva Estructura.* Buenos Aires: Siglo Veintiuno Editores Argentina.

Lanfranchi, Gabriel, and Florencia Yañez. 2018. *Urban challenges in the 21st Century: Social Capital and Innovation as Key Factors for Implementing Integrated Development Approaches.* Buenos Aires: CIPPEC.

Lewis, William Arthur. 1954. "Economic Development with Unlimited Supplies of Labour." *The Manchester School* 22 (2): 139–91.

Lucas, Robert E. 2004., "The Industrial Revolution: Past and Future." *The Region.* 2003 Annual Report of the Federal Reserve Bank of Minneapolis, pp. 5–20.

Marengo, Cecilia, and Virginia Monayar. 2020. "Urban Growth, Social-Spatial Inequalities and Housing Policy: A Case study of Cordoba, Argentina." In Urbana, *Urban Affairs & Public Policy.* 10.47785/urbana.1.2020.

Massey, Douglas S. 1990. "The Social and Economic Origins of Immigration." *The Annals of the American Academy of Political and Social Science* 510: 60–72.

MPF. 2011. *Plan Estratégico Territorial Avance I: Planificación Estratégica Territorial.* Buenos Aires: Ministerio de Planificación Federal, Inversión Pública y Servicios.

Muzzini, Elisa, Beatriz Eraso Puig, Sebastian Anapolsky, Tara Lonnberg, and Viviana Mora. 2016. *Leveraging the Potential of Argentine Cities: A Framework for Policy Action.* Washington, DC: World Bank Publications.

Nicastro, Marcela. 2016. *Quote from Dinámica de la normativa y de los precios del suelo.* http://igualdadargentina.com.ar/taller-dinamica-de-la-normativa-y-de-los-precios-del-suelo/

OECD Stat. 2021. *Metropolitan Areas: Economy.* Paris: Organization for Economic Co-operation and Development.

Oxford Economics. 2018. *Global Cities.* https://www.oxfordeconomics.com/microsites/cities

Prévôt-Schapira, M., and Sébastien Velut. 2016. "El sistema urbano y la metropolización." *La sociedad argentina hoy,* G. Kessler (comp.). Buenos Aires: Siglo 21: 61–84.

Prud'homme, Rémy, Hervé Huntzinger, and Pierre Kopp. 2004. "Stronger municipalities for stronger cities in Argentina." Paper for the Inter-American Development Bank. Available at: https://publications.iadb.org/publications/english/document/Stronger-Municipalities-for-Stronger-Cities-in-Argentina.pdf, accessed November 28, 2021.

Reboratti, Carlos. 2010. "Un mar de soja: la nueva agricultura en Argentina y sus consecuencias." *Revista de Geografía Norte Grande* 45: 63–76.

Reporte Inmobiliario. 2021. *Relevamientos.* Buenos Aires. Available at: https://www.reporteinmobiliario.com/

Rofman, Alejandro B. 1985."Argentina: A Mature Urbanization Pattern." *Cities* 2 (1): 47–54.

Schmidt-Kallert, Einhard. 2016. "Magnet Stadt." In *Urbanisierung im globalen Süden.* Hammer: Wuppertal.

Smolka, Martim Oscar. 2013. *Implementing Value Capture in Latin America: Policies and Tools for Urban Development.* Policy Focus Report. Cambridge, MA: Lincoln Institute of Land Policy.

United Nations. 2018. *World Urbanization Prospects.* New York, NY: Department of Economic and Social Affairs. Population Division.

UN-Habitat. 2014. *Construction of More Equitable Cities.* Nairobi, Kenya: United Nations Human Settlements Programme, CAF, and Avina.

———. 2016. *Slum Almanac 2015–2016.* UN-Habitat.

Velásquez GA. 2015. "El proceso de urbanización en la Argentina: de la primacia a la fragmentación socio-espacial." *Tiempo y Espacio* 9–10: 5–22.

World Bank. 2021. "Urban Population (% of Total Population)." World Bank data. Available at: https://data.worldbank.org/indicator/SP.URB.TOTL.IN.ZS, accessed November 28, 2021.

Yardley, Jim. 2011. "In One Slum, Misery, Work, Politics and Hope." *The New York Times*, December 28, 2011. https://www.nytimes.com/2011/12/29/world/asia/in-indian-slum-misery-work-politics-and-hope.html

Zysman, Guillermo. 2010. "Por una ciudad para todos." *Pagina 12*, December 17, 2010. https://www.pagina12.com.ar/diario/suplementos/rosario/9-26633-2010-12-17.html

4 How the privatization of water spurred inequality in metropolitan Buenos Aires

About three decades ago, Argentina engaged in the world's most extensive and rapid privatization of public services and state-owned companies.[1] Water and sanitation systems did not escape the privatization wave, leaving lasting scars. In metropolitan Buenos Aires today, nearly three in ten residents do not have running water inside their homes, and six in ten lack access to adequate sanitation. The differences across neighborhoods are enormous, reflecting deep socioeconomic inequalities.

Privatization of public services was a common feature in Latin America during the neoliberal economic and social transformations in the 1990s. It was heralded as a solution to the region's economic woes, including hyperinflation, rising debt levels, and disinvestment in public services. Privatization was perceived as a panacea. It could bring cash into empty government coffers and shift some of the state's responsibility to third actors (Chong et al. 2004). The idea was that it would improve the quality of services for everyone.

People's lived experiences, however, suggest a very different reality. Privatization inserted public services like water into the global circulation in exchange of capital, creating a new geometry of power and control. Rather than expanding water services at affordable rates, the commercial logic that dominated Argentina's privatization boom in the 1990s deepened territorial inequalities in access to water and sanitation by increasing their costs and prioritizing expansion in wealthy areas (Azpiazu et al. 2005).

In light of these negative experiences, it is not surprising that the privatization of public services has become one of the region's most explosive policy issues. Proposals in recent years to privatize, or keep privatized, water, health care, education, or pension systems have mobilized fierce public resistance in Bolivia, Chile, Nicaragua, Ecuador, and Argentina.[2]

Data from the regionwide annual public opinion survey Latinobarómetro[3] show that, in 2017, a clear majority of Latin Americans disapproved of the privatization process; this is true across age groups, gender, and socioeconomic class, but is strongest among low- and middle-income households. When asked whether schools should be run by the public or the private sector, 92 percent responded "the public." When asked in 2013 whether service provision improved or deteriorated during privatization, about 70 percent of

DOI: 10.4324/9781003201908-5

Latin Americans surveyed said they were less satisfied with public services after they were transferred from the public into private hands.

Alongside the shift in public opinion, the political and ideological tide of privatization seems to have turned. Many cities that rushed to sign 20-year concessions with water companies have terminated agreements and returned water provision to public control. A 2014 report by the three organizations Transnational Institute (TNI), Public Services International Research Unit, and the Multinational Observatory shows that 180 cities and communities in 35 countries, including Buenos Aires, Johannesburg, Berlin, and La Paz, have all "re-municipalized" their water systems in the past decade (Kishimoto et al. 2014).

The COVID-19 pandemic has made the need for governments to intervene in the water sector ever clearer – by suspending payments of water bills, temporarily prohibiting disconnections, and reconnecting people to services to ensure sufficient water for handwashing. At the same time, however, the risk of a new privatization wave is rising as countries struggle to pay off the mounting debt they accumulated during the pandemic.

This chapter speaks about the case of water privatization in metropolitan Buenos Aires during the 1990s, which presents a cautionary tale of how the insertion of private interests into the provision of public services disproportionally hurts low-income individuals and families.

In many ways, this case is paradigmatic of the destruction of communal rights and the transformation of public utility users into consumers who have to pay for essential services rather than enjoy their entitlements. It also discusses how corporate ownership and control of water resources have deepened inequalities in access, with direct links to economic and environmental disparities.

Inequality in access to water today

The metropolitan area of Buenos Aires, in short AMBA (área metropolitana de Buenos Aires),[4] is located in a territory with abundant water sources. Among them is the Río de la Plata, the primary source of fresh water in the region and the country's border to the east. Multiple basins, streams, and aquifers run cross AMBA, such as the Luján, Reconquista, Matanza Riachuelo river basin, and the Pampeano and Puelche aquifers, used for water extraction and supply. Unlike in other parts of Argentina, where water is scarce, in Buenos Aires, water is present everywhere.

However, the abundance of water does not translate into its universal or equitable access by the people who live in AMBA. According to the latest census data collected in 2010, about 76 percent of households living in the metro area (3,088,030 households) had access to drinking water, and 57 percent (2,339,920) had access to sanitation through the public network (INDEC 2010). The disparities in access within AMBA are staggering. Household survey data from 2018 show that in Buenos Aires city, drinking water and sanitation reach practically universal coverage (99.6 percent water and 98 percent sewage) (INDEC 2018). But in Greater Buenos Aires, access is well below the average for the region, with 67 and 41 percent, respectively. In the municipalities Ezeiza or Ituzaingó, less than 20 percent of households are connected to the public water network.

Low-income and peripheral areas are least connected. Household survey data paint a bleak picture, showing that poverty is inversely related to access to water; see Figure 4.1. Specifically, the data suggest that the higher the poverty rate in a given municipality, the lower the share of households connected to water.[5] Ituzaingó, Ezeiza, and Hurlingham have the highest percentage of the population without access to network water. They also have a large share of their population living in poverty. In contrast, in wealthier municipalities like Vicente López and San Isidro, almost all households are connected to the water network. The quality of water networks is also worse in areas with higher poverty.

Researchers Melina Tobías and Leonardo Fernández (2019) find the relationship with poverty to be even more noticeable in the case of sanitation. This is because the costs involved in the extension of sewage networks are higher than in water and because policies historically prioritized piped water above sanitation.

The World Health Organization (2019) has linked the absence of adequate or properly managed water and sanitation services to the transmission of diseases such as cholera, typhoid, and polio. Aside from the severe and preventable health risks people without access to safe drinking water and sanitation are exposed to, they also tend to pay more for these services.

Receiving water through the public network is cheaper than via private delivery mechanisms. A report by three nongovernmental organizations – ACIJ, CELS, and COHRE – (2009)[6] estimates just how large is the differential cost burden. They find that households connected to the formal network spend on average ARS$15.22 per month for water and sewer services. In sharp contrast, those who have to purchase bottled water would end up spending up to ARS$675 per month on water alone.[7]

Living in poverty without access to public water networks thus comes with substantial economic and social costs, as one gets caught in what Pedro Pírez (2013) calls the triangle of economic precarity, pollution, and segregation. Since people living in or near poverty cannot afford to purchase water in the quantity needed, they extract water directly from sources like the Pampeano aquifer, which is closest to the surface and the most polluted. The situation is different for wealthier households, who can afford to purchase water or drill deeper until they reach the Puelche aquifer with lower contamination levels.[8]

Today's inequalities in access to water and sanitation in metropolitan Buenos Aires result from long-standing political decisions and urban policies reflecting corporate interests rather than people's needs. Especially the privatization of water services in the 1990s – which Carlos Menem introduced as

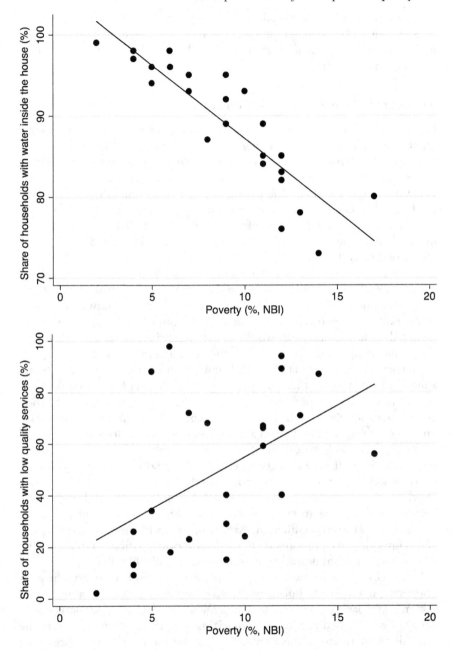

Figure 4.1 Poverty and access to water in metropolitan Buenos Aires

Data sources: Calculated from the EPH Household survey (INDEC).

Note: Each dot represents a municipality in Metropolitan Buenos Aires. NBI=Necesidades Básicas Insatisfechas (translated: Unsatisfied Basic Needs); the official methodology to assess poverty in Argentina.

"the only solution" to state modernization – poured the foundation of today's divides, as it encouraged network extensions in areas with the capacity to pay higher service rates (Azpiazu et al. 2005). Those with less economic power were left high and dry.

The world's largest privatization wave

In the early 1990s, Argentina suffered from hyperinflation and massive capital flight, with unemployment inching close to 25 percent and levels of poverty and inequality twice as high as in the early 1970s. These painful experiences opened a window to impose drastic macroeconomic reforms following the policy prescriptions of the International Monetary Fund (IMF), the World Bank, and the US Treasury. They proclaimed public spending and growing fiscal deficits as the root causes of the crisis and regarded privatization as a magic bullet to help save Argentina from a continuation of economic struggles (Cohen 2012).

Privatization was believed to have several advantages over state enterprises: to renovate old, poorly maintained, and technologically obsolete infrastructure, to promote efficiency, reduce fiscal deficits, increase consumer surplus, and create a competitive environment that would lower cost. It was also argued that the private sector would do better at bringing public services like water and sewage connections to low-income areas (Azpiazu 2010).

The privatization agenda of the IMF and World Bank could not have found a more willing partner than the government of Carlos Menem. Banking on Argentines' fear of hyperinflation, the government presented privatization as a panacea for the country's economic woes. "Shrinking the state means growing the nation" proclaimed a slogan of those years (Bosman 2005).

Fiscally, shedding state-owned companies implied shrinking the state's budget. Selling off public assets provided the capital needed to warrant the initial viability of the monetary convertibility scheme, instituted in 1991, in which one Argentine peso equaled one US dollar. The goal of the new currency scheme was to entice foreign investors. At first, it put an almost immediate end to hyperinflation. Argentina's debt became attractive again, and economic growth resumed after a decade of stagnation – GDP grew by 10 percent in 1992 and nearly 6 percent in 1993 and 1994 (ibid).

In this climate of renewed fiscal stability and economic recovery, the government quickly hatched plans to privatize water, gas, and communications systems. Two laws – 23696 (state of emergency) and 23697 (economic emergency) – were passed in a hurry, authorizing the privatization process. In the immediate aftermath of these laws, USD 23 billion flooded into Argentina from anticipated public sector sell-offs, plus billions more in foreign direct investment (Barlow and Clarke 2004).

In just two years, Menem privatized more state companies and public services than Margaret Thatcher in ten years in the United Kingdom. In a speech in 1998 to a trade delegation from the Confederation of British Industry, Menem proudly declared (Briscoe 2003): "For constitutional reasons, we did not privatize the state. But everything else that we could, we privatized."

Buenos Aires' water privatization: Profiteering at the cost of the poor

The privatization of water in AMBA was one of the most extensive privatization endeavors worldwide due to its speed and reach (Vilas 2007).[9]

The national water agency Obras Sanitarias de la Nación (OSN) began providing water across Argentina in 1912. By the 1960s, Argentina ranked second in Latin America in providing its population with water (Almansi et al. 2010). But in the 1970s, the military government began withdrawing its involvement and support for social policies and the provision of infrastructure and public services. Decentralizing such tasks was one strategy to reduce the government's role. In this bid for decentralization, provincial governments were handed the responsibility of managing, regulating, expanding, and allocating water and sanitation services (Azpiazu and Forcinito 2004).

However, the national government would not match the transfer of responsibilities with a transfer of resources, causing a financial dilemma for local governments now in charge of service provision (Clemente and Smulovitz 2004). The economic crisis affecting the country at the end of the 1980s further limited public spending and the capacity of local governments to provide services universally and at high quality.

These overlapping developments explain why the Buenos Aires province would make no investments in the water and sanitation systems since its acquisition, with enormous impacts on quality (Rey 2000). The deplorable conditions made it an appealing target for privatization. Because in many ways, OSN exemplified the weaknesses of the Argentine public sector: operational inefficiencies, weak financial management, lack of capital funds, and failure to address growing environmental pollution.

As the first step in OSN's transition from the state to a private operator, the national government set up a commission in 1991. To draw the attention from potential bidders, the government raised water and sanitation rates several times before the actual transaction. Martin Bosman (2005), Professor at the University of Florida, estimates that between 1991 and 1993 water and sanitation user tariffs increased by about 205 percent.

In 1993, the government selected a bidder, granting a 30-year concession to Aguas Argentinas S.A. (AASA), a consortium controlled by two French corporate giants, Compagnie Générale des Eaux (now Vivendi) and Lyonnaise des Eaux (now Suez).[10] While the consortium didn't pay a single peso for the concession, they promised to reduce water rates and expand services. But no precise goal to improve services to low-income households was set (Loftus and McDonald 2001).

Privatization's distributive impact: No money, no water

The ink had barely dried on the contracts when several of AASA's promises washed away. Just one year after the initial agreement, AASA solicited an increase in user fees and connection rates. The consortium claimed it had already invested US$300 million with a deficit of US$23 million and could not continue investing unless fares were raised. The government agency created to regulate the concession, ETOSS (short for Ente Tripartito de Obras de Servicios de Saneamiento, in English: Tripartite Entity for Sanitary Services), accepted the petition in exchange for a commitment to expand services sooner than originally contracted. With the new pricing regime in place, AASA went from registering deficits to reaping profits in its second year of operation, taking in US$350 million with US$50 million in net profits (Vilas 2007).

Over the years, AASA's management succeeded in pushing through various regulatory changes that altered the original contractual clauses and authorized several tariff increases at rates that exceeded inflation. Changes in water price disproportionately affected low-income households who had the most trouble shouldering the fees to begin with. Azpiazu and Forcinito (2004) estimate that, in 2002, households in the lowest-income decile spent about 9 percent of their income on water and sanitation, while the highest-earning decile spent just about 1.3 percent.

New connection fees added an additional barrier for low-income families to get hooked up. AASA's contract stipulated that financing for expansions would come exclusively from fees and rates paid by new users. While this arrangement might work in high-income countries, it is dreadfully inadequate in countries like Argentina, where incomes were low and poverty widespread. Households without water and sewage services had the lowest earnings, making them the least able to afford connection fees. Despite all its promises, AASA did not expand service to low-income areas because they saw little chance of recovering their investment, much less making profits.

User-funded approaches are generally a regressive way of funding public services and should be avoided. Instead, they should be part of government operating budgets and paid for with more progressive revenue sources.

The increase in rates and fees eventually led to public protests in the late 1990s, which erupted in the municipality Lomas de Zamora and soon spread through AMBA. Thousands of residents blocked roads into the capital to protest the US$800 charged to connect to the water and sewage systems (Tobias 2019). A congressional commission concluded that Aguas Argentinas had "committed serious and grave breaches of contract" and ordered the company to suspend the charging of connection fees.

ETOSS and AASA agreed to reduce the connection rate to US$200 while creating a new *Universal Service* fee to be paid by existing clients. "It was a cross-subsidy for the new clients who were poor," explained ETOSS director Cevallo. While the protests petered out, the real winner was Aguas Argentinas, as it succeeded in imposing fees not described in its initial contract (Santoro 2003). Despite the reduction, the fee was still hefty, considering a monthly family income of about US$400 (Almansi et al. 2010).

A group of Argentine architects and sociologists (Hardoy et al. 2005) found a salient flaw of the initial concession: the equal treatment of municipalities in a profoundly unequal metro area. Instead of stipulating that AASA should expand services to the most vulnerable and excluded areas, the contract treated all neighborhoods and municipalities the same. But low-density and low-income areas were perceived as financially unattractive to AASA since fewer people lived per square meter, and the incidence of non-payment was higher. Thus, water services were extended to the wealthier parts of the city, while low- and middle-income neighborhoods and municipalities remained underserved.

AASA's interest in profitability above all else also became apparent in its prioritizing of water at the expense of sanitation and drainage services – the costs associated with sewage service are twice those of water. Sewerage infrastructure did not keep pace with water service expansion, and AASA postponed the construction of a wastewater treatment plant. The consequences were drastic because the lack of drainage systems elevated the water table, especially in densely populated low-income parts of Greater Buenos Aires. Overflowing cesspools caused severe problems, with millions of people experiencing health and environmental harm (Vilas 2007).

Loftus and MacDonald (2001, p. 3) describe that the lack of sewage systems resulted in "over 95 percent of the city's sewage [...was] dumped directly in the Río de la Plata. Also, households with new water services are often forced to dump their sewage into makeshift septic tanks, cesspools or directly onto streets and open fields. [...] water-borne diseases are a constant concern."

Besides increasing user fees, AASA raised its external debt burden through loans from the International Finance Corporation (IFC, the private sector arm of the World Bank) – a shareholder in the concession – and the European Investment Bank. Between December 1994 and December 2000, loans given to AASA more than quadrupled from US$128.4 million to US$561.8 million. Between 1993 and 1997, the IFC alone gave US$911 million in loans. AASA also borrowed internationally, taking advantage of the interest rate differentials between Argentina and international interest rates during most of the 1990s, and the peso-dollar parity. Early in 2002, the company defaulted on about $US700 million in loans. (Vilas 2007).

While millions of people awaited the benefits of water privatization and debt accumulated, private investors raked off huge dividends and, in some cases, earned windfall profits. In 1998, AASA's profitability increased and amounted to a 20-percent return on capital, which is considerably superior to the 11 percent projected in the original contract. In most countries, acceptable limits are much lower: 6.5–12.5 percent in the United States, 6–7 percent in the United Kingdom, and 6 percent in France (Phillips 1993).

Perhaps most disturbingly, the high profits made by AASA were not invested in infrastructure but shipped off to stockholders in Europe. This can, in large, be attributed to the concession's ineffective regulatory architecture and an environment of asymmetric information, lack of transparency, and accountability in decision-making (Cohen 2012).

With the macroeconomic crisis in 2001 and the accompanying political and social turmoil, poverty and inequality increased sharply. The economic and political crisis and AASA's suspension of infrastructure expansion projects led to a cancellation of the contract in 2006. At that point AASA had met about 50 percent of the investment goals. It also fell short in improving the quality of the service, with low water pressure problems reported in 70 percent of the supply network (ETOSS 2003).

After the provision of water turned back into the hands of the public sector, the national government tried to recover some of the shortfalls and made notable investments in expanding networks to low-income areas. Between 2006 and 2016, about 3.4 million residents of metropolitan Buenos Aires received a water connection, and 2.8 million were added to the sewage network (AySA 2019).

Looking back to look forward

Thirty years have passed since Argentina's privatization rush, and it seems fair to say that the water concession's negative impacts have been most deeply felt in the poorest parts of Buenos Aires. Moving water and sanitation from the public into private hands was not a panacea for coverage and quality shortfalls, as praised by the Menem government and the Bretton Woods institutions. Instead, it turned access to water and sewers into a commodity only enjoyable to those who could pay.

As the case of AMBA demonstrates, the impacts of privatization can be far more reaching than just monetary costs. It renders explicit the tensions between public health, poverty reduction, and the conservation of resources and the environment, on the one hand, and the goals of commercial profit, on the other. It also serves as a cautionary tale that when public services meant to benefit everyone are privatized, they can morph into separate and unequal systems that divide communities and perpetuate inequality.

While noteworthy, this case is not unique, and the behavior of AASA is not unlike that of Suez's other companies throughout the world. Nor is it, in general terms, different from that of any other transnational corporation. Concessions and privatization processes have a patchy record, at best. They have been marked by bribery, corruption, breaches of contracts, public sector layoffs, rate hikes, and more (see Chong et al. 2004 and Andres and Ramlogan-Dobson 2008).

With the COVID-19 pandemic, achieving universal access to public services seems like a Sisyphean task for cash-strapped local governments, especially in rapidly growing cities with large informal sectors. With state revenues down and recovery for state and local governments slow and uneven, many governments may flirt with cost savings through contracts with private companies. The introduction of new user fees may appear to be the solution to tight budgets. However, neither of these "solutions" are long-term answers in the provision of essential services.

Governments should resist the call of privatization and combat rising inequality by adequately funding public services. Too often, privatization is touted as a way to save costs while improving the service quality. But the goals of saving costs and improving quality are at odds, and privatization efforts frequently result in either cost overruns or decreased service quality, and often both.

In Argentina, corporate control has not improved water quality or provided equitable and affordable access. Private water corporations sought to extract value from struggling systems by raising rates and, in many cases, cutting corners to reduce operating costs, negatively impacting service quality. These impacts were particularly felt by low-income households since struggling systems disproportionality serve these communities.

Meanwhile, privatization fails to address the underlying causes of why a publicly run service may have hit road bumps. In some cases, purposeful underfunding of public services is used ideologically as a "starve the beast" method for cutting public services, creating a crisis within a service, and then pitching privatization as a way to run it more effectively.

In turn, building, upgrading, and repairing needed physical infrastructure are ways that governments can create jobs and achieve equitable economic recovery. These investments create jobs and ensure that people and businesses in the future have the infrastructure needed to promote well-being and support a more equitable economy. Rather than cutting infrastructure spending and engaging in austerity, governments should invest in public services.

At the very least, when considering the involvement of the private sector, governments should look at questions beyond potential cost savings. While a rigorous cost-benefit analysis should be part of every government's "make or buy" decision, the government should examine potential impacts on workers, the community, businesses, and those who use the service or asset.

Multinational corporations are quick to argue that market forces would bring more efficiency to delivering state-run services. But the bottom line is that public goods and services like water – by their very public nature – require public oversight to ensure that people, not profits, come first.

Notes

1 In less than five years, the government privatized the following state companies and services via sale, concession, or licenses: the national oil company (YPF), the telephone service, electric power, natural gas, substantive parts of the road infrastructure, television channels, the dredging and marking of the Santa Fé-Atlantic Ocean waterway, passenger and cargo railways, port terminals, shipyards, the military aircraft factory, steel and petrochemical companies, and more. Source: Azpiazu (2010).

2 For example, in 2020, Nicaraguan lawmakers vote to open the door to water privatization, see here: https://www.reuters.com/article/uk-nicaragua-water/nicaraguan-lawmakers-vote-to-open-the-door-to-water-privatization-idUKKBN27S33N, 2019

protests in Chile were a response to the government's inaction on privatized services, see here: https://www.atlanticcouncil.org/blogs/new-atlanticist/whats-behind-chiles-protests/ or here: https://www.nrdc.org/experts/jessica-carey-webb/water-right-parallel-cop-santiago.

3   Latinobarómetro is an annual public opinion survey that involves some 20,000 interviews in 18 Latin American countries, representing more than 600 million inhabitants. Findings are based on data from 2013 and 2017: https://www.latinobarometro.org/latContents.jsp.

4   The AMBA comprises the City of Buenos Aires and the 24 municipalities of Greater Buenos Aires surrounding it in rings.

5   In Argentina, poverty is measured with the NBI (necesidades básicas insatisfechas), a multidimensional poverty index that measures income, housing, education, and other basic needs. It translates to "Unsatisfied basic needs." For more info, see https://www.indec.gob.ar/indec/web/Nivel3-Tema-4-46.

6   ACIJ= Asociación Civil por la Igualdad y la Justicia (Civil association for Equity and Justice), CELS = Centro de Estuidos Legales y Sociales (Center for Legal and Social Studies), and COHRE = Center on Housing rights and Evictions.

7   People with metered water pay $0.343 per cubic meter and have a free consumption of 10,000 liters (10 m^3) per month. According to the WHO, a person needs about 7.5 liters of water per day as the minimum consumption. The study assumes that a typical family would thus need about 900 liters per month at a minimum. If they buy 20-liter cans of water, they need to buy 45 cans per month to satisfy their basic need, equivalent to an expense of approximately $675 per month (taking as an average price of $15 each).

8   Although the degree of contamination of the Puelche is lower than that of the Pampeano, there is significant evidence of contamination mainly by organic compounds and to a lesser extent by heavy metals. Source: Auge (2006).

9   As in most Latin American cities, the metropolitan area had expanded faster than the waterworks could keep up. Of the additional nine million people living in the suburbs and shantytowns around Buenos Aires by 1993, only 50 percent were connected to water services, and 65 percent did not have sewer connections.

10 The consortium was comprised of Suez (25 percent), Aguas de Barcelona (12.6 percent), Meller S.A. (11 percent), Banco Galicia y Buenos Aires (8 percent), Companie Generale des Eaux S.A. (7.9 percent), Anglian Water Plc. (4.5 percent), and the Stock Ownership Program (10 percent).

References

ACIJ, CELS, and COHRE. 2009. *El acceso a agua segura en el Área Metropolitana de Buenos Aires. Una obligación impostergable.* Buenos Aires: Asociación Civil por la Igualdad y Justicia.

Almansi, Florencia, Ana Hardoy, and Jorgelina Hardoy. 2010. *Improving Water and Sanitation Provision in Buenos Aires: What Can a Research-Oriented NGO Do?* Human Settlements Working Paper Series Water, No 22. London, UK: International Institute for Environment and Development (IIED).

Andres, Antonio Rodriguez, and Carlyn Ramlogan-Dobson. 2008. *Corruption, Privatisation and the Distribution of Income in Latin America. No. 2008/11. Economics.* Nottingham: Nottingham Business School, Nottingham Trent University.

Auge, Miguel. 2006. *Agua subterránea: deterioro de calidad y reserva.* Buenos Aires: Facultad de Ciencias Exactas y Naturales (UBA).

AySA (Agua y Saneamientos Argentinos S.A). 2019. "Nuestros Números." https://www.aysa.com.ar/Quienes- Somos/nuestros-numeros

Azpiazu, Daniel. 2010. "Privatización del agua y el saneamiento en Argentina: El caso paradigmático de Aguas Argentinas SA." In *VertigO La revue électronique en sciences de l'environnement.*Online. Available at: https://www.erudit.org/en/journals/vertigo/2010-n7-vertigo3897/044527ar/, accessed November 28, 2021.

Azpiazu, Daniel, and Karina Forcinito. 2004. "Historia de un fracaso: la privatización del sistema de agua y saneamiento en el Área Metropolitana de Buenos Aires." In *Recursos Públicos, Negocios Privados. Agua Potable y Saneamiento Ambiental en el AMBA.* Los Polvorines, Buenos Aires: Universidad Nacional de General Sarmiento.

Azpiazu, Daniel, Martín Schorr, Emilio Crenzel, Gustavo Forte, and Juan Carlos Marín. 2005. "Agua potable y saneamiento en Argentina: Privatizaciones, crisis, inequidades e incertidumbre futura." *Cuadernos del CENDES* 22 (59): 45–68.

Barlow, Maude, and Tony Clarke. 2004. "The Struggle for Latin America's Water." *Global Policy Forum*. Online. Available at: https://archive.globalpolicy.org/social-and-economic-policy/global-public-goods-1-101/46052-the-struggle-for-latin-americas-water.html, accessed November 28, 2021.

Bosman, Martin. 2005. "Review of Privatization of Water and Sanitation Systems: The Case of Greater Buenos Aires." Unpublished manuscript.

Briscoe, Ivan. 2003. "Argentina: How Politicians Survive While People Starve." *open-Democracy*. March 17, 2003, https://www.opendemocracy.net/en/article_1167jsp/

Chong, Alberto, Florencio López-de-Silanes, Luis F. López-Calva, and Eduardo Bitrán. 2004. "Privatization in Latin America: What Does the Evidence Say?" *Economía* 4 (2): 37–111.

Cohen, Michael A. 2012. *Argentina's Economic Growth and Recovery: The Economy in a Time of Default*. London: Routledge.

Clemente, Adriana, and Catalina Smulovitz. 2004. "Descentralización, sociedad civil y gobernabilidad democrática en Argentina." *Descentralización, políticas sociales y participación democrática en Argentina*, A. Clemente y C. Smulovitz (Comps.), Buenos Aires: Instituto Internacional de Medio Ambiente y Desarrollo–IIED-AL.

ETOSS. 2003. *Informe sobre el grado de cumplimiento alcanzado por el contrato de concesión de Aguas Argentinas SA*. Buenos Aires: ETOSS.

Hardoy, Ana, Jorgelina Hardoy, Gustavo Pandiella, and Gastón Urquiza. 2005. "Governance for Water and Sanitation Services in Low-Income Settlements: Experiences with Partnership-Based Management in Moreno, Buenos Aires." *Environment and Urbanization* 17 (1): 183–200.

INDEC. 2010. Censo 2010. Database. Buenos Aires: Instituto Nacional de Estadística y Censo.

_____. 2018. *Encuesta Permanente de Hogares*. Database. Buenos Aires: Instituto Nacional de Estadística y Censo.

Kishimoto, Satoko, Emanuele Lobina, and Olivier Petitjean. 2014. *Here to Stay: Water Remunicipalisation as a Global Trend*. London, Amsterdam and Paris: PSIRU, TNI and Multinational Observatory.

Loftus, Alex, and David A. McDonald. 2001. *Lessons from Argentina: The Buenos Aires Water Project*. Johannesburg: Municipal Services Project.

Phillips, Charles F. 1993. The Regulation of Public Utilities: Theory and Practice. Arlington, VA: Public Utilities Reports, Inc.

Pírez, Pedro. 2013. Perspectivas latinoamericanas para el estudio de los servicios urbanos. *Cuaderno urbano* 14 (14): 173–92.

Rey, Osvaldo. 2000. *Saneamiento en el área metropolitana: desde el virreinato a 1993*. Buenos Aires: Aguas Argentinas.

Tobias, Melina. 2019. "Conflictos y territorios hidro-sociales en el área metropolitana de Buenos Aires." *Revista del CESLA*, núm. 23: 197–218.

Tobias, Melina, and Leonardo Fernández. 2019. "La circulación del agua en Buenos Aires: resonancias geográficas y desigualdades socioespaciales en el acceso al servicio." *Cuadernos de Geografía: Revista Colombiana de Geografía* 28 (2): 423–41.

Santoro, Daniel. 2003. *The 'Aguas' Tango: Cashing in on Buenos Aires' Privatization.* Washington, DC: Center for Public Integrity.

Vilas, Carlos. 2007. "Water Privatization in Buenos Aires." *NACLA Report on the Americas* 38 (1): 34–42.

World Health Organization (WHO). 2019. *Drinking-Water. Online. Available at:* https://www.who.int/news-room/fact-sheets/detail/drinking-water, *accessed November 28, 2021.*

Part II

Why Some Cities Are More Unequal

Evidence from Argentina's Cities

5 Determinants of intra-urban inequality

What causes inequality to rise? Where can we find the drivers of intra-urban inequality? In the different resources and capacities that individuals have? Or in political and economic structures that determine one's societal standing and place of residence? And, what can we do to keep inequality in check? Scholars and activists from different disciplines and backgrounds have long attempted to respond to such complex questions.

Historians, economists, and social scientists have connected colonial structures with inequality in the founding of countries, economic systems, global market forces, and the influence of elites in accumulating enormous amounts of wealth and power. In the eighteenth century, the Scottish philosopher and economist Adam Smith argued that legal frameworks and social privileges combined with economic power could explain some of it. For Karl Marx in the nineteenth century, inequality is the result of capitalism, as a process of exploitation, extracting surplus value from the working class. More contemporary scholars like Thomas Piketty (2014) and Anthony Atkinson (2015) argue that inequality is high when the rate of return on capital is increasing faster than the economy grows, whereas Saskia Sassen (2005) suggests that globalization is the primary driver of inequality in large cities.

Each of these perspectives sheds light on what determines inequality, and they are all interconnected to some degree.

This chapter takes a step back and identifies some of those determinants. It presents the Urban Inequality Matrix (UIM), which offers a multidimensional perspective to identify influential factors from the global, the national, and the local levels. This chapter intends not to comprehensively review all relevant theoretical contributions but rather identifies the fundamental forces impacting inequalities in cities.

The Urban Inequality Matrix

A sea of structural factors shapes economic inequality, often underpinned by policies from different levels of government. Intra-urban inequality can result from local policies, such as increases in a city's minimum

DOI: 10.4324/9781003201908-7

wage or housing policies and land-use regulations that expand or limit the supply of affordable homes. National-level policies also play a role. For instance, austerity measures that slash public spending may entice cities to cut social protection programs and housing assistance, subsequently rising inequality within their jurisdictions. Even global events or policy directions can affect intra-urban inequalities. Global economic crises, like the one that erupted with the COVID-19 pandemic, or policy prescriptions by international financial institutions like the World Bank or the International Monetary Fund (IMF), influence national and local policies, as we have seen in the case of water privatization in Buenos Aires (see Chapter 4).

Naturally, most researchers approach inequality from the point of view of their discipline or by focusing on a sector of their interest. But as Michael Walzer (2008) describes in his concept of pluralism (see Chapter 1), tackling inequality through a single lens may not just be insufficient; it may make things worse. We need multiple distributive tools for each sphere of life, suggesting that societies are more unjust if one central principle to redistribute prevails, especially if this mechanism is income.

A refreshing alternative is presented by Caroline Moser's *Asset Accumulation Framework* as it describes the pathways of addressing persistent gender-based inequalities within a context of broad driving forces (2015). In this framework, Moser, a British anthropologist, identifies interrelated national and local forces that should be considered in the fight against inequality. Moser's framework results from over three decades of research on urban poverty in a low-income community in Guayaquil, Ecuador. In her work, Moser challenges conventional approaches to measure and tackle poverty. She suggests that the most effective way to lift people out of poverty and reduce gender inequality is to create opportunities for individuals and families to accumulate assets.

Though Moser focused on gender-based inequalities, the intersect between macro- and micro-forces is relevant to urban inequality as a whole. It testifies to the complexity of the issue and the need for comprehensive analyses. It confirms that tackling intra-urban inequality through the national level alone is lacking context and depth.

The UIM is provided in Figure 5.1 and builds off Moser's framework. The matrix serves as the skeleton for the quantitative analysis of the determinants of intra-urban inequality in Argentina, which follows in Chapter 7. The national-level driving forces, depicted on the left, include broader economic trends, political change, industrial policy and institutions (e.g., labor market institutions), fiscal and social policy, inflation, and globalization.

On the right-hand side are local intermediary forces shaping intra-urban inequality. Here, the local economy plays an important role, alongside urban form (e.g., density and city size), local political attitudes, demographics, human capital (education), non-governmental actors, and the accessibility

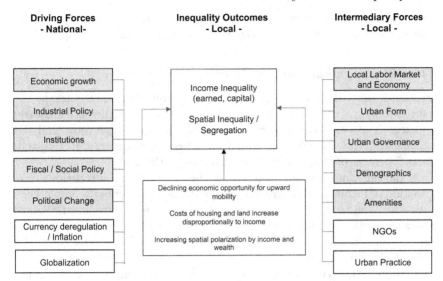

Driving Forces
- National-

Inequality Outcomes
- Local -

Intermediary Forces
- Local -

Figure 5.1 The Urban Inequality Matrix

Note: Own graphic based on Moser's (2016) Urban Asset Accumulation Framework. The fields shaded in gray are discussed in this chapter.

of urban amenities and basic services. Urban practice can shape the driving forces, turning constraints into opportunities.

In what follows, several potential drivers are grouped, and their relevance for increasing or reducing inequality is discussed, specifically: (i) economic growth, (ii) the nature of institutions, (iii) fiscal and social policy, (iv) a city's labor market, (v) urban form, and (vi) existing social inequalities.

Economic growth

Few links have been more studied in economics than the one between economic growth and inequality. Nevertheless, their relationship is the subject of a far from settled literature (see Anand and Kanbur 1993; Banerjee and Duflo 2003; and Voitchovsky 2009 for assessments).

Except for Adam Smith and Karl Marx, early theories (e.g., David Ricardo and Thomas Malthus) almost exclusively justified inequality as necessary for growth and development. Over time, however, these perspectives shifted. After the detrimental social and economic implications of the Washington Consensus and other structural reforms in the 1990s, international organizations such as the World Bank, the IMF, and the Organisation for Economic Co-operation and Development (OECD) adopted a new discourse emphasizing the harms of inequality and the need for more inclusive and sustainable development.

This debate can be organized in two broad camps; one that identifies inequality as growth-enhancing and growth-impeding. These two camps reflect the diverging perceptions about economic functioning that inevitably connect with political, social, and ideological perspectives.

Inequality as a growth-enhancing factor

Economic inequality was already a critical question when the classical political economy was born in England and France in the late eighteenth and early nineteenth century. This is perhaps not a surprise, given that most land and other natural resources belonged to a small hereditary nobility. In England, some 2 percent of the population owned most of the land.

At the time, most of the inequality studies focused on the functional distribution of income and the distribution of the net product between workers, capitalists, and landlords (the three classes Adam Smith introduced). People realized that radical transformations were underway, precipitated by sustained demographic growth coupled with a rural exodus and the advent of the industrial revolution.

Adam Smith, a witness to the English industrial revolution, would propose the first coherent theory of economic growth. In Smith's masterpiece *Wealth of Nations* (1776), he explains how production increases when workers specialize. This process can happen both within a firm and throughout a market. Increased population density and trade would help this process of specialization and thus promote economic growth. That's why Smith advocated for both domestic and international free trade and opposed government-granted monopolies, such as exclusive trading privileges. Smith observed that growth was improving workers' living standards. Meaning in his view, economic growth would eventually reduce inequality.

On the other end of the spectrum sit two British economists Thomas Malthus and David Ricardo who saw inequality as part of economic growth. Malthus (1776–1834) claimed that workers' wages would forever remain at "subsistence" because of their propensity to reproduce faster than food production could increase. Any efforts to assist the poor would be counter-productive, as they would just have more children. This logic, while pleasing to the elite as it justified the status quo, would have horrified Adam Smith.

David Ricardo (1772–1823) believed poverty wages were the only option for economies to progress. He looked specifically at land and argued that the cost of rent depends on the difference in return on a landlord's most and least profitable piece of property; the land with the high return would need to subsidize the one with low return. Ricardo's rent theory led him to propose a doomsday model. As the population grows, the landowners will take so much that there won't be enough to provide even starvation wages to workers. Only improved technology and gains from trade could stave off collapse.

In the early twentieth century, the Austrian political economist Joseph Schumpeter (1942) would argue that inequality was necessary to create incentives for individual effort. Without "winners," there would be little investment. Inequality, then, was a consequence of rewarding the winners.

However, Schumpeter was hopeful that investment and competition would reduce prices and eventually translate into a rising standard of living for the working class (Galbraith 2016).

In a similar vein, the "rising-tide hypothesis," also called the trickle-down hypothesis, emerged in the 1950s, which asserts that policies favoring the rich end up benefitting everyone, as the rewards would trickle down from the rich to the poor.

Neoclassical economics, the dominant approach to economics at the time, perceives inequality as arising from the difference in value added by labor, capital, and land. It is based on two assumptions: first, that a freely competitive capitalist economy generates full employment, and second, that income and wealth inequality is determined by the marginal productivity theory. This theory, heralded by the American economists Milton Friedman (1953) and Paul Samuelson (1958), assumes that compensation reflects an individual's contribution to society, and therefore, class differences are related to disparities in effort. In a competitive market, exploitation would not persist, and capital additions increase everyone's wages due to savings and innovations at the top.

Around the same time, the American economist Simon Kuznets (1955) would contribute to one of the most debated and influential theories on economic development and inequality. Kuznets prefaces his hypothesis amidst the backdrop of pre-industrial Britain, a country of small farmers. Here society is relatively equal since farmers make similar amounts of money. Suppose that with industrialization and urbanization, factory jobs in towns began paying more than farm jobs, attracting people to the city. As workers become specialized, their need for services they traditionally performed themselves increases, and so does the demand for new jobs. Apart from factory workers, the city now needs bankers, cleaners, and public workers filling the landscape. In this process of people moving to cities, income distribution across the country begins to vary, and inequality increases. Once more people live in cities than rural areas, according to Kuznets' theory, inequality would start to decline. The Kuznets curve would reflect an inverted U, with inequality rising at the beginning of the development process and falling, later on.

Inequality as a growth-impeding factor

The German philosopher Karl Marx (1867) rejected Malthus' wage theory and had a more revolutionary perspective. At the time of his writing, it appeared that there were no limits to (food) production, as Malthus had claimed, and despite lower costs of growing food, workers remained poor and in miserable working conditions. He recognized that the exploitation inherent to capitalism resulted in the unfair distribution of profit, resulting in inequality between the proletariat and the bourgeoisie. While Marx perceived inequality as inherent and inevitable in a capitalist economic system, he predicted that growing inequality would lead to a collapse of the capitalist system and its replacement by a new socialist society. In effect, Marx said growth increases inequality, leading to revolution followed by equality.

Between Marx's writing and the 1990s, most theories on the relationship between growth and inequality belonged to the growth-enhancing camp. It was only with the endogenous growth theory in the 1990s and new empirical evidence that this perspective shifted. It would take a century before the first statistical evidence that less inequality is good for growth would appear. First by Easterly and Rebelo in 1993 and followed shortly after by Perotti in 1996. By the 2000s, Milanovic et al. (2007) and Alvaredo and Piketty (2010) show that the decline of wealth inequality in high-income countries between 1914 and 1945 did not negatively impact their economic growth performance.

Although the Kuznets hypothesis found continued support in the 1990s and early 2000s, the more recent experience of industrialized countries – many of which encounter increasing inequality placed doubt on its validity. Consider the United States, where inequality has increased continuously since the 1970s. Harrison and Bluestone (1990) refer to this phenomenon as the "reversion of the Kuznets curve" or the "Great U-Turn." This has appeared in other industrialized countries as well in Canada, Sweden, Australia, and Germany (Milanovic 2016).

This has all but silenced the earlier claim that inequality promotes growth. Milanovic et al. (2007) found inequality to result from the concentration of political power and widened income gaps through rent-seeking and rent-keeping. Stiglitz (2012) found labor productivity to be lower in more unequal societies and shows that inequality affects aggregate demand, as the wealthy spend a smaller fraction of their incomes. And Galor and Moav (2004) provide evidence that low health outcomes and the struggle to finance education can generate social discontent and political instability, harming economic stability.

Rather than presenting a linear causal relationship, economic growth and its relationship with inequality depend on several components, such as macroeconomic stability, physical and human capital investment, a robust legal system, the structural composition of the economy, and competent institutions (Galbraith and Berner 2001).

The role of institutions

No country experienced steady economic well-being without state involvement in the form of subsidies, tariffs, and sector-level support. In their book *Industrial Policy and Development*, Mario Cimoli, Giovanni Dosi, and Joseph Stiglitz (2009) convey that industrial policies are essential to address the market's shortcomings (alias market failures), such as knowledge coordination problems. The institutions that allow for the generation and coordination of knowledge and ensure that policies follow equity objectives rather than aspirations of rent-seeking government officials are key.

In the book *Why Nations Fail*, Daron Acemoglu and James Robinson (2012) present a very compelling case for the relevance of institutions, which they classify as either inclusive or extractive. Inclusive institutions enable individuals to start businesses, create incentives for long-term investments, and improve their skills through education. They are intrinsically pluralistic, seeking a broad spread of political power. Extractive institutions, on the contrary, benefit the few at the expense of the many.

Societies with extractive institutions are often referred to as having been "captured" by elite powers (Cañete 2018). In Guatemala, for instance, political power is highly concentrated in the hands of few families, who represent the top 1 percent of the population. Extractive institutions like the ones in Guatemala are not conducive to shared economic growth, as the ruling elite is free to bask and protect their power, regardless of the population's interests (Acemoglu and Robinson 2012).

Stiglitz (2012) describes the link between inequality and institutions as a double relationship. With inequality causing the subversion of institutions by the politically powerful wealthy elite. Plus, low institutional quality renders a higher degree of inequality. Writing about political structures in the United States, Stiglitz (2012) describes this relationship as follows:

> Politics have shaped the market, and shaped it in ways that advantage the top at the expense of the rest. Any economic system has to have rules and regulations; it has to operate within a legal framework. There are many different such frameworks, and each has consequences for distribution as well as growth, efficiency and stability. The economic elite have pushed for a framework that benefits them at the expense of the rest, but it is a system that is neither efficient nor fair (...) Given a political system that is so sensitive to moneyed interest, growing economic inequality leads to a growing imbalance of political power, a vicious nexus between politics and economics. And the two together shape, and are shaped by, societal forces—social mores and institutions—that help reinforce this growing inequality.

The relevance of inclusive institutions is also apparent in the labor market, where they regulate the workplace via collective bargaining arrangements or a minimum wage. These institutions are vital for quality jobs that provide fair wages and safe and healthy working conditions. As New School Professor David Howell (2015) writes, "institutionally driven bargaining power is a critical piece of the [inequality] story, whether it is the noncompetitive "rents" earned by top managers and financiers, or the collapsing power of hourly wage employees."

The erosion of labor market institutions, or in some countries the lack thereof, has added to rising inequality across North America, Europe, Asia, and parts of Africa. The financial crisis of 2008, the austerity measures imposed in many parts of the world, and the deregulation of labor laws and collective bargaining are all manifestations of weakening labor market institutions. In Latin America, on the other hand, the decline in inequality in the early 2000s coincided with their strengthening (ILO 2020).

The impact of institutions on inequality is not limited to the national level but transcends all levels of government. The American geographer Neil Brenner (2013) argues that city-level institutions play a particularly relevant role, as they are the sites in and through which global forces such as the accumulation of capital, the regulation of political-economic life, the reproduction of social relations, and the contestation of the future occur. With that, city-level institutions play an essential role in addressing these interrelated forces.

Fiscal and social policy

Fiscal and social policies can intervene at different stages in the inequality generating process, which broadly can be categorized as pre-market, market, and post-market; see Table 5.1 for an overview. Investing in quality public services for example would be a pre-market intervention as it creates a more equal playing field for everyone. Here, it matters how these services are financed. For instance, a progressive inheritance tax could spread wealth more evenly, addressing inequality from the top. In some of the world's most unequal nations (Brazil, South Africa, and India), inheritance tax is almost inexistent (Alvaredo et al. 2018).

Other policies can intervene in the labor market, via wage-setting mechanisms, bargaining possibilities of workers, or antitrust laws. Unions play a critical role at this stage as they can influence policies to improve working conditions and pay, particularly for those at the bottom of the income distribution. Such policies include the minimum wage, which ensures a minimum level of earnings above the poverty line. But the impact of a fair minimum wage can go further. In the words of Heather Boushey, who currently serves as a Member of the Council of Economic Advisers, (2014): "[r]aising the minimum wage will have positive economic effects above and beyond

Table 5.1 Fiscal and social policy areas that can combat inequality

Area of intervention	Policy areas
Level playing field, pre-market	Investment in quality public services (education, health care, etc.)
	Paid for via progressive revenue generation measures (e.g., inheritance tax)
In the labor market	A minimum wage equivalent to a living wage
	Job guarantees
	Labor protections, including collective bargaining
Post-market	Strong social protection systems
	Progressive taxation (e.g., income or wealth taxes)

Source: Take-aways from a conference held in 2019 at the Peterson Institute for International Economics called "Combating Inequality." See Blanchard and Rodrik (2019).

lowering the poverty rate (…), [it] boosts productivity, and addresses the growing problem of rising income inequality."

Almost all countries have a minimum wage. However, this does not protect all workers, especially in countries where informality is high or enforcement is scarce. Although the minimum wage tends to be most effective for formal sector workers, it can serve as a bargaining tool for informal workers – which scholars refer to as the "light-house effect" (Maurizio 2014). In Brazil, where nearly half of the urban workforce is informal, the implementation of the minimum wage benefitted formal and informal workers alike (ibid).

Post-market policies, meaning after labor has been provided and was compensated for, generally aim to redistribute unequally held wealth and income. Progressive income and wealth taxes, income support policies, and other forms of social protection fall into this category. In most rich countries, tax progressivity drastically declined from the 1970s to the mid-2000s. In the United States, the ultra-rich have seen their taxes drop from 70 percent in the 1950s to just 23 percent in 2018 (Saez and Zucman 2020).

Social protection systems and social transfers are also critical at this last stage, as they protect people at the bottom from falling into poverty by supplementing their disposable income, subsequently reducing inequality. Social protection is most impactful when non-contributory, so even those who did not pay into the system are protected. Transfers positively affect school enrollment while also improving access to health services and participation in the workforce (Bárcena and Cimoli 2018).

The inequality-reducing effect of social protection systems is largest if financed with revenue from progressive taxation. In the words of Lustig et al. (2013), "[w]hat prevents Argentina, Bolivia, and Brazil from achieving similar reductions in inequality is not the lack of revenues but the fact that they spend less on cash transfers—especially transfers that are progressive in absolute terms—as a share of GDP."

Although social transfer policies are generally designed and financed at the national level, cities can play a relevant role in expanding social protection. During the COVID-19 pandemic, several local governments distributed emergency relief and broadened the reach of social registries to protect people from going hungry or losing their homes. Some even addressed the shortfalls of national support systems. For example, with a US$20 million donation from the Open Society Foundation to the Mayor's Fund, New York City provided direct monetary support for immigrant workers and their families who were ineligible for federal relief and unemployment insurance, providing a lifeline to about 76,000 individuals (NYC 2020).

A city's labor market

One of the potentially most influential factors on inequality in cities is the structure and composition of their labor markets. Cities thrive because people enjoy their bounty in culture and food or are drawn to some fixed geographic characteristic, such as a port. But many people move to cities because of the opportunities to make a living.

Historically, urban economists have argued that large cities imply a thicker labor market with more economic activities. For example, labor markets like Mexico City and Buenos Aires offer more job opportunities than Oaxaca or Salta. It can be mutually beneficial for workers and employers since workers can choose between jobs, and for employers, it is easier to find specialized workers in a large labor pool. This idea is based on so-called agglomeration theories, which suggest that firms move to cities because it reduces their costs of moving goods, people, and ideas (see Marshall 1890; Krugman 1991; or Glaeser and Gottlieb 2009).

Globalization and subsequent changes in the labor market have complicated early agglomeration theories. By bridging cities across continents through phone cables and high-speed internet, globalization has created opportunities and challenges for highly skilled workers (primarily in advanced economies) and foreign (and cheaper) labor. According to the sociologist Saskia Sassen (2005), the economic restructuring contains the potential for great conflict, expressed in cities' spatial and socioeconomic arrangements such as the polarization of jobs and the associated expansion of gentrified areas alongside long-neglected low-income neighborhoods.

Some recent theories by Duranton and Puga (2005) have emphasized the role of spatial proximity in facilitating learning and innovation. An example is Silicon Valley's computer cluster and its ripple effect on the information and communication technology. But Enrico Berkes and Ruben Gaetani (2019) find that innovation and an expansion of the knowledge economy positively correlate with income segregation in cities. Using empirical evidence, they demonstrate that innovation intensity is responsible for about 20 percent of the overall increase in urban segregation in the United States between 1950 and 2010.

The dominant industry or type of job in a given city may also influence inequality. Estimating the effect of specialization takes us back to Adam Smith. His insight on the impact of division of labor on economic growth ranks among his most important contributions to the field of economics. During his time, specialization was generally perceived as desirable, increasing productivity and economic growth. Like the Canadian economist Mario Polèse (2013), others ascertain that the dominance of a particular industry or sector leaves "its imprint on a city—and it isn't always a good one."

All things considered, the effect of specialization on inequality is somewhat inconclusive. Abdel-Rahman and Fujita (1990) find that the relationship depends on the prevalent sector because not all sectors are equally productive or lend themselves to extractive behavior fueling inequality. Thus, the composition of industries within the urban economy matters for productivity, growth, and inequality.

At a granular level inequality, especially wage inequality, is determined by pay differences within companies. Here, company size and the prevalence of small, medium, or large firms in a city are relevant. Some scholars like Mueller et al. (2015) find that the largest firms in an economy drive inequality. Similarly, Cobb and Lin (2017) find that wage inequality within firms is higher in large companies with more than 500 employees. Wage differentials between high- and medium- or low-skill jobs increase with firm size, while those between medium- and low-skill positions are invariant to firm size or, if anything, slightly decrease. As firms expand in size, the wages of top managers and CEOs grow. At the same time, compensations in lower-level jobs are stagnant, widening the wage gap between managers and workers.

Rising inequality is also often blamed on the growing demand for workers with higher levels of education – the more schooling you have, the better you'll get paid. The notion that skills and training determine individual wage rates has a strong foothold in the human capital theory that formed in the 1960s (see Katz and Murphy 1992). The theory suggests that the largest jumps in earnings come, first, for those completing secondary education and then, more markedly, for those embarking upon tertiary and postgraduate education.

But more recent research indicates that the rising gulf in income has little to do with returns to education alone. Evidence from the United States shows that the demand for college graduates has grown far less in the period since the mid-1990s than it did before. The rise in inequality between 2000 and 2018 is thus not a story of a growing differential of wages between college and high school graduates, but one of growing inequality between the top relative to the vast majority of workers (Gould 2019).

The more salient story is that wage inequality is driven by changes within education groups (among people with the same education) and not between education groups. Despite similar education levels, rates of return as measured by earnings favor men over women or non-indigenous over indigenous people.

ECLAC (2018) find that the most striking differences exist in the formal-informal segmentation in labor markets. Average earnings in most forms of informal employment are well below yields for formal work, and households depending on informal employment have a higher risk of living in poverty (Chen 2003). In Argentina, the average incomes of formal workers are about twice as high as those with informal jobs.

Urban form

A city's labor market and level of inequality can also relate to its morphology. Within the literature on urban form and inequality, the part that has received the most attention is population density and city size, but the findings are unsettled. Some argue that the biggest cities are the most unequal and segregated (see Nord 1984 or Gordon and Monastiriotis 2006), while others offer justifications for a negative or a more nuanced relation. Glaeser et al. (2009) find a positive correlation between city size, density, and income inequality, whereas Angel et al. (2016) argue that density is like cholesterol, with "good and bad" types.

Studies by urban economists Duranton and Puga (2005) and Rosenthal and Strange (2004) begin with the premise that productivity rises with city size and density. The reasons put forward are thicker labor markets, the transmission of knowledge spillovers, and infrastructure sharing. As productivity and earnings rise with city size, so do household incomes. However, not everyone may benefit from the increase in income. Rosenthal and Strange (2004) document that higher-income earners benefit more from the productivity-city size-density link than lower earners.

Another potentially influential factor are the amenities that shape the attractiveness of cities and neighborhoods. If one amenity is particularly attractive or in short supply, such as a waterfront, rich people are generally the only ones to afford to live in such locations. Goytia and Dorna (2016) find that the rich live in the most desirable neighborhoods in Argentinian cities, with a higher concentration of quality schools, fitness centers, walkable areas, or organic grocery stores. The difference in amenities shapes the cost of housing and land, limiting the options for low-income families who have no choice but to live in areas with low-quality amenities where housing is more affordable. Segregation is thus higher in cities where the options for people in poverty are limited.

Reinforcing social inequalities

We live in a world where individual characteristics such as age, sex, ethnicity, race, or migrant status shape our economic possibilities. Men tend to earn more than women, and a person's nationality may influence their pay. For example, in the Gulf region, Filipino day laborers are among the lowest-paid groups of migrant workers (Segall and Labowitz 2017).

Racial inequality is one of the structuring axes of the matrix of social inequality, along with socioeconomic, gender, territorial, and age inequalities. About 48 million indigenous people and an estimated 125 million Afro-descendants live in Latin America, most of the former residing in Brazil (ECLAC 2016). Taken together, one in every four Latin Americans is indigenous or Afro-descendent. They often face discrimination and are more likely to live in poverty than the non-Afro-descendent, non-indigenous population – more than twice as high in Brazil and Uruguay and about 1.5 times in Ecuador and Peru. This racial inequality manifests in socioeconomic segregation in cities, where low-income minority groups find themselves in more run-down or marginalized parts of town.

The share of migrants in a city has a curious bimodal effect on inequality with clustering at the top and the bottom of the skill distribution and indications to widen the overall income distribution (Orrenius and Zavodny 2018). International migration can have different effects from internal and inter-metropolitan migration, which can mix with processes that operate based on stigma, deepening social and economic inequality.

In terms of gender inequality, some countries have made notable progress in reducing differences in access to health care, education, and financial services. But worldwide, men still have more economic opportunities than women and often earn more for the same job. Women do considerably more unpaid domestic work, from housekeeping to caring for children and older people. They are underrepresented in high-level positions and overrepresented in low-paying jobs. As women move into higher-paying employment, they tend to have fewer children, which may explain why lower-income families tend to have more children than those with higher incomes (Bloom et al. 2013).

The last factor to discuss is age. In recent decades, Latin America's age structure has changed due to a pronounced fall in fertility rates and improved life expectancy, with a sustained process of aging (ECLAC 2016). But incomes are lower among older people, and the dispersion of income by age takes on a hump shape, peaking around the 50s, the concavity becoming more pronounced over the years (Guvenen et al. 2015). As most older people are retired, the distributional impact does not go through the labor market but rather through private savings and social security returns. These changes elevate new needs and aspirations among different age groups, which ought to be addressed and resolved through public policies that guarantee social and economic inclusion for everyone.

References

Abdel-Rahman, Hesham, and Masahisa Fujita. 1990. "Product Variety, Marshallian Externalities, and City Sizes." *Journal of Regional Science* 30 (2): 165–83.

Acemoglu, Daron, and James Robinson. 2012. *Why Nations Fail: The Origins of Power, Prosperity, and Poverty.* London: Profile Books.

Alonso, Rosa Cañete. 2018. "Captured Democracy: Government for the Few. How Elites Capture Fiscal Policy, and Its Impacts on Inequality in Latin America and the Caribbean (1990–2017)." In *Oxfam and CLACSO Policy Paper.* Nairobi: Oxfam International.

Alvaredo, Facundo, Lucas Chancel, Thomas Piketty, Emmanuel Saez, and Gabriel Zucman. 2018. *World Inequality Report 2018.* Paris: World Inequality Lab - Paris School of Economics.

Alvaredo, Facundo, and Thomas Piketty. 2010. "The Dynamics of Income Concentration in Developed and Developing Countries: A View from the Top." In *Declining Inequality in Latin America: A Decade of Progress?* edited by Luis F. López-Calva and Nora Lustig, 72–99. Washington, DC: Brookings Institution Press.

Anand, Sudhir, and Ravi Kanbur. 1993. "Inequality and Development A Critique." *Journal of Development Economics* 41 (1): 19–43.

Angel, Shlomo, Alejandro Blei, Jason Parent, Patrick Lamson-Hall, Nicolas Galarza Sanchez, Daniel L. Civco, Rachel Qian Lei, and Kevin Thom. 2016. *Atlas of Urban Expansion.* 2016 Edition, Volume 1: Areas and Densities. New York: New York University, Nairobi: UN-Habitat, and Cambridge, MA: Lincoln Institute of Land Policy.

Atkinson, Anthony. 2015. *Inequality: What Can Be Done?* Cambridge, MA: Harvard University Press.

Banerjee, Abhijit and Esther Duflo. 2003. "Inequality and Growth: What Can the Data Say?" *Journal of Economic Growth* 8 (3): 267–99.

Bárcena, Alicia, Mario Cimoli, and United Nations, eds. 2018. *The Inefficiency of Inequality: 2018, Thirty-Seventh Session of ECLAC, Havana, 7–11 May*. Santiago, Chile: United Nations publication.

Berkes, Enrico, and Ruben Gaetani. 2019. "Income Segregation and Rise of the Knowledge Economy." Rotman School of Management Working Paper No. 3423136, Available at SSRN: https://ssrn.com/abstract=3423136 or http://dx.doi.org/10.2139/ssrn.3423136

Blanchard, Olivier, and Dani Rodrik. 2019. "We Have the Tools to Reverse the Rise in Inequality." Reflection paper. Peterson Institute of International Economics. Available at: https://www.piie.com/commentary/speeches-papers/we-have-tools-reverse-rise-inequality, accessed November 28, 2021.

Bloom, David E., Salal Humair, J.P. Sevilla Larry Rosenberg, and James Trussell. 2013. *"A Demographic Dividend for Sub-Saharan Africa: Source, Magnitude, and Realization."* IZA Discussion Paper. Bonn: IZA Institute of Labor Economics.

Boushey, Heather. 2014. *Understanding How Raising the Federal Minimum Wage Affects Income Inequality and Economic Growth*. Washington, DC: Washington Center for Equitable Growth.

Brenner, Neil. 2013. "Theses on Urbanization." *Public Culture* 25 (1): 85–114.

Chen, Martha Alter. 2003. "Rethinking the Informal Economy: From Enterprise Characteristics to Employment Relations." in Neema Kudva and LourdesBenería, eds. *Rethinking Informalization*. New York: Cornell University.

Cimoli, Mario, Giovanni Dosi, and Joseph Stiglitz. 2009. *Industrial Policy and Development: The Political Economy of Capability Accumulation*. Oxford, UK: Oxford University Press.

Cobb, J. Adam, and Ken-Hou Lin. 2017. "Growing Apart: The Changing Firm-Size Wage Premium and Its Inequality Consequences." *Organization Science* 28 (3): 429–46.

Duranton, Gilles, and Diego Puga. 2005. "From Sectoral to Functional Urban Specialisation." *Journal of Urban Economics* 57 (2): 343–70.

Easterly, William, and Sergio Rebelo. 1993. "Fiscal Policy and Economic Growth." *Journal of Monetary Economics* 32 (3): 417–58.

ECLAC. 2016. *Horizons 2030: Equality at the Centre of Sustainable Development (LC/G.2660/ Rev.1)*, Santiago, Chile: United Nations.

Friedman, Milton. 1953. *"The Methodology of Positive Economics."* in Essays in *Positive Economics*, edited by Milton Friedman. Chicago: University of Chicago Press.

Galbraith, James K. 2016. *Inequality: What Everyone Needs to Know*. Oxford, UK: Oxford University Press.

Galbraith, James K., and Maureen Berner, eds. 2001. *Inequality and Industrial Change: A Global View*. Cambridge: Cambridge University Press.

Galor, Oded, and Omer Moav. 2004. "From Physical to Human Capital Accumulation: Inequality and the Process of Development." *The Review of Economic Studies* 71 (4): 1001–26.

Glaeser, Edward L., and Joshua D. Gottlieb. 2009. "The Wealth of Cities: Agglomeration Economies and Spatial Equilibrium in the United States." *Journal of Economic Literature* 47 (4): 983–1028.

Glaeser, Edward L., Matt Resseger, and Kristina Tobio. 2009. "Inequality in Cities." *Journal of Regional Science* 49 (4): 617–46.

Gordon, Ian, and Vassilis Monastiriotis. 2006."Urban Size, Spatial Segregation and Inequality in Educational Outcomes." *Urban Studies* 43 (1): 213–36.

Gould, Elise. 2019. "Higher Returns on Education Can't Explain Growing Wage Inequality." *Economic Policy Institute*. Available at: https://www.epi.org/blog/higher-returns-on-education-cant-explain-growing-wage-inequality/, accessed August 22, 2021.

Goytia, Cynthia, and Guadalupe Dorna. 2016. *What Is the Role of Urban Growth on Inequality, and Segregation? The Case of Urban Argentina's Urban Agglomerations.* Working Paper N° 2016/12. Buenos Aires: CAF.

Guvenen, Fatih, Fatih Karahan, Serdar Ozkan, and Jae Song. 2015. "What Do Data on Millions of US Workers Reveal about Life-Cycle Earnings Risk?" *National Bureau of Economic Research*, no. w20913.

Harrison, Bennett, and Barry Bluestone. 1990. *The Great U-Turn: Corporate Restructuring and the Polarizing of America.* New York, NY: Basic Books.

Howell, David. 2015. "What Are the Links between Institutions and Shared Growth?" *World Economic Forum*. Online. Available at: https://www.weforum.org/agenda/2015/02/what-are-the-links-between-institutions-and-shared-growth/, accessed November 28, 2021.

ILO. 2020. *2020 Labour Overview: Latin America and the Caribbean.* Lima: ILO Regional Office for Latin America and the Caribbean.

Katz, Lawrence F., and Kevin M. Murphy. 1992. "Changes in Relative Wages, 1963–1987: Supply and Demand Factors." *The Quarterly Journal of Economics* 107 (1): 35–78.

Krugman, Paul R. 1991. *Geography and Trade.* Cambridge, MA: MIT Press.

Kuznets, Simon. 1955. "Economic Growth and Income Inequality." *The American Economic Review*, Volume XLV.

Lustig, Nora, Carola Pessino, and John Scott. 2013. "The Impact of Taxes and Social Spending on Inequality and Poverty in Argentina. Bolivia, Brazil, Mexico, Peru and Uruguay: An Overview." Working Papers 1313. Tulane University, Department of Economics.

Marshall, A. 1890. *Principles of Economics.* London: Macmillan.

Marx, Karl. 1959. *Das Kapital, a Critique of Political Economy 1867.* Chicago, IL: H. Regnery.

Maurizio, Roxana. 2014. "Labor Formalization and Declining Inequality in Argentina and Brazil in the 2000s: A Dynamic Approach." *ILO Research Paper No. 9.* Geneva: International Labor Office.

Milanovic, Branko. 2016. *Global Inequality: A New Approach for the Age of Globalization.* Cambridge, MA: Harvard University Press.

Milanovic, Branko, P.H. Lindert, and J.G. Williamson. 2007. "Measuring Ancient Inequality." *Working Paper, no. 13550.* Cambridge, MA: National Bureau of Economic Research.

Moser, Caroline. 2015. *Gender, Asset Accumulation and Just Cities: Pathways to Transformation.* Oxfordshire: Routledge.

Mueller, Holger M., Paige Ouimet, and Elena Simintzi. 2015. "Wage Inequality and Firm Growth." In *Working Paper No. 20876.* Washington, DC: Center for Economic Policy and Research.

New York City (NYC). 2020. "NYC COVID-19 Immigrant Emergency Relief Fund." https://www1.nyc.gov/site/fund/initiatives/covid-19-immigrant-emergency-relief-fund.page

Nord, Stephen. 1984. "Urban Income Distribution, City Size, and Urban Growth: Some Further Evidence." *Urban Studies* 21 (3): 325–9.

Orrenius, Pia M., and Madeline Zavodny. 2018. *Does Migration Cause Income Inequality?*

Perotti, Roberto. 1996. "Growth, Income Distribution, and Democracy: What the Data Say." *Journal of Economic Growth* 1 (2): 149–87.

Piketty, Thomas. 2014. *Capital in the Twenty-First Century.* Cambridge, MA: Harvard University Press.

Polèse, Mario. 2013. "Five Principles of Urban Economics." City Journal. Online. Available at: https://www.city-journal.org/html/five-principles-urban-economics-13531.html,

Rosenthal, Stuart S., and William C. Strange. 2004. "Evidence on the Nature and Sources of Agglomeration Economies." In *Handbook of Regional and Urban Economics, 4: 2119–2171.* Amsterdam: Elsevier.

Saez, Emmanuel, and Gabriel Zucman. 2020. *Trends in US Income and Wealth Inequality: Revising After the Revisionists. No. w27921.* Cambridge, MA: National Bureau of Economic Research.

Samuelson, Paul A. 1958. "Evaluation of Real National Income." *Oxford Economic Papers* 2: 1–29.

Sassen, Saskia. 2005. "The Global City: Introducing a Concept." *Brown Journal of World Affairs* 11: 27–43.

Schumpeter, Joseph. 1942. *Capitalism, Socialism, and Democracy.* London: Routledge.

Segall, David, and Sarah Labowitz. 2017. *Making Workers Pay: Recruitment of the Migrant Labor Force in the Gulf Construction Industry.* New York, NY: NYU Stern Center for Business and Human Rights.

Smith, Adam. 2000. *The Wealth of Nations (1776).* New York, NY: Modern Library.

Stiglitz, Joseph E. 2012. *The Price of Inequality: How Today's Divided Society Endangers Our Future.* New York, NY: WW Norton & Company.

Voitchovsky, Sarah. 2009. "Inequality and Economic Growth." In *The Oxford Handbook of Economic Inequality.* Oxford: Oxford University Press.

Walzer, Michael. 2008. *Spheres of Justice: A Defense of Pluralism and Equality.* New York, NY: Basic Books.

6 The income sources that determine inequality in Argentina's cities

Over the last two decades, income inequality and poverty reduced in cities across Argentina. Following the years of economic crisis at the turn of the century, Argentina's economy surged forward until 2008 before the global financial crisis would curtail its growth and affect commodity prices. The macroeconomic performance occurred alongside improvements in socioeconomic spheres: unemployment dropped, poverty and inequality improved, and incomes recovered. From small cities like Resistencia or Jujuy in the north to the oil cities Neuquén and Comodoro Rivadavia in Patagonia, to the capital city Buenos Aires, income became more equally distributed. Key to these gains was the Kirchner administration's strengthening of labor policies, their support of unions, and the expansion of social protection programs (Maurizio 2014).

However, the achievements were not felt equally across all cities. Resistencia and Córdoba, for example, had a similar income distribution pattern in 1996 with a Gini coefficient of 55. Since then, the Gini dropped to 38 in 2018 in Resistencia. But in Córdoba, the Gini remained higher at 43.

The dispersion of inequality across cities (see Figure 6.1) raises several interesting questions: Why is inequality high in some cities while it remained stagnant or sharply declined in others? What policies have led to an increase (or decrease) in income inequality since the 1990s? What is the contribution of the different factor sources to income inequality?

This chapter addresses these questions by analyzing data from 32 Argentinian cities between 1996 and 2018, decomposing inequality by its income sources. The analysis uses a methodology developed by Lerman and Yitzhaki (1985) that identifies income factors contributing positively and negatively toward inequality. By looking at income inequality this way allows us to identify some of the determining factors into the local and national policies that could curtail inequality. More importantly, it could serve as an example for neighboring cities and countries to learn and emulate from.

The reasons that can explain the dispersion across cities are of course complex because the distribution of income results from an interaction between economic, social, demographic, institutional, and historical factors.[1] At the global and national levels, some of the factors driving income inequality relate to technological changes affecting employment, trade and globalization, or

DOI: 10.4324/9781003201908-8

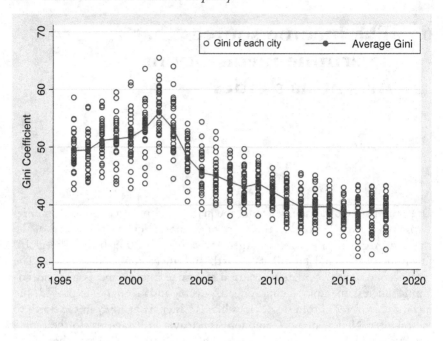

Figure 6.1 Income inequality in Argentina's cities (32 cities, 1996–2018)

Data sources: Calculated from EPH Household survey data (INDEC).

Note: Each dot represents inequality in one city in a given year, showing the inequality dispersion across cities.

redistributive policies. At the city level, the structure of the local economy and the availability of formal and well-paying jobs or the implementation of social protection programs play a role.

This chapter builds on previous studies that used the decomposition methodology of Lerman and Yitzhaki to analyze the decline in Latin America's inequality in the early 2000s. For example, Medina and Galván (2008) applied the method of Lerman and Yitzhaki to decompose the Gini coefficient for 17 Latin American countries for 1999 and 2005. Trujillo and Villafañe (2011) used the method to dissect the income distribution in Argentina in the early 2000s.

What is new about this analysis is that it takes the assessment to the city level. Despite the plethora of studies focusing on inequality in Argentina's cities, few have applied a quantitative approach to assess the role of income sources on inequality in urban areas.

Method for decomposing income inequality

For decades, economists have been interested in studying how income sources shape inequality. The most influential studies that developed methodologies to decompose income inequality by its sources are by Rao (1969), Shorrocks

(1982), and Lerman and Yitzhaki (1985). Rao (1969) created a first method to decompose the Gini coefficient by measuring the relation of an income source in total income and weighing the coefficients by their relative share. Shorrocks went a step further, using the inequality measure Coefficient of Variation, and dissected it by income across subgroups like single persons, married couples, and families with children, and other common characteristics like age, household size, region, or occupation.

Lerman and Yitzhaki (1985) followed it up by focusing on the decomposition of the Gini coefficient. While both the methods of Shorrocks and Lerman and Yitzhaki are qualitatively similar, the widespread use of the Gini coefficient led to a qualitative and quantitative jump in the decomposition literature using the approach of Lerman and Yitzhaki, which is now the most frequently used methodology for decomposing inequality (Box 6.1; Figure 6.2).

Box 6.1

The Gini coefficient

The most widely used measure of inequality is the Gini coefficient. The Gini has a value between 0 and 100 (or 0 to 1), which makes it well suited to comparing countries or cities with each other and their own experiences through time. A Gini of 0 represents perfect equality; the closer the Gini is to 100, the more unequal is a society.

The easiest way to understand the Gini is to envision the Lorenz Curve (see Figure 6.2), a simple plot that can be drawn for any distribution. In a perfectly equal society, the poorest 20 percent of the population would earn 20 percent of the total income; the bottom 50 percent would make 50 percent of total income, and so forth (Maio 2007). Perfect equality is painted by a straight line known as the "line of equality," which has a slope of 45 degrees. As inequality increases, the Lorenz Curve deviates farther from the line of equality.

The Gini (G) is the ratio of the area between the Lorenz Curve and the line of equality (numerator), and the whole area under the line of absolute equality (denominator), or:

$$G = A/(A + B)$$

The Gini coefficient has the advantage of being invariant concerning scale so that larger or richer areas do not necessarily have larger or smaller Gini coefficients. A 10-percent increase in everyone's income will not impact the Gini coefficient. While the actual computation of the Gini coefficient may include taking an integral or using a slightly more complex formula, the visual description is elegant and easy to understand.

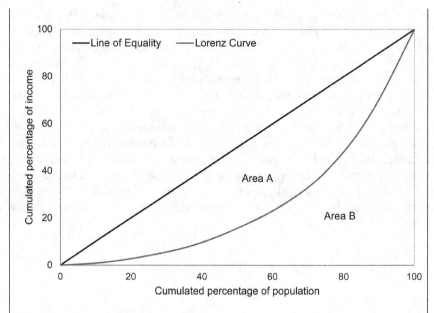

Figure 6.2 The Gini coefficient and the Lorenz Curve

The fact that the Gini converts all the data from the Lorenz curve to a single number is sometimes seen as a limitation, as it does not differentiate between different kinds of inequality. Two very different income distributions can have the same Gini coefficient. Also, the Gini is most sensitive to disparities in the middle part of the income spectrum (Cowell and Fiorio 2011).

According to Lerman and Yitzhaki (1985), the Gini coefficient for total income inequality, G, can be expressed as

$$G = \sum_{k=1}^{k} R_k \ G_k \ S_k \qquad (1)$$

R_k is the component referred to as the coefficient of correlation, as it measures the correlation between the income source k and total income. The coefficient ranges between −1 and +1, with −1 indicating that the income source would be mainly received by lower-income households and +1 when higher-income households receive it. One would assume, for example, that social transfers by the state, such as public pensions, would have a negative correlation with the Gini. Capital incomes, on the contrary, would have a positive correlation indicating an inequality-increasing effect.

The component G_k, also referred to as the relative Gini coefficient of income source k, determines how equally or unequally distributed the

Table 6.1 Interpretation of the elasticity of each income stream and its effect on inequality

Income stream	Elasticity <1	Elasticity >1
Marginal increase of income stream k	Decrease	Increase
Marginal reduction of income stream k	Increase	Decrease

income source is. The third component, S_k, indicates how important the source k is for total income.

The product of $R_k \star G_k \star S_k$ represents the absolute contribution of a given income source k in the Gini coefficient, and $(R_k\, G_k\, S_k)/G_k$ is the relative contribution of each income stream to total inequality.

The approach of Lerman and Yitzhaki also offers a way to examine how marginal changes in income sources alter inequality using the elasticity of the Gini. The authors derive a relationship that allows quantifying the effect e (for elasticity) that occurs in inequality due to variations in the source of income k. E is the difference between the ratio of the contribution of the source to the overall Gini before the income change, and the share of that income source before the change. We can estimate the effect that a 1-percent change in income from source k will have on total income inequality through the elasticity.

An elasticity of 1 indicates that the income source positively correlates with total income but that a marginal change of its contribution will not affect inequality in a meaningful manner. An elasticity level larger than 1 suggests that changes in the source would increase inequality, and an elasticity smaller than 1 would have a redistributive and inequality-reducing effect (Table 6.1).

Income sources

As detailed in Figure 6.3, Argentina's household survey provides data for 16 income sources, which were clustered into six categories for the analysis. The income variable is per capita household income, constructed by the household income from each source, divided by the household size.

The first category is *labor income*, broken down into wages from *formal employment*, *informal employment*, and *informal self-employment*. The latter refers to informal individual contractors or owners of small shops.[2] *Formal self-employment* has been omitted in the analysis because only very few (less than 0.5 percent) of workers fall into this category.

For non–labor income, *capital income*, *social transfers*, and *others* are the main categories. *Capital income* stems from renting housing, profits from companies in which the person does not work, financial interests from investments, and other rents. *Social transfers* include pensions, unemployment insurance, and other benefits from social protection programs or support by the church and charity organizations. *Other* incomes include financial assistance from other persons

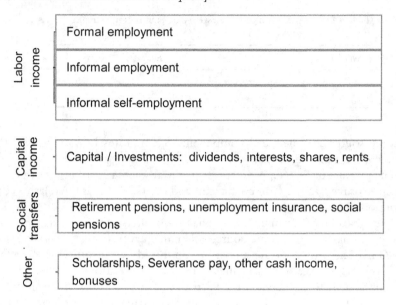

Figure 6.3 Income components used in the analysis

who do not live in the same household, cash incomes from gambling, bonuses (such as Christmas bonus or retirement bonus), and severance pays.

All of these sources include income from both primary and secondary jobs. These sources cover about 98 percent of all incomes.

A note on data – disputes about Argentina's household survey

The analysis draws from microdata of the Encuesta Permanente de Hogares, Argentina's permanent household survey (referred to as EPH), conducted by the National Statistics Institute INDEC.[3] The EPH was first carried out in the early 1970s, bi-annually in May and October (EPH puntual). In 2004, the EPH transitioned into its *continua phase*, surveys carried out over the whole year would be published quarterly. The analysis uses the round "May" from the EPH puntual (1996–2003) and the 2nd quarter from the EPH continua (2004–2018).[4]

In 2018, the EPH covered 32 cities of more than 100,000 people, home to 71 percent of Argentina's urban population. Since 91 percent of the population lives in urban areas, the EPH represents around 64.6 percent of the country's total population.[5]

Like most household surveys, the EPH effectively captures labor incomes and cash transfers but is weaker for capital income. Besides the usual problems of household surveys (e.g., underreporting), official statistics in Argentina have been contested, especially between 2007 and 2015, due to methodological changes in the survey design. Although the most questioned information produced by INDEC corresponds to that referring to the evolution of prices, scholars and politicians have raised doubts, objections, and suspicions about possible manipulations of the EPH. In 2013, the IMF declared a breach of Argentina's minimum reporting requirements because of allegedly inaccurate CPI (Consumer Price Index – used to determine inflation) and GDP data (Wroughton 2013).

These accusations are indisputably serious. The distortion of the CPI and a lack of transparency in internal decisions and procedures harmed the credibility of data produced by INDEC, including the EPH. But a rigorous study by Sol Minoldo and Diego Born (2019) published by the Center for Sociological Studies (Centro de Investigaciones y Estudios Sociológicos, CIES) suggests that despite its deficiencies, the EPH is of great value. Analyzing the EPH between 2007 and 2015, Minoldo and Born find that data concerns emerged from management inefficiencies in the production of information rather than a deliberate manipulation of data. The authors find that the quality of social indicators did not deteriorate during this period, as the IMF suggested.

The composition of income in Argentina's cities

The first component in the decomposition method of Lerman and Hitzhaki (1982) is the share of each income source in total income (S_k).[6] The analysis shows that labor income (the sum of formal wages, informal wages, and income from informal self-employment) in Argentina's cities makes up the largest piece, with about 70 percent on average, see Figure 6.4. Mendoza

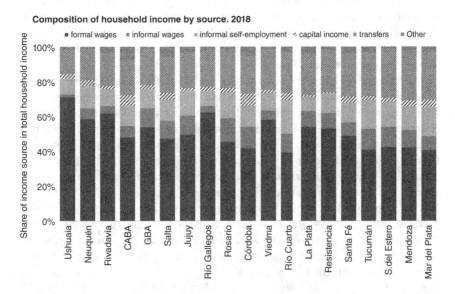

Figure 6.4 Most income stems from the labor market (2018)

Data sources: Calculated from EPH Household survey data (INDEC).

and Buenos Aires city have the lowest share of income stemming from labor (65 percent), Ushuaia and Neuquén have the highest (80 percent).

Depending on the city, social transfers make up a considerable part of total income. In San Juan, Mar del Plata, and Mendoza, transfers account for about 30 percent of total income, while in Ushuaia, Neuquén, and Comodoro Rivadavia, it varies between 13 and 19 percent. Pensions and unemployment benefits rank among the most prominent social transfers.

Capital incomes are relatively low, with about 3 percent on average. In 2018, Córdoba, Paraná, and Buenos Aires city had the highest share of capital incomes (6–7 percent), La Rioja, Corrientes, and La Plata had the lowest shares of 1 percent or less. In 1996 and 2004, this share was slightly higher with 5 percent; by 2015, it decreased to 3 percent. It's important to caveat these findings since capital incomes are systematically underreported (Gasparini 2004).

High informality, low pay

To get a more refined picture of labor income, I look at formal and informal sources. Considering the "formality" of labor income is critical because close to half of Argentina's urban workforce (47 percent in 2018) is informal. Informal employment tends to be more precarious and lower paying than formal sector work.

Figure 6.5 depicts the discrepancy between formal and informal sector income over time. While formal incomes recovered in the post-crisis years and even exceeded 1996 levels in real terms, wages from informal work did not recover to the same extent. The gap between informal and formal wages even widened in the post-crisis years. In 2018, the mean income from formal employment was ARS14,818, about twice that of informal work (ARS7,291) – almost equivalent to social transfers.

The Argentine labor economist Roxana Maurizio (2014) describes these disparities between formal and informal earnings as *income segmentation.* Maurizio argues that the workers' attributes (skills, education, etc.) cannot explain such wage differences. Informal wages are lower because firms employing informal workers face less pressure from unions and do not abide by regulations such as the minimum wage. Workers often have little to no choice but to accept lower wages and precarious working conditions because there are not enough jobs in the formal sector.

Maurizio (2014) also finds a positive correlation between informality and poverty, with poverty among informal sector workers two to five times higher than formal workers. In 2012, about one-third of informal workers were considered poor in Argentina, compared to just 5 percent of formal sector workers. Informality, however, should not be viewed as a cause of poverty. Rather, it is the scarcity of formal jobs and the limits of policies aimed at addressing social deprivation and guaranteeing labor protections (Beccaria and Groisman 2008).

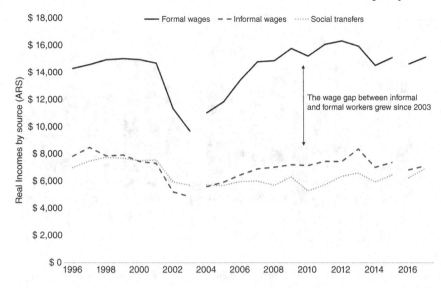

Figure 6.5 The evolution of formal and informal wages and social transfers (1996–2018)

Data sources: Calculated from EPH Household survey data (INDEC).

The informal sector is not equally large across the 32 cities, see Figure 6.6. Cities in the north have higher informality, with about 54 percent engaged in informal activities, compared to cities in the south with about 31 percent. In Ushuaia and Rio Gallegos, cities in southern Patagonia, only 10 percent of the workforce was informal in 2018; in Salta and Tucuman in the north, 58 percent worked informally. In cities with larger informal economies, the relevance of informal income is larger too: Ushuaia, Rio Gallegos, and Comodoro Rivadavia have very low shares of informal income (13–18 percent), it is much more prominent in Rosario, Tucumán, and Río Cuarto (about 40 percent).

Informal employment is higher in cities with a large share of domestic workers or activities in construction and commerce. For example, in Salta and Santiago del Estero, the three sectors make up close to 40 percent of all employment, and the informal sector employs close to 56 percent of all workers. Cities with high unemployment also tend to have more informal workers. In Córdoba and Greater Buenos Aires, unemployment was 13 percent in 2018, and about half the workforce was informal (Figure 6.6).

On the contrary, cities with a larger share of public sector employees tend to have a smaller informal economy. In Ushuaia and Rio Gallegos, where the public sector employs 34.3 and 46.8 percent of the respective populations, informal employment is low with 18 and 26 percent. A country-level study by the ILO supports these sector-level findings (Bertranou and Casanova 2013). It also finds informal employment is most prevalent among domestic workers (22.8 percent) and in commerce (15.4 percent), manufacturing (12.8 percent), and construction (12.6 percent).

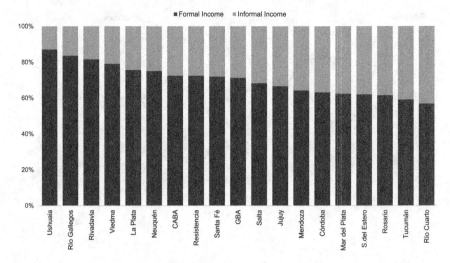

Figure 6.6 Across cities about 30 percent of labor income was informal in 2018

Data sources: Calculated from EPH Household survey data (INDEC).

Over time, the share of informal employment fluctuated alongside changes in income and inequality. Between 1996 and 2003, informality was high and increased in nine out of ten cities. In Tucuman and Mendoza, about 60 percent of the workforce was informal. Although labor informality remains high, it declined after the 2001/02 crisis by about 0.6 percent per year during strong employment growth, creating new jobs registered in the social security system (Maurizio 2014). Protecting quality formal sector jobs requires constant state support and intervention, which started to loosen in 2015. Between 2015 and 2018, informality increased again in two-thirds of the cities.

It is important to note that the share of informal income in total income dropped more than informal employment. This suggests that compensations in the informal sector deteriorated, and workers in the informal sector are paid less than they were two decades ago.

Increasing social protection to fight poverty and inequality

In contrast to informal income, the share of social transfers increased over time, especially after 2004, when such payments contributed, on average, 14 percent to total income. Transfers would then increase substantially until 2018, with an astonishing annual average growth of 4.3 percent. This increase in social transfers coincides with the return of a *justicialista* administration, which engaged in fiscal expansion and redistribution policies on a large scale.[7]

Between 2004 and 2013, consolidated government spending increased from 26 to 45 percent of GDP (Gómez Sabaíni et al. 2013).[8] Social spending alone accounted for more than half of the increase. This increase was almost evenly distributed between health and education, noncontributory pensions, and other forms of social spending (Lustig and Pessino 2014). Table 6.2 presents an overview of the leading social spending programs introduced or expanded after 2003 (ibid).

Considering the spending behavior over time, the year 2003 was somewhat unusual. For instance, as indicated in Table 6.2, the total amount spent on direct cash transfers as a share of GDP was 1.3 percent in 2003 and dropped to 0.7 percent in 2006 and 0.8 percent in 2009. This may be due to the dire economic situation that followed the 2001/02 crisis when unemployment climbed to 17 percent and poverty skyrocketed. To cushion the economic fallout, the government expanded direct cash transfers. As the economy recovered and unemployment declined, fewer people relied on these programs, and spending needs eased.

The extraordinary increase in social programs after 2004 was accompanied by exceptional growth in the tax burden, from 23.4 percent of GDP in 2003 to 32.5 percent in 2014, which Darío Rossignolo (2016, p.4) describes as "the greatest increasing and continuing tax burden [...] in its history." A hybrid of introducing and expanding taxes financed these programs, including a tax on financial transactions and primary exports.

Despite these efforts to grow revenue, it was insufficient to cover spending, and the government tapped international reserves and profits from the Central Bank to fill the gap (ibid). Argentina also took active fiscal policy measures to respond to the Global Recession in 2008/09. An assessment by Hanni et al. (2016) shows that Argentina provided the most comprehensive social protection measures across Latin America. Over 90 percent was allocated to boost spending under public works program.

Figure 6.7 presents the increase in the share of social transfers between 2004 and 2018 in the 32 cities. The x-axis displays the percentage of transfers in total income in 2004, and the y-axis shows the 2018 share. In all 32 cities social transfers increased, except Jujuy where it remained stagnant. Mendoza had the largest jump, with 8 percent annually. Mar del Plata and San Juan had the highest contributions in 2018, with 28.2 and 29.5 percent, respectively. Social transfers were of lower significance in Ushuaia and Neuquén, where 13.4 and 19.3 percent of incomes constituted social transfers. On average, social transfers represented about one-fourth of total income in the cities in 2018.

A correlation analysis of the 32 cities shows that the share of transfers in total income is higher in cities that have more households headed by a (single) woman and a larger population older than 65 or younger than 18; see Table 6.3. Household size matters too; in cities with larger average households, the share of transfers is higher. These demographic variables speak to the target beneficiaries of the social programs described in Table 6.2.

Table 6.2 An overview of social protection programs

Name of program	Year launched	Brief description	Target population	Spending on program (% of GDP)	Beneficiaries 2009
Direct cash transfers					
Jefes y Jefas de Hogar Desocupados (JJHD, Unemployed heads of households)	2002	Workfare program until beneficiary finds job in the formal sector	Unemployment households with dependents	2003: 1% 2009: 0.03%	450,000 individuals
Programa Familias para la Inclusión Social (family allowances for social inclusion)	2006	Conditional cash transfer	Head of households with less than secondary education and at least two children	2003: 0.08% 2009: 0.05%	695,177 families
Programa Nacional de Becas Estudiantiles (Scholarship programs)	1997, expanded 2002	Increase school retention, primary and secondary education	Poor families	2003: 0.04% 2009: 0.02%	500,000 individuals
Seguro de Empleo (Unemployment insurance)	1993	Contributory program, basic unemployment benefit	Unemployed	2003: 0.23% 2009: 0.08%	147,000 individuals
Asignación Universal por Hijo (AUH) (universal per child allowance)	2009	Conditional cash transfer	Families with children, head of household unemployed/working in informal sector earning less than min wage	2009: 0.6%	1.87 million households (3.5 million children)

(Continued)

Table 6.2 An overview of social protection programs (*Continued*)

Name of program	Year launched	Brief description	Target population	Spending on program (% of GDP)	Beneficiaries 2009
Noncontributory pensions					
Pensiones Graciables y Asistenciales (Social Assistance Noncontributory Pension)	1948	Old-age pensions and other special benefits		2003: 0.2% 2009: 0.5%	719,597 individuals
Moratoria Previsional (Pension Moratorium)	2004	early retirement program through a moratorium for those who had not completed 30 years of service	Women aged 60 and men aged 65 who have not fulfilled the requirement (30 years of contributions)	2003: 0.4% 2009: 2.4%	2.2 million individuals
Contributory pensions	1904	Basic pension + additional pension based on earnings over last 10 years		2003: 5.7% 2009: 7.2%	3.3 million individuals
Education and health		70% enrolled in public educational institutions; public health services include hospitals and other facilities		2003: 3.4% 2009: 5.9% 2003: 2.9% 2009: 2.6%	

Social Spending Programs: direct cash transfers, noncontributory and contributory pensions, and spending on education and health.

Source: Overview based on Novick and Villafañe 2011.

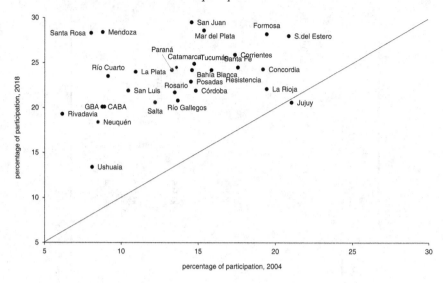

Figure 6.7 The share of social transfers in total household income (2004 and 2018)

Data sources: Calculated from EPH Household survey data (INDEC).

Table 6.3 Correlation coefficients between transfers and city characteristics (2018)

	Female headed household	Average income	Population over 65	Children under 18	Household size	Informal employment
Transfers	0.1748	−0.4443	0.275	0.2461	0.2051	0.5086

Data sources: Calculated from EPH Household survey data (INDEC).

The most significant relationship appears with informal employment. This may be due to the Asignación Universal por Hijo (AUH; universal per child allowance), a large-scale targeted, conditional cash transfer program launched in November 2009. Its primary beneficiaries are families with children (18 or younger) whose head of household is working in the informal sector or is unemployed. Transfers appear to be negatively correlated with average incomes, which signals that the need for social transfer payments is lower in economically prosperous cities.

Income sources that drive income inequality

The other two factors that shape income inequality, according to Lerman and Yitzhaki, are the correlation of each income source to the Gini coefficient (R_k) and the Gini of each source (G_k). The three factors combined (with S_k) are what compute the relative participation of each income stream to total inequality.

Table 6.4 presents an overview of the contribution of the income sources to the Gini coefficient for 2004 and 2018. It shows that formal labor income

Table 6.4 Relative participation of income sources in the Gini coefficient (%)

Urban area	Formal salaries		Informal salaries		Informal self-employed		Capital incomes		Transfers	
	2004	2018	2004	2018	2004	2018	2004	2018	2004	2018
Bahía Blanca	57	86	10	11	17	12	10	8	4	10
CABA	58	63	6	8	31	15	8	10	3	19
Catamarca	54	63	3	2	19	10	5	2	14	17
Concordia	44	54	7	2	16	20	10	6	14	8
Córdoba	38	51	12	10	22	11	17	13	8	15
Corrientes	45	96	6	9	23	16	7	0	15	19
Formosa	58	64	1	3	6	15	5	5	21	18
GBA	57	83	14	11	19	14	4	5	3	16
Jujuy	45	64	13	6	18	11	4	2	15	16
La Plata	73	80	9	7	9	9	5	0	4	22
La Rioja	46	86	3	7	11	11	7	1	20	16
Mar del Plata	51	68	11	12	23	28	13	8	11	15
Mendoza	57	51	8	7	19	16	7	6	3	20
Neuquén	76	79	2	2	10	14	6	6	8	14
Paraná	54	55	6	1	27	15	0	15	9	20
Posadas	57	66	8	3	18	16	6	6	8	11
Resistencia	63	80	7	5	13	11	1	0	10	10
Río Cuarto	56	49	6	6	26	26	8	7	4	14
Río Gallegos	77	81	3	3	7	11	6	4	7	24
Rivadavia	74	83	2	1	18	12	6	1	2	10
Rosario	49	64	8	14	36	18	8	5	3	16
S.del Estero	53	61	3	5	12	13	6	5	19	24
Salta	65	63	4	5	16	8	6	6	8	10
San Juan	51	45	5	9	18	19	9	5	14	16
San Luis	61	59	9	3	11	21	8	12	10	11
Santa Fé	48	73	6	4	21	6	12	8	6	14
Santa Rosa	54	68	4	3	41	19	3	4	2	19
Tucumán	49	57	8	7	22	15	10	4	10	17
Ushuaia	67	78	4	-1	9	10	11	2	6	10
Simple average	56	68	7	5	19	14	7	5	9	16

Data sources: Calculated from EPH Household survey data (INDEC).

contributes most to inequality, irrespective of the city. This effect has become more influential since 2004, increasing the relative participation of labor income to the Gini coefficient from 53 to 68 percent. This finding corroborates with evidence from country-level studies in Latin America (see Medina and Galván 2008). The correlation between labor income and the Gini is positive and significant, suggesting that labor income has increased inequality.

Figure 6.8 illustrates the changes in the contribution of formal employment to inequality between 2004 and 2018. Formal sector wages explain between 45 percent (in San Juan) and 93 percent (in Corrientes) of total inequality in 2018. These findings suggest that disparities in the formal labor market have increased and are essential to address. While education and skills

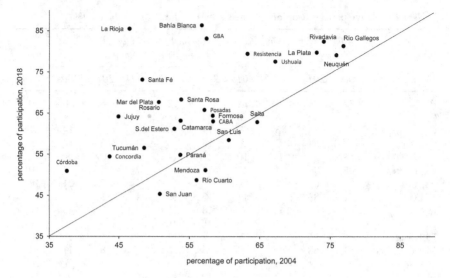

Figure 6.8 Participation of formal salaries in total inequality (2004 and 2018)

Data sources: Calculated from EPH Household survey data (INDEC).

are vital for social mobility, unequal compensation even within the same skill groups is a challenge.

Besides labor income, social transfers have the second-largest impact on the Gini and have increased from 9 percent in 2004 to 16 percent in 2018. This increase can be traced back to the expansion of social security programs after 2004, when the share of transfers in income doubled from 10 percent in 2004 to 20 percent in 2015. In five cities (Rio Gallegos, Santiago del Estero, La Plata, Paraná, and Mendoza), transfers explained more than 20 percent of inequality. The correlation coefficient is negative and exceeds 0.5, which means it is inequality reducing but weaker than formal income.

The correlation between the Gini and informal income (both salaries and self-employment) is weak and negligible. On the other hand, capital incomes have a positive and strong correlation coefficient.

The redistributive capacity of income sources

Information on how income sources affect changes in inequality is particularly relevant from a public policy perspective. The Gini elasticity provides a valuable indication of how potential changes in a given income source would affect inequality based on how an income source is distributed across the population.

Figure 6.9 presents the elasticity of the Gini for each of the components of total income in 2018 for 21 selected cities. While there are fluctuations across cities – see Buenos Aires city (CABA) and Rio Gallegos versus Resistencia and Santa Fe – three general trends appear:

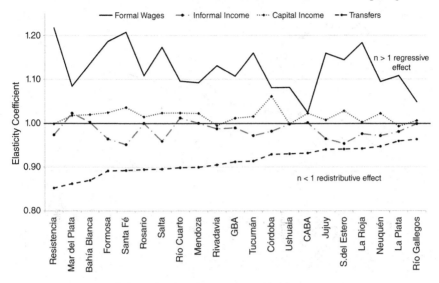

Figure 6.9 Elasticity of income sources in 2018

Data sources: Calculated from EPH Household survey data (INDEC).

1 Formal incomes have elasticities greater than 1 in all cities, indicating an inequality increasing effect.
2 Informal incomes (both from informal salaries or self-employment) and capital incomes have values close to 1, suggesting that a marginal change of these incomes will not significantly alter the Gini.
3 Social transfers have elasticity levels below 1, indicating a redistributive and inequality reducing effect. The effect is most potent in cities where more people rely on such transfers (e.g., Resistencia and Mar del Plata).

Figure 6.10 illustrates the changes in elasticity of formal income between 2004 and 2018, showing that its relevance in the Gini increased in 28 of the 32 cities (except Buenos Aires city, Neuquén, Rio Gallegos, and La Plata), by an average of 4 percent. The cities with the largest increase are La Rioja, Santa Fe, Corrientes, and Jujuy, with changes exceeding 10 percent. The cities with large and increasing elasticities are located in the Pampas region and in the northern parts of the country, which tend to be cities with overall higher inequality. These cities also have a larger share of the population working in the informal sector, where wages are lower and employment is more precarious.

Social transfers present the opposite trend (see Figure 6.11). In all cities except five (Río Gallegos, La Plata, Santa Fé, Rosario, and Córdoba), the elasticity coefficient of transfers declined since 2004, suggesting that a marginal increase in transfers today has a higher redistributive effect than it used to. In Mar del Plata, Resistencia, and La Rioja, transfers have become particularly critical.

The redistributive relevance of transfers corroborates findings from country-level analyses. In a study on social spending in Argentina, Lustig and

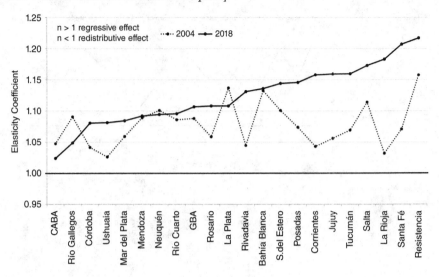

Figure 6.10 Elasticity of formal incomes to the Gini (2004 and 2018)

Data sources: Calculated from EPH Household survey data (INDEC).

Pessino (2013) compare pre- and post-transfer inequality and poverty before and after the implementation and expansion of transfer programs between 2003 and 2009. The findings indicate that social spending accounts for 12 percent of the change in the inequality in disposable income over this period. The analysis further shows that the economy's improvement was a decisive factor.

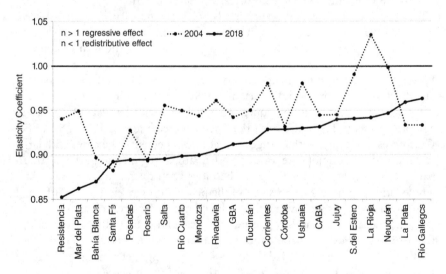

Figure 6.11 Elasticity of social transfers to the Gini (2004 and 2018)

Data sources: Calculated from EPH Household survey data (INDEC).

Social spending was particularly relevant between 2006 and 2009, where 40 percent of the change in the Gini was due to transfer programs. The story of poverty is very similar and perhaps even stronger. Between 2006 and 2009, 90 percent of the decline in poverty results from redistributive policies and social transfers.

The expansion of noncontributory pensions drastically reduced poverty, with coverage increasing from 3.6 to 6.3 million between 2003 and 2009. In 2009, 88.6 percent of the population aged 65 or older received a pension (69.6 in 2003). Benefits also became more generous. Since 2002 pensions increased by about 70 percent in real terms.

Aside from pensions, cash transfers (e.g., the AUH child cash transfer) reduced poverty and inequality. In 2009, more than 90 percent of people living in extreme poverty and more than 80 percent of those in poverty received at least one cash transfer program or noncontributory pensions (Gómez Sabaíni et al. 2013).

Public spending on education and health care also increased during this time, with more low-income families participating in the schooling and health care systems.

An analysis of the impact of taxes and public spending on poverty and inequality by Rossignolo (2016) finds that direct taxes (personal income tax, social security contributions, etc.) also reduced inequality. He finds that the combination of taxes and transfers reduced extreme poverty by 65 percent and income inequality by 16 percent. In-kind transfers in education and health further reduced poverty and inequality, with a decline in the Gini by 24 percent. However, spending for tertiary-level education tends to be regressive, as it benefits wealthier households more than poorer ones (ibid).

But more can be done to reduce inequality. Lustig and Pessino (2013) and Puig and Salinardi (2015) find much of government spending on essential services like water and electricity is regressive, suggesting that the richest receive more subsidies than people with lower incomes. For example, the richest 20 percent captured about 30 percent of electricity subsidies, while the poorest 20 percent accounted for just 12 percent.

The regressive nature of subsidies should not be interpreted as a call for cutting subsidies altogether. Instead, it should serve as a call to redirect transfers to lower-income people and establish a more progressive tariff system. The subsidy cuts in 2015 failed to consider such nuances and disproportionately affected those at the lower end of the income spectrum.

Results of a 2018 survey of 1,500 households in Metropolitan Buenos Aires by the Center for Metropolitan Studies (CEM 2019) after the subsidy cut indicate that 65 percent of households consider tariffs too high for public services. About a quarter of families cannot pay the increased prices. This share is even higher for some services: 37 percent could not afford the increased electricity costs, 27 percent said water became unaffordable.

The difference across cities is likely the result of the local economic conditions and social inequalities. Since some programs, like the AUH, specifically

Table 6.5 Impact of marginal changes in income sources on inequality (2004 and 2018) (number of cities by source)

Effect on inequality	Formal labor income		Informal labor income		Capital incomes		Transfers	
	2004	2018	2004	2018	2004	2018	2004	2018
Regressive	27	31	–	–	3	1	–	–
Neutral	5	1	30	30	29	31	7	2
Progressive	–	–	2	2	–	–	25	30

target households with children, the transfer payments are larger in cities where more people fall into those groups. In a study on the impact of transfer programs across Argentina's five regions, Maurizio (2008) finds that the effect of transfer programs is greater where economic hardship is higher.

Table 6.5 summarizes the marginal effects of each income source on inequality in Argentina's cities in 2004 and 2018. With a few exceptions, informal employment and capital incomes had a negligible impact on inequality across all cities and over time. Formal work had regressive effects in 2004, which increased over time and was true for all cities except Buenos Aires in 2018. Finally, the potential marginal impact of transfers on inequality has also been significant for most cities in 2004 and all cities except La Plata and Rio Gallegos in 2018.

Conclusions

The blend of economic recovery and expanded social protection reduced inequality and poverty across Argentinian cities after the 2001/02 crisis. These improvements were, however, not equally felt across all places and income earners. While people working in the formal sector saw their incomes recover after the crisis, informal sector incomes remained low.

This chapter applies the decomposition methodology of Lerman and Yitzhaki (1985) to analyze the income sources that shape inequality for a more informed discussion about its driving forces and policies to address inequality moving forward. Five conclusions can be drawn from this study.

First, labor income represents the largest income source for households. In some cities – San Nicolas, Paraná, and Mendoza – the share of labor income in total income is slightly lower at about 65 percent; in others – like Ushuaia and Neuquén, it makes up 80 percent of total income. Within this bracket, the share of income from formal employment has increased over time, and so has their contribution to inequality. Between 2004 and 2018, the relative participation of income from formal work to total inequality has increased in eight out of ten cities, explaining on average 68 percent of inequality. Moreover, a marginal increase in formal employment had an inequality-increasing effect in 2018 in all cities except Buenos Aires.

Second, the increasing discrepancy between the share of informal income in labor income (30 percent) and the share of informal workers in total employment (47 percent) suggests that people working in the informal sector are worse off today than in 2004. This so-called informality wage gap persists despite the employment generation and labor formalization in the early 2000s and a context of better labor protections. The increased participation of registered wage earners in total employment has been a positive phenomenon because it induced higher wages and expanded the social security system coverage. However, informal workers have not seen their wages improve sufficiently.

Third, the share of capital incomes in total income has declined since 1996, from about 6 to 3.8 percent in 2018. The share of capital incomes is largest in cities with ballooning housing prices like Córdoba (7 percent) and Buenos Aires city (6 percent), and lowest in La Rioja, Resistencia, and Corrientes (less than 1 percent). Although capital incomes are extremely unequally distributed and strongly correlate with the Gini, the elasticity of capital incomes indicates that an increase in capital incomes has an insignificant effect on inequality. However, studies have found that capital incomes are prone to underreporting, even more than other types of income. Thus, the unequal distribution of capital incomes may play a more vital role than the results suggest.

Fourth, social transfers are the second most important source of income in Argentinian cities. The share of social transfers in total income increased after 2004. Between 2003 and 2009, the federal government increased social spending by about 13.5 percentage points. In 2018, transfers constituted about 24 percent of all incomes and explained 16 percent of total inequality. The correlation with inequality is negative, and the elasticity is high, suggesting that an increase in transfers has a redistributing, inequality-reducing effect. The transfer programs introduced and expanded between 2004 and 2015 lowered inequality notably.

The findings suggest that inequality in the formal job market needs to be reduced, formal employment generation must be strengthened, and complemented with a social protection system that expands noncontributory components. Informal workers are often excluded from social protection owing to the challenges inherent in collecting contributions and determining subsequent entitlements to services. The evolution of the real minimum wage, for instance, might have contributed to the growing wage gap between formal and informal workers. Empirical literature (see Maurizio 2014) suggests that the minimum wage almost exclusively helped formal workers in Argentina, resulting in a widening wage gap between workers subject to the effects of such labor institutions and those who are not.

Ensuring access to essential services for everyone can best be achieved by providing universal access, delinked from one's employment status. Given that, by definition, informal workers lack protection, universal policies can address this gap, thereby contributing to incremental formalization. Distributive mechanisms encompassing the entire labor market are particularly essential in times of macroeconomic difficulties like the COVID-19 pandemic caused in 2020.

Since transfers represent a vital tool for reducing poverty and inequality, it is crucial to ensure sustained financing of transfers in the future. Already in 2009, Cetrangolo and Gómez Sabaíni warned about the imbalances in the tax system and the erratic revenues and dependence on the economic cycle. The authors state that the current system leans too heavily on direct taxation and is too cautious of taxing personal income and equity.

Finally, the differences in informal employment and the share in transfers across the cities in this study suggest that social and labor policies and economic strategies should consider local and regional differences. For example, the *Programa Familias para la Inclusión Social*, which targets low-income families with at least two children, could be most effective in cities with larger average households, like Salta or Santiago del Estero. Reinforcing and adjusting transfer programs by local characteristics and needs of a city might thus help reduce inequality and poverty nationally.

Notes

1 The analysis in Chapter 7 speaks to a series of these underlying factors that may influence inequality.
2 Following studies by the Ierullo (2019) at the Centro de Estudios de la Ciudad, a research center on urban issues at the University of Buenos Aires, *informal employment* is calculated based on the following criteria: workers not covered by labor legislation, generally working in small private enterprises of less than five workers, with low qualifications.
3 Instituto Nacional de Estadísticas y Censos.
4 Using the same quarter throughout the years minimizes the risk of distortions from seasonal employment or complementary salaries like the *Aguinaldo* (Christmas Bonus).
5 In 1974, the EPH was extended from Gran Buenos Aires to 31 large urban areas. This geographical extension has taken place gradually over time. Some conglomerates were included in the 1980s, while others have been added in the 1990s. The last conglomerates to join the EPH were San Nicolás-Villa Constitución, Trelew-Rawson, and Viedma-Patagones in 2002. Source: World Bank (2021).
6 Throughout this chapter, "income" refers to monthly real per capita household income, which considers inflation. Since Argentina is infamous for high inflation levels, real incomes have been calculated to compare trends over time more accurately.
7 Justicialismo, also known as Peronism, was first instituted by Juan Domingo Peron in the 1940s and turned into a mass movement with strong populist underpinnings (Lustig and Pessino 2014).
8 Referring to spending by federal, state, and municipal governments.

References

Beccaria, Luis, and Fernando Groisman. 2008. "Informalidad y pobreza en Argentina." *Investigación económica* 67 (266): 135–69.
Bertranou, Fabio, and Luis Casanova. 2013. *Informalidad laboral en Argentina: segmentos críticos y políticas para la formalización.* Buenos Aires: Oficina de País de la OIT para Argentina.

Centro de Estudios Metropolitanos (CEM). 2019. "XI Monitor del Clima Social." Online. Available at: http://estudiosmetropolitanos.com.ar/2019/10/08/xi-monitor-del-clima-social/, accessed November 30, 2021.

Cetrángolo, Oscar, and Juan Carlos Gómez Sabaíni. 2009. *La imposición en la Argentina: un análisis de la imposición a la renta, a los patrimonios y otros tributos considerados directos.* CEPAL - Serie Macroeconomía del desarrollo No 84. Santiago de Chile: United Nations.

Cowell, Frank A., and Carlo V. Fiorio. 2011. "Inequality Decompositions—a Reconciliation." *The Journal of Economic Inequality* 9 (4): 509–528.

Gasparini, Leonardo. 2004. *Poverty and Inequality in Argentina.* La Plata: Departamento de Economia. Universidad Nacional de La Plata.

Gómez Sabaíni, Juan Carlos, Harriague, Marcela, and Darío Rossignolo. 2013. "La situación fiscal en Argentina y sus efectos sobre la distribución del ingreso. Una estimación para el año 2008." *Desarrollo económico: revista de ciencias sociales* Vol. 52, No. 207-208, pp. 339–380.

Hanni, Michael, Ricardo Martner Fanta, and Andrea Podesta. 2016. "The Redistributive Potential of Taxation in Latin America." *CEPAL Review.* Santiago de Chile: United Nations.

Ierullo, Martin. 2019. "*Informe de Coyuntura n° 16 – Restricción de la asistencia alimentaria en tiempos de hambre.*" Buenos Aires: *Centro de Estudio de la Ciudad (CEC).*

Indec. 2020. *Bases de Datos.* Argentina: INDEC.

Lerman, Robert I., and Shlomo Yitzhaki. 1985. "Income Inequality Effects by Income Source: A New Approach and Applications to the United States." *The Review of Economics and Statistics*, Vol. 67, No.1, pp. 151–56. Cambridge, MA: MIT Press.

Lustig, Nora, and Carola Pessino. 2014. Social Spending and Income Redistribution in Argentina during the 2000s: The Increasing Role of Noncontributory Pensions. *Public Finance Review.* 2014;42(3):304–325.

Maio, Fernando G.De. 2007. "Income Inequality Measures." *Journal of Epidemiology & Community Health* 61 (10): 849–52. https://doi.org/10.1136/jech.2006.052969.

Maurizio, Roxana. 2008. "Políticas de transferencias monetarias en Argentina: Una evaluación de su impacto sobre la pobreza y la desigualdad y de sus costos." Buenos Aires: Universidad Nacional de General Sarmiento.

———. 2014. "Labor Formalization and Declining Inequality in Argentina and Brazil in the 2000s: A Dynamic Approach." In *ILO Research Paper No. 9.* Geneva: International Labor Office.

Medina, Fernando and Marco Galván. 2008. *Descomposición del coeficiente de Gini por fuentes de ingreso: Evidencia empírica para América Latina 1999–2005.* CEPAL - Serie Estudios estadísticos y prospectivos No 63. Santiago de Chile: United Nations.

Minoldo, Sol., and Diego Born. 2019. "*Claroscuros. 9 años de datos bajo sospecha.*" Buenos Aires: ESEditora.

Novick, Marta, and Soledad Villafañe. 2011. *Distribución del ingreso: enfoques y políticas públicas desde el Sur.* Buenos Aires, Argentina: *UNDP Argentina, Ministerio de Trabajo, Empleo y Seguridad Social, Presidencia de la Nación.*

Puig, Jorge Pablo, and Leandro Hipólito Arnoldo Salinardi. 2015. *Argentina y los subsidios a los servicios públicos: un estudio de incidencia distributiva.* Documentos de Trabajo del CEDLAS, No. 183. La Plata: Universidad Nacional de la Plata.

Rao, V.M. 1969. "Two Decompositions of Concentration Ratio." *Journal of the Royal Statistical Society. Series A (General)* 132 (3): 418–25.

Rossignolo, Darío. 2016. "Taxes, Expenditures, Poverty and Income Distribution in Argentina." Commitment to Equity (CEQ) Working Paper Series 45, Tulane University, Department of Economics.

Shorrocks, A.F. 1982. "Inequality Decomposition by Factor Components." *Econometrica* 50 (1): 193–211.

Trujillo, Lucía, and Soledad Villafañe. 2011. "Dinámica distributiva y políticas públicas: dos décadas de contrastes en la Argentina contemporánea." In *Distribución del ingreso. Enfoques y políticas públicas desde el Sur, by Novick and Villafañe*, 227–62. Buenos Aires: PNUD, Ministerio de Empleo, Trabajo, y Seguridad.

World Bank. 2021. "Urban population (% of the total population) – Argentina." World Bank data. Available at: https://data.worldbank.org/indicator/SP.URB.TOTL.IN. ZS?locations=AR, accessed November 28, 2021.

Wroughton, Lesley. 2013. "IMF Reprimands Argentina for Inaccurate Economic Data." *Reuters.* February 1, 2013. https://www.reuters.com/article/us-imf-argentina/ imf-reprimands-argentina-for-inaccurate-economic-data-idUSBRE91019920130202

7 A data-driven approach to assess determinants of income inequality in Argentina's cities

With more than half the global population living in urban areas, addressing the growing income gap in cities is ever more urgent. Not only does inequality compromise the cities' function as an economic engine of growth, but it also compromises the fragile social stability that holds these cities together. As Glaeser et al. (2009) point out, city-level income inequality has different implications from national-level income inequality. It neither responds to the same factors nor creates the same policy responses.

The high cross-sectional variability of intra-urban income inequality observed in Argentina suggests the need to investigate possible determinants of income inequality further, taking into account specific local factors. Argentinian cities are highly diverse in size, economic structure, and demographic composition. Yet to date, just a handful of studies look at the local dimension of income inequality (e.g., Cuenin 2002; Glaeser et al. 2009).

This chapter builds on the analysis of income sources affecting inequality in Chapter 6. So far, the findings show that social transfers were essential in reducing inequality; and the widening income gap between formal and informal employment contributes to inequality in cities. Building on these findings and the existing literature on the topic (e.g., Cuenin 2002; Glaeser et al. 2009; Gasparini et al. 2014), this chapter aims to generate further evidence for the thesis that apart from national social and fiscal policy, local context matters. Understanding local specificities and their interaction with inequality can help officials craft more effective policies at the national and city level. The national is thus not the only entry point to address disparities. Local policies and practices are just as relevant.

This chapter takes a closer look at a series of city-specific variables and their relationship with inequality. In total, the association between the Gini coefficient and 35 variables was reviewed and tested. Based on the findings of the descriptive analysis, I adopt a fixed-effects regression model, which presents the effects of 14 variables on inequality. The majority of data stems from Argentina's household survey (Encuesta Permanente de Hogares, or short EPH) for 29 cities from 1996 to 2018. The conclusions of this chapter aim to provide a more nuanced understanding of local drivers of income

DOI: 10.4324/9781003201908-9

inequality, an essential piece in formulating effective public policies to curve disparities in cities.

Understanding the determinants for distributive structures in cities is a methodological and conceptual challenge but a necessary step for designing policy solutions aimed at reducing inequality and poverty. At least two obstacles challenge the empirical analysis of the drivers of distributive changes. The first is theoretical. Atkinson and Bourguignon (2000) recognized two decades ago that there is no unified and consistent theory about the determinants of changes in income distribution. No matter the number of variables included in an analysis, it will never be all-encompassing. However, Caroline Moser's Asset Accumulation Framework (2015) discovered a path forward using different influential factors which provides researchers and practitioners alike a more holistic view. The Urban Inequality Matrix (UIM) proposed in Chapter 5 learns from this and uses it to create an umbrella for the analysis of this chapter, laying out the inter-related national and local processes, structures, and dynamics that shape inequality in cities.

A second obstacle is specific to Argentina. In a single generation, about 30 years, the country has experienced two periods of drastic distributive change. A study of the drivers of these changes may thus face an identification problem. In the first period, from 1996 to 2003, numerous economic transformations occurred; nearly all state companies were privatized, deregulation was common practice, and the social security system was slashed. In the second period, beginning in 2003, many of these transformations were scaled back and, in some cases, overturned. The new government halted privatization, renationalized companies providing public services, overhauled trade policy to protect the local market, and extended social protection measures to people working in the informal economy. All these processes, many of which are interrelated, affected the income distribution in cities. Given that many variables are in flux, it is challenging to extract clear evidence in favor of any possible hypotheses about distributive changes.

With these challenges in mind, this chapter makes an effort to integrate the literature on inequality and available data to present evidence on the potential drivers of income inequality in Argentinian cities. This evidence is illustrative, but in no way should it be considered conclusive given the limitations noted.

The chapter builds on inequality research done first by Cuenin (2002) and then followed by Gasparini et al. (2009) and Glaeser et al. (2009). Fernando Cuenin's analysis in 2002 appears to be the first and only study that assesses determinants of inequality in Argentinian cities quantitatively. Cuenin used panel data to determine the trends and levels of inequality between 1996 and 2000. His fixed-effects model discovered that cities with lower inequality have fewer differences in educational achievements, a stable sectoral composition of the economy, low unemployment, and a higher level of economic development. Gasparini et al. (2009) estimate the role of unemployment, structural changes, education and skills, trade liberalization, and technological change in income inequality across Latin American countries. Glaeser et al. (2009) apply a regression analysis on the disparities in the return to skills in US cities, which they then related to local industrial patterns.

This chapter makes several additions to Cuenin's and Glaeser et al.'s analyses. First, it assesses a much more extended period, from 1996 to 2018. Inequality shifted considerably since Cuenin's study nearly two decades ago. A follow-up study is valuable to identify how and what drivers have changed. Moreover, both prior analyses exclude variables on informal employment, migration, educational achievements disaggregated by gender, political variables, the degree of economic specialization, or the size of firms, variables that the literature deemed as potentially significant factors.

Data and methodology

The analysis uses public data from 29 cities, home to 71 percent of Argentina's urban population (INDEC 2020a; INDEC 2020b, INDEC 2020c). The data are presented in a balanced panel, meaning all cities had data for every year (1996–2018).

Localized inequality data are often missing in the official statistics for many countries, Argentina is no exception. As a first step in the analysis, microdata from Argentina's household survey (EPH) was used to calculate three income inequality measures for each city every year: the Gini coefficient, the Theil Index, and the Palma Index. As shown in Table 7.1, the correlation between the inequality indicators is very high, suggesting that the measures indicate similar results, especially between the Gini and the Theil Index.[1]

Table 7.2 is an overview of the variables included in the analysis. The variables were selected based on the UIM and grouped into four subgroups: (i) city structure, (ii) politics, (iii) demographic characteristics, and (iv) the local labor market. While the macroeconomic situation is relevant too, country GDP is strongly correlated with local incomes and the dummy for a progressive federal government and therefore omitted to avoid multicollinearity.

Table 7.1 Correlation matrix of inequality measures for Argentina (2018)

Index	Gini	Theil	Palma
Gini	1		
Theil	0.9008	1	
Palma	0.6814	0.5122	1

Data sources: Calculated from EPH Household survey data (INDEC).

Table 7.2 Definitions, sources, and descriptive statistics of the explanatory variables included in the analytical model[2]

Variable	Definition	Mean	Std	Expected effect
(i) City structure				
Average income (Y)	Per capita mean income logs (in real terms)	8.54	0.38	?
High-income cities (HY)	Interacting variable of a dummy for high-income cities with average per capita income	1.26	3.16	?
Large city (L)	Dummy for cities with a population larger than 500,000	0.31	0.46	+
(ii) Politics				
Family allowance (F)	Share of total GDP spent on family allowances, logs	−0.33	0.37	−
Progressive government (PG)	Dummy for PGs at local and national level	0.38	0.49	−
(iii) Demographic factors				
Female secondary education (FSE)	Share of women that have completed secondary education, logs	3.08	0.20	−
Female primary education (FPE)	Share of women that have completed primary education, logs	4.49	0.06	−
Household size (HS)	Average household size, logs	1.23	0.13	+
Older household member	Share of households with a family member aged 65 or older, logs	3.10	0.28	−
Immigrants	Share of population not born in the city (internal and international migration)	3.34	0.37	?
(iv) Local labor market				
Diversity (D)	The inverse of the Herfindahl-Hirschman Index (HH), to estimate the participation of each sector in the city's total employment, logs	2.49	0.19	?
Unemployment rate (U)	Share of the 18–65-years-old population that is unemployed, logs	2.07	0.62	+
Informal employment (I)	Share of workforce in informal employment situations, logs	3.81	0.23	+
Medium firms (M)	Share of medium sized companies, with employees between 40 and 200 workers (exact size depends on the sector), logs	2.44	0.53	−

Data sources: Calculated from EPH Household survey data (INDEC).

Model specification: Fixed-effects regression model

In the empirical analysis, I first establish my base model, which includes variables on *city structure* (S), such as proxies for economic development and city size. After that, I add variables that speak to *politics* (P), *demographic characteristics* (D), and the *local labor market* (L). These variables suggest:

$$I_{it} = S_{it}, P_{it}, D_{it}, L_{it} \tag{1}$$

where I_{it} is the level of inequality of the urban agglomerate i in year t, S, P, D, and L are vectors of characteristics and variables that are assumed to relate with inequality. The dependent variable – inequality – is measured with the Gini coefficient, the Theil Index, and the Palma Index.

Econometric models using panel data allow for greater information since they involve a combination of time series and cross-section models. The availability of data in panel form makes it possible to consider both types of information simultaneously, allowing to estimate a component model of errors. All variables (except the dummy variables) have been converted to natural logs so that their estimated coefficients can be interpreted as elasticities:

$$Log\ (l_{it}) = \beta_0 + \beta_1 \log S_{it} + \beta_2 \log X_{it} + U_{it} \tag{2}$$

U_{it} is the error term, and $i = 1, \ldots, 32$; $t = 1996, \ldots, 2018$,

where I is the log of each of the three inequality measures across i and t. All variables of the base model (S) vary over time and across cities. Following the base model, I control for a series of explanatory variables (see Vector X). β represents the coefficients that the model intends to predict; U is the idiosyncratic error, because it changes across t and i.

The regression is estimated assuming that the individual specific constant terms are randomly distributed across the urban agglomerations. How this model is estimated will depend on the specification of the error term. If it is assumed that there is no unobservable heterogeneity ($v_i = d_t = 0$), then it is valid to estimate the model by using Ordinary Least Squares (OLS):

$$Log\ (l_{it}) = \alpha + \beta_1 \log S_{it} + \beta_2 \log X_{it} + e_{it} \tag{3}$$

Subsequently, I consider the existence of unobservable factors that only vary by agglomerates, estimating the model (4) by fixed and random effects:

$$Log\ (l_{it}) = \alpha + \beta_1 \log S_{it} + \beta_2 \log X_{it} + v_i + e_{it} \tag{4}$$

The results of the F-test of fixed effects and the Breusch and Pagan test favor the presence of unobservable factors that vary by agglomerate (*log gini (city, t)* $= Xb + u(city) + e(city, t)$). Consequently, since unobservable heterogeneity exists, estimating the model (3) by OLS would not be correct. In addition, according to the Hausman test, the explanatory variables are correlated with the random term, and therefore, only the estimators of the fixed-effects model are consistent.

The fixed-effects model is appropriate to study city-specific variables that affect changes in inequality over time because it allows controlling for unobservable city-specific characteristics. It also helps alleviate potential heteroscedasticity problems stemming from possible differences across cities (Greene 2003).

The fixed-effects model has n different intercepts, one for each entity. A set of variables can represent these intercepts. These variables absorb the influences of all omitted variables that differ from one entity to the next but are constant over time. The fixed-effects estimator, also called the within-estimator, is appropriate to assess variables that affect change over time. It allows one to focus on how changes in within-city characteristics are related to changes in within-city inequality. The fixed-effects model is also more suitable when focusing on a specific set of cities, and the inference is restricted to these places (Baltagi 2008).

Therefore:

$$Log\ (l_{it}) = \beta_0 + \beta_1 \log S_{it} + \beta_2 \log X_{it} + \beta_3 Z_i + U_{it} \qquad (5)$$

where Z is an unobserved variable that varies from one city to the next but does not change over time. I want to estimate β_{1-2}, the effect of Y on X holding constant the unobserved city characteristics Z. Because Z varies from one city to the next but is constant over time, the Gini regression model in equation (5) can be interpreted as having n intercepts, one for each city. Specifically, let $\alpha = \beta_0 + \beta_3 Z_i$. Then, equation (5) becomes:

$$Log\ (l_{it}) = \beta_1 \log SD_{it} + \beta_2 \log X_{it} + \alpha_i + u_{it} \qquad (6)$$

Equation (6) is the fixed-effects regression model, in which $\alpha_i \dots \alpha_n$ are treated as unknown intercepts to be estimated, one for each city. Because the intercept α_i in equation (6) can be thought of as the "effect" of being in city i, the terms $\alpha_i \dots \alpha_n$ are known as entity fixed effects. The variation in the entity fixed effects comes from omitted variables that, like Z, in equation (5), vary across cities but not over time.

To check for robustness, several tests were conducted to avoid multicollinearity, stationarity, and endogeneity. An F test was used to detect whether the independent variables predict the dependent variable, R-squared helps identify how well the model suits the data. Standard errors were robustified and clustered to avoid issues of autocorrelation and heteroskedasticity.

Intra-urban inequality models[3]

This chapter aims to generate findings on the city characteristics that shape intra-urban income inequality. Ideally, the results give insight into the national and local policies that create more just and equal societies and economies.

Table 7.3 presents the estimation results obtained using equation (6). The models are specified in log-log terms to facilitate interpretation. All coefficients (except the dummy variables) represent the elasticity of the Gini for the independent variables. In other words, the coefficients present the estimated percent change in the Gini for a percent change in the independent variables.

Table 7.4 presents the results of model 6 for the Gini coefficient, the Theil Index, and the Palma Index. Although the model has the strongest explanatory power with the Gini, the Theil and the Palma models have an R^2 of 0.687 and 0.661 (respectively), indicating high predictability and consistency of the findings across inequality measures.

The following sub-sections discuss the model results, organized in the four categories city structure, politics, demographics, and the local labor market.

City Structure – the base model

The "city structure" presents the base model in the analysis and includes population size and economic development variables. Although much work has been done analyzing the relationship between city size, development, and income distribution, it remains hotly contested (see, e.g., Kuznets 1955; Milanovic 2016).

The regression results show that income is the strongest predictor in the base model and has the expected sign: as incomes increase, inequality reduces. This finding is consistent with descriptive findings on the evolution of inequality in Argentina; when the economy recovered from the 2001 crisis, average incomes across all cities grew steadily until 2012. At the same time, inequality reduced. Figure 7.1 depicts the sudden and large fall in inequality following the 2001 crisis, showing a negative association between incomes and the Gini coefficient during the episodes of crisis and recovery.

High-income cities recovered much more rapidly from the crisis than middle- and low-income cities, as Figure 7.2 depicts. After 2013, however, average incomes stagnated and even dropped in some cities. Although

Table 7.3 Income inequality determinants – Gini coefficient

	(1) Gini	(2) Gini	(3) Gini	(4) Gini	(5) Gini	(6) Gini
Average income	-0.442***	-0.401***	-0.130***	-0.134***	-0.095***	-0.070**
	(0.020)	(0.022)	(0.038)	(0.037)	(0.032)	(0.033)
High-income city	0.195***	0.204***	0.113***	0.031	0.134***	0.086**
	(0.041)	(0.046)	(0.043)	(0.042)	(0.040)	(0.038)
Large city (D)	-0.087***	-0.098***	-0.077***	-0.026	-0.025	-0.037**
	(0.020)	(0.021)	(0.021)	(0.025)	(0.020)	(0.018)
Econ diversity		0.439***	0.355***	0.260***	0.149***	0.085**
		(0.063)	(0.054)	(0.047)	(0.044)	(0.040)
Progressive Gov (D)			-0.082***	-0.068***	-0.028***	-0.029***
			(0.009)	(0.009)	(0.008)	(0.008)
Family allowances			-0.177***	-0.133***	-0.062***	-0.052***
			(0.018)	(0.017)	(0.016)	(0.015)
Informal employment			0.154***		0.065*	0.055
			(0.041)		(0.036)	(0.036)
Immigration				0.245***	0.105***	0.055**
				(0.030)	(0.029)	(0.028)
Household size					0.277***	0.371***
					(0.097)	(0.093)
Female SE					-0.091***	-0.063***
					(0.026)	(0.024)
Female PE					-0.118	-0.258**
					(0.139)	(0.128)
Older hh member					-0.088***	-0.080***
					(0.024)	(0.023)
Medium firms					-0.059***	
					(0.011)	
Unemployment						0.074***
						(0.010)
Obs.	638	638	638	638	638	638
R-squared	0.532	0.577	0.658	0.695	0.766	0.784

Standard errors are in parenthesis.
*** $p<0.01$, ** $p<0.05$, * $p<0.1$.

Data sources: Calculated from EPH Household survey data (INDEC).

Table 7.4 Regressions with three inequality measures

	Gini coefficient		Theil Index		Palma Index	
	Coefficient	Standard error	Coefficient	Standard error	Coefficient	Standard error
City structure						
Average income	−0.070★★	0.033	−0.176★★★	0.062	−0.169★★★	0.064
High-income city	0.086★★	0.038	0.167★★★	0.063	0.212★★★	0.069
Large city	−0.037★★	0.018	−0.059★	0.032	0.026	0.052
Politics						
Progressive Gov	−0.029★★★	0.008	−0.043★★★	0.014	−0.016	0.015
Family allowance	−0.052★★★	0.015	−0.070★★	0.028	−0.123★★★	0.032
Demographic factors						
Female SE	−0.063★★★	0.024	−0.034	0.042	−0.077	0.049
Female PE	−0.258★★	0.128	−0.193	0.191	−0.386	0.311
Older hh member	−0.080★★★	0.023	−0.122★★★	0.039	−0.187★★★	0.053
Immigration	0.055★★	0.028	0.085★	0.045	0.074	0.090
Household size	0.371★★★	0.093	0.357★★	0.141	0.119	0.208
Local labor market						
Diversity	0.085★★	0.040	0.109★	0.062	−0.018	0.094
Informal empl	0.055	0.036	0.073	0.063	0.234★★★	0.075
Unemployment	0.074★★★	0.010	0.108★★★	0.017	0.128★★★	0.020
Obs.	638		638		638	
R-squared	0.784		0.687		0.661	

Standard errors are in parenthesis.
★★★ $p<0.01$, ★★ $p<0.05$, ★ $p<0.1$.

Data sources: Calculated from EPH Household survey data (INDEC).

less notable, middle-income cities experienced a similar stagnation of incomes after 2013. Low-income cities, in contrast, recovered more slowly from the crisis and experienced a steady increase in average income throughout the years.

Taking a closer look at the cities with higher incomes, it appears that the inequality-reducing effect of income growth ceases after a certain threshold. The findings suggest that an increase in income among high-income cities might even be inequality increasing.[4] This is the case in Buenos Aires, the city with the highest average per capita incomes (ARS 11,917 in December 2018) and a high Gini of 42.4. ARS - Argentine peso.

The notion that income growth reduces inequality, up to a certain threshold after which inequality increases again, goes against Kuznets' hypothesis. He believed that inequality would first increase alongside

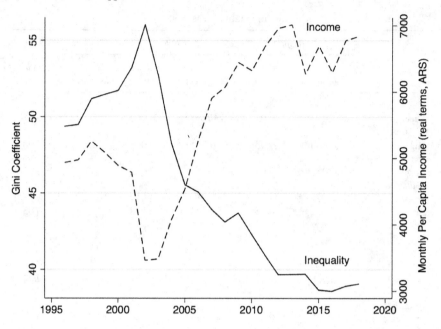

Figure 7.1 As incomes increased, inequality declined. Averages for 29 cities

Data sources: Calculated from EPH Household survey data (INDEC).

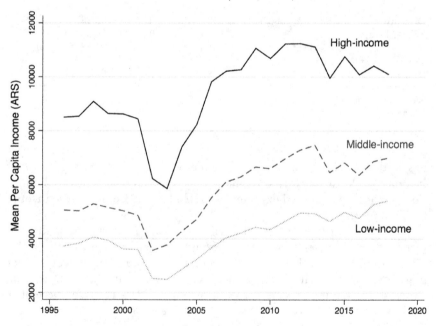

Figure 7.2 Changes in income across high-, middle-, and low-income cities (1996–2018)

Data sources: Calculated from EPH Household survey data (INDEC).

economic growth and drop after a certain point. To further explore the relationship between inequality and economic growth (measured by average income), the Gini was plotted against per capita income, using data from 1996 to 2018 for the 29 cities. The result, depicted in Figure 7.3, seems to confirm a U-shaped relationship: the Gini is notably higher in lower-income cities, declines as incomes increase, and resurges after a certain point.

To further test the link, income and income squared are regressed, and the Lind and Mehlum test is applied.[5] Table 7.5 presents the results, confirming the U-shaped relationship, although the shape is not very pronounced. The regression analysis suggests that the income threshold after which inequality resurges corresponds to around ARS10,900, a value that only the four cities Rio Gallegos, Ushuaia, Rivadavia, and Buenos Aires exceed. These tests suggest that, to a certain degree, Argentinian cities follow an inversed Kuznets' pattern of inequality: inequality improves as income expands and deteriorates after a certain threshold.

Regarding city size (measured in population), the models show that large cities have lower inequality than small- and medium-sized cities.[6] According to the literature on agglomeration economies (see, e.g., Duranton and Puga 2005), increases in a city's economic activity boost firms' productivity and the wages they pay. However, the wage premium of larger cities does not seem to

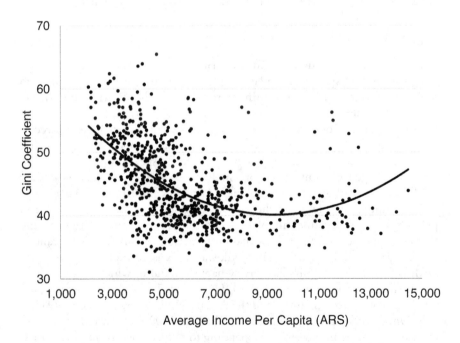

Figure 7.3 Inequality and development: a U-shaped relationship (1996–2018)

Data sources: Calculated from EPH Household survey data (INDEC).

Table 7.5 The Gini coefficient and per capita income

	(1)
Income (log)	−2.367***
	(0.400)
Income (log squared)	0.127***
	(0.023)
Costant	14.742***
	(1.722)
Obs.	667
R-squared	0.280
Lind and Mehlum test for U shape	
$\mid t \mid$	1.41
p-value	0.0801

Standard errors are in parenthesis.
*** $p<0.01$, ** $p<0.05$, * $p<0.1$.

Data sources: Calculated from EPH Household survey data (INDEC).

apply in Argentina. The cities with the highest average incomes are generally not the cities with the largest population. This is because, except Buenos Aires, all high-income cities (Ushuaia, Rio Gallegos, Neuquén, Rawson-Trelew, and Rivadavia) are based on extractive economies, mainly gas and oil. Figure 7.4 depicts the negative relationship between city size and average incomes.[7]

Politics

A city's economic structure and redistributive character are guided by a broader political system that plays a quintessential role in producing and reproducing inequalities as administrators dictate the drafting and enactment of policies and regulations affecting distribution (Rodrik 2008). Public spending, social transfers, and the progressivity of taxes, directly and indirectly, affect income inequality. Inequality may also depend on factors related to political alignments. Generally speaking, progressive or left-leaning governments are more inclined to reduce inequality as they tend to promote redistributive policies (Atkinson and Brandolini 2010).

The empirical model (6) includes two variables speaking to such systems: public spending on family allowances and the progressiveness of governing parties. The model findings show that both variables are highly significant. A larger share of GDP spent on family allowances is associated with lower inequality. This finding coincides with Chapters 4 and 6, which describe how public spending increased after the 2001/02 crisis. The Programa Jefes y Jefas de Hogar introduced in 2003, and the Asignación Universal por Hijo (AUH, The Universal Child Allowance) launched in 2009 were among the most critical milestones in government spending to reduce poverty and inequality.

The AUH, a conditional cash transfer program, expanded social transfers to previously excluded sectors, mainly informal, unemployed, and low-wage workers. As part of the AUH, families receive a monthly stipend for

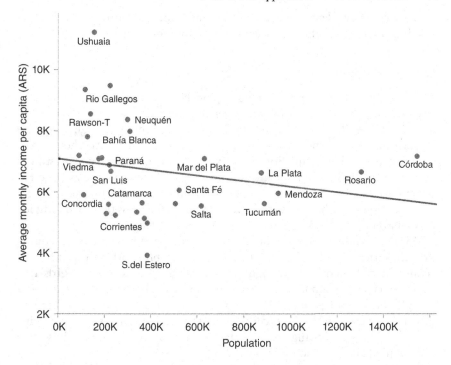

Figure 7.4 In Argentina, larger cities are not necessarily richer (2018)

Data sources: Calculated from EPH Household survey data (INDEC).

each child. The cash transfer quickly became a vital source of income for economically vulnerable households (Alvaredo et al. 2018). Trujillo and Villafañe (2011) find that between 2008 and 2009, incomes of the poorest decile increased from 10 to 26 percent – in part due to social transfers. The authors estimate that the AUH alone reduced the Gini by three percentage points.

The analysis shows no statistically significant relationship between inequality and general expenditures on social assistance, which may seem contradictory at first. After looking more closely at the components of public spending, the reason may be that most spending is in-kind (i.e., health care or infrastructure) and may not directly reflect income. However, these investments are crucial from a redistributive perspective because they ensure that all people have access to quality public services regardless of their income.

Interestingly, the dummy variable for PGs at the local and national levels is statistically significant. The negative coefficient suggests that city inequality is lower when a progressive party is ruling at the national and the city level simultaneously. Two reasons might be at play. First, in Argentina, progressive national governments have a track record of strengthening labor market policies, a central pillar in the distributive dynamics. Second, some local left-leaning administrations expanded national social security and support systems at the city level and invested in public infrastructure and affordable housing at a much higher rate than conservative counterparts.

Demographic factors

The literature deems several demographic factors influential in shaping a city's income distribution, including gender, migration status, education, or household size (HS). The model findings provide some new and exciting insights into those aspects. For instance, cities with more large households tend to have higher inequality. This finding confirms country-level studies that identified HS to be indicative of poverty. In Argentina, the average HS among people in poverty is 6.1 people, with more than two children younger than 12. Non-poor households are much smaller, with less than two individuals on average and 0.3 children (Maurizio et al. 2008).

HS also relates to aspects of informal employment and female education. In cities with larger households, more people work in the informal economy, and inequality is higher. In turn, more women and girls finish primary and secondary education living in smaller families. While the completion rate of primary education for girls is generally very high in urban Argentina, with 89 percent, the completion rate for secondary education is lower. Investing in secondary education for girls can thus have critical inequality-reducing effects.

The share of households with at least one member older than 65 years appears to be inequality reducing, indicating the redistributive character of Argentina's pension system. Belloni and Fracchia (2016) find that income from pensions was the most crucial factor in explaining favorable changes in income distribution since 2004. The contribution came thanks to the increase in retirement credit and the extension of social protection to people working in the informal sector. Benefits also became more generous, increasing their participation in social transfers and total household income.

Results further suggest that cities with a larger share of migrants tend to have higher inequality. The variable is strong and significant. However, adding the variable *immigration* to the model cancels the significance of high-income cities and large cities. Interestingly, the correlation analysis shows a positive correlation (0.74) between a city's income and the share of residents born elsewhere. One explanation may be that the average income of migrants is higher than that of the locally born population.

However, not all migrants earn more. Table 7.6 lists the average incomes by migrant groups. Migrants from Bolivia, Paraguay, Brazil, Chile, and Uruguay earn the lowest incomes. The second-lowest earners are those born in the respective city, with slightly below-average income. On the contrary, migrants born in other cities and provinces and who moved to the city tend to have higher incomes. The same is true for immigrants from other countries, other than those neighboring Argentina.

Table 7.6 Average incomes in 2018, by migration background, in ascending order

Migration background	Average per capita income (ARS)
Average across all urban areas	*9,225*
Migrated from a neighboring country (Bolivia, Paraguay, Brazil, Chile, Uruguay)	8,090
Born in the city	8,740
Migrated from another country	11,202
Migrated from a different city in Argentina	11,293

Data sources: Calculated from EPH Household survey data (INDEC).

The local labor market

At the beginning of the analysis, the local labor market was considered the most critical category. Indicators such as unemployment, the share of part-time and informal workers, the size of the manufacturing sector, public sector employment, or a city's sectoral specialization were assumed to provide insight into inequality and shed light on potential policies for remedy. The model results show that local labor market characteristics are indeed significant and profoundly impact inequality in Argentina's cities.

Rotondo et al. (2016) find that cities with a strong industrial, commercial, and service sector base tend to have more economic diversity than cities based on agricultural and extractive activities. Since 1996, there is a tendency toward a greater specialization of productive activity in urban Argentina, with more jobs concentrating on a smaller group of activities. Many cities thus became more specialized. This process took place with different intensities over the last 20 years. The trend toward specialization was most rapid in the 1990s and slowed down after 2003. A cross-sectional analysis of the 29 cities in 2018 indicates that the degree of economic diversity per se does not directly link to higher or lower inequality. The effect found in the empirical model (6) is thus the result of the time variable, which indicates a decline in inequality throughout specialization in Argentina.

What matters, however, is the sector specialization has occurred in. Grouping the cities in five sectors – agriculture and farming, manufacturing, trade and services, extractive industries, and tourism – cities specialized in agriculture and farming have higher inequality. The descriptive statistics show that they also have the lowest incomes.

Figure 7.5 is a box plot chart showing the average Gini coefficient among cities specialized in the five sectors. Cities running on agriculture, trade, and services have higher inequality. While manufacturing cities have lower inequality (except the heavy manufacturing metropolitan Buenos Aires and Rosario). Cities based on extractive industries have the lowest inequality levels and the highest incomes.

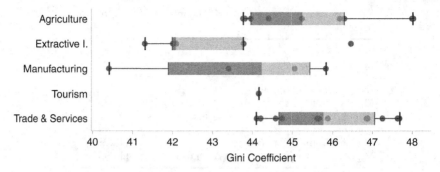

Figure 7.5 Cities by specialized activity and inequality (1996–2018)

Data sources: Calculated from EPH Household survey data (INDEC).

The model further finds that cities with higher unemployment have higher inequality; see Table 7.7. Córdoba, Buenos Aires, and Salta had high inequality in 2018 (with Ginis exceeding 40) and 8.3 to 10.5 percent unemployment rates. On the contrary, San Luis, Rivadavia, and Formosa had less than 4 percent unemployment, and Ginis of about 35. This finding corroborates country, and urban-level studies by Gonzalez-Rozada and Menendez (2000) and Santos (2005), who found that in Argentina, unemployment accounted for a large part of the increase in income inequality between in the 1990s.

Another relevant characteristic of the urban labor market is the share of the informal sector. Cities with a larger informal economy tend to have higher inequality. In Argentina, informal employment is most prominent in low-income professions. The Argentine economist Agustin Mario (2013) finds that informal employment reduces average income between 53 and 71 percent in cities, depending on the region. Meanwhile, the formalization of previously informally employed workers reduced poverty between 10 and 16 percent (ibid).

Finally, the size of firms in a local labor market seems to matter too, with a larger presence of medium-sized firms having an inequality-reducing effect. While the analysis shows that large companies also have an inequality-reducing effect, it was less significant and less strong. Thus, only the variable medium-sized firms were included in the regression model. Micro and small firms, on the contrary, show an inequality increasing effect, which may be

Table 7.7 Unemployment and inequality (2018)

Cities with higher inequality	Gini	Unemployment (%)	Cities with lower inequality	Gini	Unemployment (%)
Córdoba	43.3	10.5	San Luis	35.3	3.5
CABA	42.4	8.3	Rivadavia	35.4	3.8
Salta	41.5	10	Formosa	35.9	3.7

Data sources: Calculated from EPH Household survey data (INDEC).

because they are more likely to employ informal workers. Besides, medium and larger firms are subject to more scrutiny to follow labor laws and pressures by labor unions.

A typology of cities: Discussion and conclusions

Considerable research has focused on the factors leading to the increase and subsequent decline in inequality in Argentina since the 1990s. However, little has been said on intra-urban inequality and the elements making some cities more unequal than others. There is a general belief that the northern cities and Greater Buenos Aires have higher levels of inequality. However, the causes of this difference in inequality have not been isolated.

This chapter provides new empirical evidence by examining panel data of 29 cities in Argentina from 1996 to 2018 using more than 35 variables. These shed light on the relationship between city characteristics and income inequality. The analysis paid close attention to the role of national-level social spending and changes in labor market policies. The increase in public spending since 2009 had an essential redistributive effect, which was felt in all the cities included in the analysis.

The analysis intended to advance the debate around local characteristics that shape intra-urban income inequality, such as its economy, size, labor market and demographic characteristics, and political attitudes. It was expected that large cities would be more unequal, and the share of informal workers, unemployment, larger households, and households with an older person induced higher inequality. Inversely female education, a larger share of medium-sized firms, and the political proxy variables would reduce inequality.

The findings suggest that there are shared characteristics among cities with high/low inequality. Table 7.8 summarizes such typologies of intra-urban inequality.

The following paragraphs discuss five overarching findings in the typology matrix in more depth and place them within the context of Argentina and related literature.

First, the economic development of a city seems to play a crucial role in inequality. The first observation from the data is that lower-income cities are more unequal than middle-income cities, and the difference is quite large. There can be several reasons for this. One possible factor is the lack of appropriate infrastructure in poorer cities which may impede productivity and growth. Infrastructure, such as roads, electricity, and transportation, is crucial to economic development and redistribution. Less investment in public infrastructure and services in low-income cities may also explain why they have fewer medium-sized firms, which have an inequality-reducing effect.

A study by the Inter-American Development Bank (Grazzi and Pietrobelli 2016) found that labor agencies limited labor inspection to registered large- and medium-sized forms. The directive to comply was not enforced to micro and small enterprises. City officials will need to reevaluate first before closing

Table 7.8 A typology of intra-urban inequality

	Cities with high Inequality	Cities with low inequality
City structure	Cities where incomes are very low, or very high Smaller and medium sized cities	Medium income cities Larger cities
Politics	Low social spending Low investment in quality public services	PGs with redistributive agendas High investments in social protection and quality public services
Demographic factors	Large households Large share of migrants	Higher completion rate of primary and secondary education for girls Larger share of households receiving social transfers
Local Labor Market	Large informal economy Specialized in agriculture, and trade and services High unemployment	Large share of public sector employment Specialized in manufacturing and extractive industries Many medium-sized firms

firms that employ informal workers. Understanding why employers and independent workers continue to opt out of the formal system for economic or administrative reasons and adopt appropriate policies to remedy the problem could be a first step toward a solution.

Most low-income cities in Argentina have economies specialized in agriculture and farming. Even during periods of macroeconomic growth (as during the recovery post-2003), it is challenging to sustain growth driven primarily by agriculture. But attention should be given to the agricultural sector even if it grows more slowly than the rest. Annez et al. (2009) suggest that increasing productivity in the agricultural sector frees up labor to work in manufacturing and services.

In relation to this, this chapter's assessment found a U-shaped relationship (an inversed Kuznets curve) between inequality and income. In Argentina's cities, inequality decreases as average incomes rise, yet only up to a certain point, after which inequality rises again. Earlier studies (e.g., Cuenin 2002) found a Kuznets' relationship in Argentina's cities with an inverted U-shape. Cuenin's study focused on pre-crisis years (before 2003) when the inequality and growth relationship differed significantly. This, however, suggests the prevalence of *Kuznets waves*, a term used by Milanovic (2016) to describe inequality trends over extended periods. Recognizing this, it would be interesting to conduct more research into Argentina's high-income cities, especially those reliant on extractive economies such as gas and oil, that were unable to reduce inequality. The only high-income city outside of this portfolio is Buenos Aires, based on trade and services. In 2018, Buenos Aires had the third-highest inequality in the country.

Second, education remains key to the development of individuals, households, communities, and societies. The analysis finds that education, and especially female education, is crucial to reduce income inequality. Cities with higher primary and secondary school completion rates among girls have lower income inequality. Several studies have demonstrated that low levels of education and poor skill acquisition hamper economic growth and slow down poverty reduction. In Argentina, the gender wage gap remains a challenge where the greater gaps are in jobs requiring lower educational levels (UNDP 2011).

The analysis further finds that female education is directly related to the size of a household. This echoes previous studies showing that the higher a woman's educational attainment, the fewer children she is likely to bear. In Argentina, larger households are more likely to live in poverty than smaller households, especially when headed by a single woman (Maurizio et al. 2008).

Since 1996, female education has improved notably, and almost all women now complete primary education. Significant differences, however, remain among cities in terms of the completion of secondary education. From a policy perspective, promoting FSE in the cities with the lowest completion rates might positively affect the labor market and reduce income (and gender) inequality.

This leads to the third conclusion, on the informal economy. In Argentina, about 45 percent of the workforce operate informally, a share that varies across cities. In some, such as Ushuaia and Rio Gallegos, informality is as low as 18 percent, while in others, more than 58 percent find employment in the informal sector (e.g., Salta, Tucuman). The data show that informal workers tend to have lower education and that cities with higher informality have more internal migrants and people from neighboring countries.

Cities with high informality have higher income inequality, which is likely due to the vast income differences between informal and formal salaries (see Chapter 6). A study by Agustin Mario (2013) on wage differences finds that being employed in the informal sector implies a 65-percent lower wage than that obtained by registered workers in the same sector. While informal employment reduced after 2003, it resurged after 2015 and remained high. A study by Luis Beccaria et al. (2015) shows that the income gap between informal and formal workers has in fact increased despite the overall fall in informal employment. Workers who "formalized" were those with higher incomes and better jobs than those who remained informal.

Fourth, expanding the social protection system is vital to prevent people from falling into poverty. The pension moratorium[8] and the AUH (universal child cash transfer), which deepened the non-contributory nature of the social security system, were necessary steps in reducing inequality. National and local administrations should ensure that the systems in place are not subject to austerity cuts in the future, even in times of debt restructuring or economic crisis. Instead, a steady expansion of the social policy paradigm to informal sector workers is an essential step to tackle inequality. Future research may be necessary to understand better the linkages between informality and other demographic and labor market variables.

Fifth, the two variables included in the regression model that speak to the political landscape suggest that PGs and policies reduce income inequality in cities. At the national level, aside from the AUH and approaches to reduce informal employment, three streams of policies have been particularly influential in reducing inequality between 2003 and 2015. All three were launched during the Kirchner government.

In 2004, the government reintroduced the minimum wage after ten years of dormancy, raising pay for some of the lowest earners (MTEySS[9] 2013). The government also invested in creating jobs. Between 2003 and 2009, 4.9 million jobs were created in cities, reducing unemployment from 21.5 percent in 2002 to 7.9 percent in 2010. The third component is the expansion of social protection schemes. Between 2002 and 2009 seven million individuals became beneficiaries of a social protection program such as the pension scheme, the AUH, or other programs. In 2009, 84 percent of older persons and 86 percent of minors received social assistance (Kessler 2014).

Despite these achievements, the gap between workers protected by regulations and those in precarious working conditions – mainly informal workers – has increased since 2003. Actis di Pasquale (2010) finds that in 2010, 42 percent of the working population are in critical conditions, which is an 8-percent increase from 32 percent in 2003.[10]

In summary, the findings suggest that the economic reactivation of cities reduced income inequality. As local economies recovered from the macroeconomic crisis and a series of social and labor market policies were introduced, incomes increased, and poverty and inequality declined. However, the degree to which cities were able to reduce inequality depends on the sector they have specialized in, which relates to average incomes, the share of informal employment, and educational attainments. Cities heavily based on agricultural activities may benefit from increased productivity as they diversify their economy. Moreover, it would be important to support schooling in cities where FSE completion rates are low, in addition to addressing equity issues in reaching other public services. Similarly, adopting localized approaches of transitioning workers from informality to formality may help address the increasing wage gap between them, which threatens the accomplishments in reducing inequality since 2003.

Notes

1 For explanatory reasons, only the results for the year 2018 are presented in Table 7.1. However, the conclusions derived here are extensible to the rest of the period considered.

2 The workforce includes workers between 18 and 65 years old.

3 Unless indicated, all figures, tables, and calculations in this section are the author's.
4 The categories for low-, middle-, and high-income cities have been established via a frequency density analysis based on the December 2018 data from the EPH for 29 cities. At that time of analysis, low-income cities had average monthly per capita incomes of less than ARS 6,499. In middle-income cities, average incomes ranged from ARS 6,500 to ARS 9,299, and in high-income cities, average incomes were larger than ARS 9,300.
5 As Lind and Mehlum (2010) write in their methodological paper on U-shape testing, "to test…for the presence of a U shape…we need to test whether the relationship is decreasing at low values…and increasing at high values (p. 110)." Lind and Mehlum (2010) accompanied their (economics) paper with a STATA module, utest, that runs their proposed U-shape test. The program was executed after running a regression.
6 To address the concern around urban primacy, I dropped the city population variable and replaced it with a dummy variable for large cities with more than 500,000 people.
7 The decline of incomes in high-income cities in 2013 could be related to discovering new unconventional gas and oil deposits and the re-nationalization of Fiscal Oilfields (YPF).
8 The pension moratorium is a pension reform introduced during Cristina Kirchner's government that created access for more than three million people to a minimum retirement, including those that have worked in the informal sector. This pension reform was particularly important for women who disproportionally work in the informal sector.
9 MTEYSS is the abbreviation for "Ministerio de Trabajo, Empleo y Seguridad Social," equivalent to the labor department.
10 A worker in critical condition is classified as someone in an unstable working condition and paid below the minimum wage.

References

Actis Di Pasquale, Eugenio, 2010. "El mercado de trabajo argentino entre 2003 y 2009: un análisis a través de los indicadores complementarios a la tasa de desempleo abierto," FACES. Revista de la Facultad de Ciencias Económicas y Sociales, Universidad Nacional de Mar del Plata, vol. 16(34-35), pages 85–110.
Alvaredo, Facundo, Lucas Chancel, Thomas Piketty, Emmanuel Saez, and Gabriel Zucman. 2018. World Inequality Report 2018. Paris: World Inequality Lab.
Annez, Patricia Clarke, Robert M. Buckley, and Michael Spence. 2009. *Urbanization and Growth. Commission on Growth and Development.* Washington, DC: World Bank.
Atkinson, Anthony B., and Andrea Brandolini. 2010. "On Analyzing the World Distribution of Income." In *SSRN Scholarly Paper ID 1556151.* Rochester, NY: Social Science Research Network.
Atkinson, Anthony B., and François Bourguignon. 2000. "Introduction: Income Distribution and Economics." *Handbook of Income Distribution* 1: 1–58.
Baltagi, Badi Hani. 2008. *Econometric Analysis of Panel Data.* Vol. 4. Chichester:John Wiley & Sons.
Beccaria, Luis, Roxana Maurizio, and Gustavo Vázquez. 2015. "Recent Decline in Wage Inequality and Formalization of the Labour Market in Argentina." *International Review of Applied Economics* 29 (5): 677–700.
Belloni, Carlos, and Eduardo Fracchia. 2016. *Distribucion de l Ingreso en Argentina Durante El Kirchnerismo.* Buenos Aires: IAE Universidad Austral.

Cuenin, Fernando Gabriel. 2002. "Diferencias regionales en la distribución del ingreso: Argentina 1992–2000." In *Documentos de Trabajo* Nro.41. La Plata: Universidad Nacional de La Plata.

Duranton, Gilles, and Diego Puga. 2005. "From Sectoral to Functional Urban Specialisation." *Journal of Urban Economics* 57 (2): 343–70.

Gasparini, Leonardo, Guillermo Cruces, Leopoldo Tornarolli, and Mariana Marchionni. 2009. "A Turning Point? Recent Developments on Inequality in Latin America and the Caribbean." CEDLAS, Working Papers 0081, CEDLAS, Universidad Nacional de La Plata.

Gasparini, Leonardo, Martín Cicowiez, and Walter Sosa Escudero. 2014. "Pobreza y desigualdad en América Latina: conceptos, herramientas y aplicaciones." In *Documentos de Trabajo del CEDLAS*.

Glaeser, Edward L., Matt Resseger, and Kristina Tobio. 2009. "Inequality in Cities." *Journal of Regional Science* 49 (4): 617–46.

Gonzalez-Rozada, Martin, and Alicia Menendez. 2000. "The Effect of Unemployment on Labor Earnings Inequality: Argentina in the Nineties," Working Papers 216, Centro de Investigación de Finanzas. Buenos Aires: Universidad Torcuato di Tella.

Grazzi, Matteo, and Carlo Pietrobelli. 2016. *Firm Innovation and Productivity in Latin America and the Caribbean: The Engine of Economic Development.* London: Springer Nature.

Greene, William H. 2003. *Econometric Analysis.* New York, NY: Macmillan/McGraw-Hill School Division.

INDEC. 2020a. *Bases de Datos.* INDEC Argentina. https://www.indec.gob.ar/indec/web/Institucional-Indec-BasesDeDatos

⸻. 2020b. *Bases de la EPH Puntual (1974–1994).* INDEC. https://www.indec.gob.ar/indec/web/Institucional-Indec-bases_EPH_puntual

⸻. 2020c. *Cuadros Regulares – EPH Continua2003–2006 y 2016–2019.* INDEC. https://www.indec.gob.ar/indec/web/Institucional-Indec-BasesDeDatos

Kessler, Gabriel. 2014. *Controversias Sobre La Desigualdad.* Buenos Aires, Argentina: Fondo de Cultura Económica.

Kuznets, Simon. 1955. "Economic Growth and Income Inequality." *The American Economic Review*, Vol. XLV, No.1, pp. 1–28.

Lind, Jo Thori, and Halvor Mehlum. 2010. "With or Without U? The Appropriate Test for a U-shaped Relationship." *Oxford Bulletin of Economics and Statistics* 72 (1): 109–18.

Mario, Agustín. 2013. "Informalidad laboral y pobreza en Argentina: una comparación inter–regional." In Centro De Estudios Urbanos Y Regionales 20898. Consejo Nacional de Investigaciones Científicas y Técnicas. https://www.conicet.gov.ar/new_scp/detalle.php?keywords=&id=20898&inst=yes&congresos=yes&detalles=yes&congr_id=1771029

Maurizio, Roxana, Bárbara Perrot, and Soledad Villafañe. 2008. "Dinámica de la pobreza y el mercado de trabajo en Argentina post-convertibilidad." In *Ministerio de Trabajo*.

Milanovic, Branko. 2016. *Global Inequality: A New Approach for the Age of Globalization.* Cambridge, MA: Harvard University Press.

Moser, Caroline O.N. 2015. *Gender, Asset Accumulation and Just Cities: Pathways to Transformation.* London: Routledge.

MTEySS. 2013. "Diagnóstico de la informalidad laboral, a partir de los datos relevados por la Encuesta Nacional de Protección y Seguridad Social (ENAPROSS)." In *Ministerio de Trabajo, Empleo y Seguridad Social, presentación realizada en las Jornadas sobre Análisis de Mercado Laboral, Buenos Aires 25 y 26 de setiembre de 2013.*

Rodrik, Dani. 2008. *One Economics, Many Recipes: Globalization, Institutions, and Economic Growth*. Princeton, NJ: Princeton University Press.

Rotondo, Sebastián, Carla Daniela Calá, and Leandro Llorente. 2016. "Evolución de la diversidad productiva en Argentina: análisis comparativo a nivel de áreas económicas locales entre 1996 y 2015." In *LI Reunión Anual de la Asociación Argentina de Economía Política*.

Santos, María Emma. 2005. "Factors influencing income inequality across urban Argentina (1998-2003)," Ibero America Institute for Econ. Research (IAI) Discussion Papers 126. Available at: https://ideas.repec.org/p/got/iaidps/126.html, accessed November 30, 2021.

Trujillo, Lucía, and Soledad Villafañe. 2011. "Dinámica distributiva y políticas públicas: dos décadas de contrastes en la Argentina contemporánea." In *Distribución del ingreso. Enfoques y políticas públicas desde el Sur*, 227–262.

UNDP 2011. *Aportes Para El Desarrollo Humano En Argentina/. 2011género*. En Cifras: Mujeres Y Varones En La Sociedad Argentina.

Part III
Closing the Gap

8 Slum upgrading in Buenos Aires – Fighting fire with fire

Few urban initiatives have greater potential to advance equity and improve the well-being of people in poverty in Latin American cities than participatory slum upgrading. Slum dwellers often face multiple overlapping challenges, from overcrowded houses to tenure insecurity, crime and violence, and deficient infrastructure, all of which intersect with income poverty. They also experience stigmatization and discrimination, which translate to spatial, political, and economic exclusion, affecting their ability to participate in the urban decision-making process and the chances of socioeconomic mobility.

The inadequate living conditions in informal settlements also impact people's health, increasing their risk of exposure to infectious diseases, as the COVID-19 pandemic has demonstrated so painfully. In Buenos Aires, slum dwellers represent about 9 percent of the city's population, but they contributed 40 percent of the first wave of COVID-19 cases between March and July 2020. They also had higher mortality rates, despite being younger on average (Macchia et al. 2021).[1]

Lockdown or quarantine guidelines are unimaginable for people living in informal settlements, whose livelihoods depend on working outside their homes and who have little to no savings to ride out the pandemic. Most work in the informal economy and lack access to paid sick leave or unemployment benefits that many formal workers take for granted. Even basic hygiene recommendations like handwashing are difficult to follow in the absence of water and sanitation in one's house. Overcrowded conditions are yet another accelerator for transmission.

In May 2020, the Buenos Aires based community organization of slum dwellers *La Garganta Poderosa* accused city authorities of failing to protect slum residents during the COVID-19 pandemic. Their allegation received national attention after Ramona Medina, a community leader and resident of the slum Villa 31 died from COVID-19. In a video she recorded before her hospitalization, she called on the city and national governments to restore drinking water in her barrio. She asked, "How do they want us to stay home if I have to go buy water?" (Peoples Dispatch 2020).

The growth of informal settlements in Latin American cities results from a lack of affordable housing and land, one of their grandest challenges. In

DOI: 10.4324/9781003201908-11

Buenos Aires, land is 30 percent more expensive than in other capital cities in the region, which results in high financial burdens for low-income households, rendering it challenging to access housing in the formal market (IVC 2018).

In the absence of sufficient adequate public or subsidized social housing, informal settlements often present the only solutions for those with low incomes. Buenos Aires' slum population has been growing steadily over the past 20 years. Between 2001 and 2010 alone, the number of slums in the city grew by 17 percent and its population by 52 percent. Most of the slums are located in the southern parts of the city, where poverty is high and access to adequate infrastructure low.[2]

Upgrading these settlements can improve people's lives via enhanced access to housing, drinking water, or electricity and may help reduce intra-urban inequality. Yet, it depends a great deal on how upgrading projects are designed, implemented, and maintained. It also depends whether such initiatives challenge the hegemonic neoliberal market logics and models of state action. Applying a market approach to fix a housing affordability crisis that has pushed low-income people to live in slums seems like fighting fire with fire.

In this chapter, I reflect on recent developments in Villa 20, an informal settlement in Buenos Aires that has undergone profound transformations as part of a citywide effort to "integrate slums into the urban fabric" (IVC 2018). These are based on my work with The New School's Observatory on Latin America where we designed a monitoring framework for the city's housing authority to assess and monitor the upgrading process. I look at both the achievements and limitations in providing adequate housing, and at what threatens the inequality-reducing effect of slum upgrading and the sustainability of the initiative overall. These are all lessons that can inform the design of future policies in the region and beyond.

Housing inequality and the growth of Villa 20

Villa 20 is located in the Villa Lugano neighborhood in District 8 (Comuna 8) in Buenos Aires's south. It is the city's fourth most populous slum, with close to 30,000 inhabitants stretched across 30 blocks ("manzanas") and 4,559 housing units, almost 20 percent of the city's total slum population. More than two-thirds of the population live in poverty – of which one-third lives in extreme poverty (DGEyC 2015).[3]

Education levels are lower in Villa 20 than in the rest of the city. Only 32 percent of adults complete high school, compared to 76 percent in the rest of Buenos Aires. Nearly one-fifth of the school-age population does not or never attended school; it is 4 percent in the rest of the city. People's health outcomes are much lower too. More people suffer from chronic diseases, and infant mortality is 25 percent above the national average (Motta and Almansi 2017).

Villa 20 has, like most informal settlements, low quality or informal water and sanitation networks and chaotic and often pirated electricity connections.

Most roads are in bad condition or unpaved, and there are minimal waste collection and few public health and education services provided. It is generally up to the residents to maintain the few public spaces that exist. Overcrowding led to buildings of three or four stories with minimal ventilation and natural light and subpar safety standards.

Today, three sectors are distinctively marked in Villa 20. About a third of the population lives in a consolidated section subject to various upgrading projects up to the mid-2000s. Another half of the population lives in an area that remains almost entirely informal, without adequate infrastructure, and primarily makeshift houses (see Figure 8.1). The rest of the population lives in a section called Papa Francisco, once a car graveyard that the city government turned into a new housing block with nearly 1,700 new units that are connected to quality infrastructure and public services (Motta and Almansi 2017). Papa Francisco is part of the most recent slum upgrading initiative, with some units still under construction.[4]

The socioeconomic disparities that persist between Villa 20 and the rest of the city result from decades of unmanaged urbanization processes that left slum residents or *vecinos* (translates to neighbors) without access to adequate public services; and for many years they had had to face public policies that were openly hostile toward the neighborhood.

Figure 8.1 A typical street in the informal part of Villa 20 (taken 2019)

Credit: Lena Simet

Slum redevelopment in Buenos Aires:
From eradication to participation to?

Villa 20 began as a thinly populated settlement in 1910. By the 1940s, as global and local events pushed populace across border and new territories, the settlement expanded toward an adjacent plot owned by the federal police where abandoned cars leaked poisonous lead and mercury onto the land. The population would continue to grow until the 1970s when the civic-military dictatorship turned their gaze toward the slums. The 1976 administration adopted a national policy of eradication. Almost immediately police and military destroyed makeshift houses and displaced residents, nearly erasing Villa 20. Its population dropped from 21,305 inhabitants in 1976 to 3,608 in 1983 (Bellardi and De Paula 1986).

The harsh slum-clearance policies eventually became politically untenable. After the fall of the military regime in 1983 and subsequent democratization, no candidate could afford to alienate the large electorate that had become increasingly vocal and organized social movements.

In a less hostile environment, a process of repopulation in Villa 20 began in the 1980s that continues today: from 7,460 inhabitants in 1991 to 19,195 in 2010, and to 27,990 in 2016 (INDEC 2010; IVC 2018). Instead of eradication, the focus turned to upgrade settlements, in part to avoid social conflicts. In 1984, a new law (Ordinance No. 39,753) brought a substantive change in the orientation of public policies toward slums. It postulated the need to regulate their fabric and grant land titles to the residents. In this way, the new government radically reversed the approach of the military dictatorship.

Since then, local and central governments have suported in situ slum upgrading, based on the notion that it is both socially and economically preferable to allow residents to remain in their communities. They keep people's social networks and the community's cohesiveness intact while improving their living standards (Abdenur 2009). Additionally, the investments already made by the families in their homes are capitalized and incentivized, leaving them in better economic positions. Although Argentina supported the idea of such programs, in practice upgrading remained limited in scope and resulted in just a few isolated housing improvements.

The 1996 Constitution of Buenos Aires city was a milestone for the housing movement because it ratified several economic and social rights, including the right to housing. It confirmed the city's obligation to resolve the housing deficit, which included upgrading informal settlements. While this legal landmark triggered new regulatory frameworks and led to housing improvements in Villa 20, it did not yield the much-needed urban infrastructure overhaul and lacked the input and participation of the residents (Jauri 2011).

Fast forward to 2015. Under the leadership of Horacio Rodríguez Larreta, a new city government stepped in, promoting the upgrading of infrastructure in slums and regularizing housing ownership as part of a citywide approach to tackle the housing deficit. Instead of upgrading houses, the emphasis was on integrating slums into the rest of the urban fabric, reducing segregation and the many territorial inequalities that present clear divides between formal and informal neighborhoods.

Villa 20 was placed under the responsibility of the city's housing institute, short IVC (Instituto de Vivienda de la Ciudad), which kicked off the urban integration process in 2016 by approaching neighborhood leaders in search of dialogue. The IVC would introduce an experiment by involving residents from the ground up. They would help define the intervention objectives collectively and involve residents in the decision-making process, the monitoring, and the implementation.

This approach presented a fundamental break with prior upgrading initiatives that lacked meaningful resident participation. Throughout the first engagements between the IVC and Villa 20 residents, a sense of mistrust from the residents quickly crystallized, understandably so after decades of hostile policies or upgrading interventions that did not meet or respect their needs. The few upgrading initiatives that governments had launched but never completed.

The IVC introduced a series of neighborhood meetings (so-called "mesas") reoccurring at regular intervals for residents and neighborhood representatives to join. It also organized a micro-census and a socio-spatial survey (Relevamiento Socio-Espacial, RELSE) together with residents and community boards to capture the deficiencies and priorities across the neighborhood. Throughout this participatory process, which became institutionalized in several ways, IVC staff and residents defined the intervention's parameters. Through these participatory initiatives, the IVC achieved the unimaginable: they brought together local social-political groups that were previously in conflict with one another. For the first time, they put their disagreements aside and sat down to discuss the future of the neighborhood collectively.

Another aspect that suggested a break with past upgrading initiatives is the IVC's definition of Villa 20's redevelopment strategy as a *process project*. This new approach signals a recognition that complex interventions into people's lives and the urban fabric are never linear but change and evolve, which requires flexibility in the policy response. For instance, it may happen that some families do not want to relocate because they feel safe in their apartment or have strong ties to neighbors or because they do not approve of the substitute location or house. Instead of forcing people to leave, a process project would reevaluate, recalibrate, and find alternative pathways that work for everyone to move forward.

The upgrading of Villa 20, which was named the PIRU (Proyecto Integral de Re-urbanización de la Villa 20, which translates to "Comprehensive Re urbanization Project of Villa 20"), came with three components:

1 **Urban integration**. By improving the neighborhood's connective tissue, its water networks, drainage, sanitation, and streets, what was once narrow was widened to increase airflow between buildings (see Figure 8.2). Other initiatives like improvements to public spaces and providing residents with security of tenure were a central part of slum upgrading programs.

Figure 8.2 A house was removed in Villa 20 to open the airflow between buildings and to create a street (taken 2019)

Credit: Lena Simet

2 **Housing integration**. Simple improvements to housing units such as windows to improve airflow and light, upgrading wall and roof material, and the construction of safe staircases. Housing units were also connected to the trunk infrastructure. It also included the construction brand-new dwellings.

3 **Socioeconomic integration**. The final piece of the puzzle meant to enhance people's education and health and lift people out of poverty by providing people with microcredits for small shops and other commercial activities.

Taking the temperature

The primary objective of most slum upgrading initiatives is to reduce urban poverty and improve people's living standards. UN Habitat (2011) finds that upgrading programs can also reduce intra-urban inequalities by abating social segregation. But how can we tell whether an upgrading initiative has been successful, and how should we define success? Are all three components as established by the IVC equally important? Can we expect them to improve simultaneously, or is there a chronology of improvements that should be considered in the intervention and subsequent analysis? And, how do we account for unintended negative consequences, such as indebtedness and the gentrification of a slum?

As part of a team of architects, economists, public policy analysts, and social scientists at The New School's Observatory on Latin America, I spent two years developing a system for the IVC that could measure and monitor slum upgrading in the city, starting with Villa 20. We developed a comprehensive monitoring system that is mindful of the timing and sequencing of interventions by measuring immediate results and long-term impacts. For example, we can detect access to urban services in the short run, but health and child development effects take longer to manifest (if they ever occur).

The monitoring system is organized by the three components that guide the PIRU (urban integration, housing integration, and socioeconomic integration), 11 subcomponents, and 133 indicators. Table 8.1 provides an overview of the ingredients of the monitoring matrix.[5] We developed a fourth dimension to assess the "citizen integration," to monitor the inclusiveness of participatory systems and their impact.

To gauge the level of socio-spatial segregation between Villa 20, District 8, and the rest of the city, we used the Dissimilarity Index based on Duncan and Duncan's (1955) segregation measure. We adopted it to Buenos Aires and combined 16 variables, including access to public services and infrastructure, overcrowding, access to transport, poverty, unemployment, and other labor market variables.

Our findings suggest that there are deep divides that require careful consideration in the upgrading process and beyond. As of February 2020, dissimilarities were highest in terms of trunk infrastructure and access to public services. In 2019, just about 26 percent of the housing blocks in Villa 20 had water and sanitation, and just 3 percent had an electricity connection. This is in contrast to an eye-popping 99 percent of the city that is connected to the electricity grid, and about 97 percent have a water and sanitation network (OLA 2020).[6]

Almost half of Villa 20 currently reside in overcrowded substandard housing conditions, compared to just 9.4 percent in the city, where the average number of people per dwelling is 2.63; in Villa 20, it amounts to an average of six. Commonly, several families live in the same apartment.

People's economic realities are vastly unequal too. More than 80 percent of Villa 20's residents live in poverty. Of them, 37.19 percent live in extreme

Table 8.1 Overview of the framework to assess and monitor slum upgrading in Buenos Aires

Dimension	Subdimension	Indicators
Urban integration	Infrastructure	Water, electricity, sanitation, drainage
	Public space	Streetlight, availability of green space, waste collection
	Accessibility and mobility	Opening and improvement of streets, access to public transport, accessibility for people with disabilities
	Unexpected dynamics	Gentrification, displacement, re-informalization
Housing	Housing quality	Overcrowding, unit quality
	Access to basic services inside the house	Water, electricity, sanitation, gas
	Tenure security	Housing title or lease, gentrification
	Maintenance	Resident satisfaction, payment of shared bills, and upkeep
Socioeconomic integration	Health	Chronic disease, drug addiction, access to health services
	Education	School completion, accessibility/availability of schools
	Labor market	Poverty, type of work (informal/formal), unemployment

Source: Based on monitoring framework developed with the Observatory on Latin America (2020).

Note: this is not a comprehensive and all-encompassing presentation of the monitoring framework but intends to provide an overview of its main components.

poverty. Extreme poverty is much lower in the rest of the city (3.1 percent); about 12 percent live in poverty. The share of workers in the informal economy is also much higher in Villa 20: 70 percent compared to 47 percent in the rest of the city.

Even within Villa 20, poverty concentrates in specific sectors. In five of the 15 blocks that we had census data for, almost everyone lives in poverty. In block 21, for example, 97 percent live in poverty, of whom close to 58 percent are extremely poor. We measured a similar situation in blocks 3, 5, 17, and 20. In all these blocks, poverty exceeds 90 percent. Many of the families we spoke with said they rely on soup kitchens and social organizations to have a warm meal.

Even in Villa 20 housing is driven by the market logic of the more money you have, the better housing you can afford. Data from the micro-census show that overcrowding is worse in blocks with higher poverty, and houses are in worse conditions.

Slums often have social and economic problems and limited employment opportunities restricted to informal jobs that are precarious and offer lower pay than in the formal economy. Besides, the stigma attached to living in slums is pervasive and affects residents psychologically and economically, for instance, by denying them job opportunities. Janice Perlman (2010) provides evidence from slums in Rio de Janeiro (Brazil) that suggest that the stigma of possessing a residential address in a squatter settlement adversely affects the probability of finding a job.

Reducing poverty and inequality via socioeconomic integration should be front and center in upgrading projects and inform all other dimensions since they directly affect the sustainability of any intervention. But upgrading projects focus on providing the service and often neglect the affordability of the services offered. Making infrastructure work for people in poverty requires affordability of the infrastructure in the long run. Governments can ensure affordability by offering social tariffs or lifelines where a certain usage per capita is free of charge. Considering the no-win decisions people living in extreme poverty face, expecting people to start paying for the electricity they previously used for free does not make any sense.

Our assessment of Villa 20 suggests while the participatory nature of the process-project is laudable, economic integration seemed to come as an afterthought, as an expectation that it will happen once the infrastructure is in place, housing is upgraded, and streets are paved. However, the experiences in the housing complex Papa Francisco suggest that doing so can leave people worse off than before the intervention.

Barrio Papa Francisco: Housing financialization and economic precarity

In the redevelopment of Villa 20, some families had to give up their apartments to make room for a public space, a health center, or to widen one of the many narrow streets so ambulances could pass through and eventually a school bus. Other houses had to be destroyed because they were too deficient to be fixed. In these cases, the IVC offered people three options. They could:

- Leave Villa 20 and move to another part of the city (the local government provided access to special mortgages).
- Move into one of the brand-new apartments in Barrio Papa Francisco (PF).
- Swap apartments with another Villa 20 resident who moved out of their previous dwelling.

The Barrio Papa Francisco, named after Argentina's first Pope, is a section of Villa 20 that used to be the car graveyard until the city appropriated the land to construct 90 four-story buildings with 1,671 units, co-financed by the nation's housing and urban development department and the development bank of Latin America (CAF) (Buenos Aires Ciudad 2016) (see Figures 8.3 and 8.4). The city then offered the units for sale to Villa 20 residents. Since most residents in Villa 20 live in poverty, lack a bank account and have limited access to credit, the city government negotiated special 30-year

Figure 8.3 Freshly painted housing units in Papa Francisco, with the rest of Villa 20 in the background (taken 2019)

Credit: Lena Simet

Figure 8.4 A view at Villa 20, from Papa Francisco, divided by a gate (taken 2019)

mortgage rates for them; every family would pay a monthly installment of about ARS 6,000 (2019 pesos; ~ USD136) or not more than 20 percent of their income. The loans complemented the original value of people's houses, and some families received extra subsidies. The first round of people moved into PF in 2018.

In May 2019, we surveyed 60 households (201 people) who had moved in 2018 to learn how they cope, emotionally and financially, with their new living situations.[7] The findings were striking. While resident participation was high – 90 percent said they participated and voted in neighborhood workshops – and almost all families said they liked their new apartment (93 percent) and building (85 percent), their economic situation was alarming (OLA 2020).

Just one year after moving into their new home, most families reported difficulty paying the negotiated mortgage, and more than half (53 percent) said they were behind on installments. Close to 90 percent of people surveyed make income below the city's poverty line, even when including the social transfers many receive from the local or national government. For most, it is impossible to put 20 percent of their low income aside for a mortgage, plus account for expenses such as electricity, gas, and water (ibid).

On average, people said they spent about 13.8 percent of their income on the mortgage and another 14.7 percent on utilities; 10.6 percent goes to transport costs to travel to work or bring the children to school. About 60 percent of people's incomes cover essential expenses such as food (35 percent), hygiene products (7 percent), health and medicine (4 percent), and education (4 percent) (ibid).

We find that about a third of families spent more than what they earn. Some use other types of loans or credits to make ends meet. Sixty-two percent said they did not have enough for mortgage payments (ibid). More importantly nearly 72 percent of the families reported they did not have enough money for food at least once in the last three months.

The survey also suggests that the new units insufficiently accommodated residents' economic activities before moving to PF. Many people used to have small shops selling food or services in their apartments. Some housed a tailor studio or hair salon in their apartment. But many of the new units do not accommodate these commercial activities; some have gates controlling who can enter. For others, having to pay for higher electricity or water use made the business unsustainable. After the move, about half of the residents who had commercial activity in their homes abandoned it permanently (ibid).

The financial situation plays a significant role in the sustainability of the PIRU in Villa 20. In the case of the Papa Francisco neighborhood, the formalization of essential services entails a cost for residents that they previously did not have. Although the neighbors show a willingness to pay and, in some cases, have lower and subsidized tariffs, the cost of services and the mortgage payment are high compared to their income.

The notion that private finance and household debt would be the solution to conditions of inadequate housing and chronic poverty suffered by residents of slums like Villa 20 follows an economic and ideological logic of capitalism, where the emphasis is on private individual home ownership and the extension of credit to groups who previously had little access. The solution to housing for those with low incomes is seen to lie in devising market-based regulatory frameworks and financial mechanisms to enable home ownership on the basis of household debt, with little attention to the underlying flaws of this logic, and the risks it bears.

In a world where the rich get richer by the day, why not redistribute their wealth to ensure that every family has a roof over their head?

Conclusion

The upgrading and integration of informal settlements into the urban fabric have enormous potential to reduce intra-urban inequalities, both in terms of spatial divisions and economic inequality. Yet, programs encounter a myriad of challenges. What's more, they are often based on an intrinsically flawed and dangerous logic: inserting a slum into the private housing market would lift all boats.

In Buenos Aires, government approaches to informal settlements have come a long way, from eradication to in situ upgrading that involves residents and touches on aspects beyond the physical infrastructure. However, one shouldn't take such achievements for granted, as the recent evictions in Villa 31 suggest, a highly contested slum in Buenos Aires city center. As families struggle to make ends meet due to the economic impact of the COVID-19 pandemic, more people moved to Villa 31 and set up makeshift homes in between newly upgraded units. The city government perceived the new squatters as interfering with the upgrading project and asked the people to leave. But seeing they had nowhere else to go, the families asked the government for a conversation to find common ground. On September 30, 2021, at 7 am, the city police bulldozed and burned their houses (Vales 2021).

The IVC team in Villa 20 has worked hard to prevent such displacements during the pandemic, following a national decree (No. 320/2020) that suspended all evictions in 2020 due to nonpayment.[8] They facilitated conversations between landlords and tenants to find solutions and placed a moratorium on mortgage payments for residents in the barrio Papa Francisco.

One cannot deny that the participatory slum upgrading program that the IVC launched in Villa 20 in 2016 has improved housing and infrastructure conditions for thousands of people. The achievements in bringing residents and local groups together, some had been in opposition for decades, are admirable and positively affected the upgrading process. For the first time, the voices of the *vecinos* were heard and respected in the project design and implementation.

However, the participatory process alone cannot guarantee the financial sustainability of the process. The upgrading inserted low-income households into the private housing market, exposing them to the risk of nonpayment of mortgage rates and utility bills.

The economic struggles that the new residents of the Papa Francisco housing complexes experienced before the pandemic are telling because the financial repercussions of owning a home in the formal market are huge. Homeownership comes with new expenses, including mortgage payments and water, electric, and other service payments. Overall, moving to PF resulted in a net loss of household income for many families.

The OLA/IVC survey results show that just one year after moving to PF, most families said they were behind on their mortgages and utility payments; many had to take no-win decisions of paying loans or putting food on the table. The financialization of housing and the formalization of utilities exposed residents to new financial obligations many could not muster.

Another problem that may arise is the prospect of gentrification and real-estate speculation. In Peru, some slum residents refuse to accept a title on their homes and resist upgrades out of fear that rising values or the prospect of taxes will ultimately force them to leave their communities (Dubé 2015).

Integrating slums into the rest of the city shouldn't mean exposing residents to the same whims of the market that contributed to their precarious living situations to begin with. Creating housing solutions for people in poverty requires thinking outside the box of market solutions.

There are alternative pathways governments can follow. Villa 20 and Papa Francisco could adopt a community land trust model where it is owned by the community rather than privately owned. This arrangement effectively protects homes from real-estate speculation and gentrification. Or, the city government could remain as owner and rent them at affordable rates to residents, helping them through difficult financial times via rent assistance or other forms of social protection. Or, instead of offering private debt as a solution, financing upgrading programs via redistributing wealth or progressive taxes on high income seems a more just option.

The experiences in Villa 20 further confirm that removing slum upgrading programs from broader economic and housing policies fail to tackle deepseated inequality. Without bridging the divide between low pay, precarious employment, and exorbitant housing costs, slums will never be a part of the past. Unless inequality becomes front and center in slum upgrading initiatives and housing policies start working for those with low incomes, they risk further entrenching the urban divide.

Notes

1 More information about Buenos Aires' slum population is available at: https://www.estadisticaciudad.gob.ar/eyc/?p=50392 (accessed 12 June 2020).
2 In Argentina, the National Registry of Informal Neighborhoods (RENABAP) has recorded 4,400 informal neighborhoods in the country (Argentina Gob 2021), with more than four million inhabitants living in informal conditions and without basic services. In Buenos Aires, slums are defined as unplanned settlements char-

acterized by a high population density and precarious housing with high levels of unsatisfied basic needs. The following government sources portray the shape and location of the city's slums: https://www.estadisticaciudad.gob.ar/eyc/?p=45322 and https://www.buenosaires.gob.ar/areas/educacion/dirinv/pdf/villas_nht_y_ nuevos_asentamientos.pdf.

3   In May 2019, the poverty line for a one-person household was ARS11,126/ month (USD 252/month or USD 8.43/day) and ARS4,824/month (USD109/month or USD3.65/day) for extreme poverty, according to the General Directorate of Statistics and Censuses of the Government of the City of Buenos Aires (DGEyC).

4   The current state of the units can be reviewed here: https://www.buenosaires.gob. ar/baobras/barrio-papa-francisco.

5   The monitoring framework includes outcome and result indicators. Outcome indicators measure the immediate improvement, while a result indicator measures the impact that the intervention aims to achieve. For example, take improvements in the electricity grid, in the urban integration dimension. An outcome indicator would measure the share of housing blocks within Villa 20 that have formal electricity, whereas result indicators would measure the number of blackouts or fires due to unsafe electricity connections.

6   There were several reasons for the delays in the implementation, which explains the little progress in infrastructure works between 2016 and 2019. For one, it took longer than anticipated to decontaminate the land, that had high levels of lead and mercury due to its prior use as a car graveyard.

7   The survey has a +/- 10% sampling error and a confidence level of 90%.

8   See here for the decree No 320/2020: https://www.boletinoficial.gob.ar/ detalleAviso/primera/227247/20200329.

References

Abdenur, A. 2009. *Global Review of Political Economy of Slum Improvement Schemes: Constraints and Policy Orientations.* Washington, DC: World Bank.

Argentina Gobierno (Gob). 2021. Informes y estadísticas. RENABAP. Available at: https://www.argentina.gob.ar/desarrollosocial/renabap/informesyestadisticas, accessed November 30, 2021.

Bellardi, Marta, and Aldo De Paula. 1986. *Villas miseria: origen, erradicación y respuestas populares.* Vol. 159. Buenos Aires: Centro Editor de América Latina.

Buenos Aires Ciudad. 2016. "Se aprobó el financiamiento de 552 viviendas para el predio Papa Francisco." *Buenos Aires Ciudad noticias,* 8 September 2016, https://www. buenosaires.gob.ar/noticias/se-aprobo-el-financiamiento-de-552-viviendas-para-el-predio-papa-francisco

_____. 2019. *Porcentaje de viviendas habitadas, hogares Y población en villas de emergencia sobre El total de la Ciudad.* Años 2006/2018.

DGEyC (Dirección General de Estadística y Censos). 2015. *Villa 20: Ciudad de Buenos Aires.* Database. Available at: https://www.estadisticaciudad.gob.ar/eyc/?p=53796, accessed November 30, 2021.

Dubé, Ryan. 2015. "To Have & to Hold. Property Titles at Risk in Peru." *Land Lines, April.* Cambridge, MA: Lincoln Institute for Land Policy.

Duncan, Otis Dudley, and Beverly Duncan. 1955. "A Methodological Analysis of Segregation Indexes." *American Sociological Review* 20 (2): 210–17.

Instituto de la Vivienda de Buenos Aires (IVC). 2018. "Addressing Buenos Aires's Housing Challenge Housing Institute of the City of Buenos Aires". In *Presentación de Martín Motta, coordinador del proyecto de reurbanización de Villa 20 en.* New York, NY: The New School.

Instituto Nacional de Estadísticas y Censos (INDEC). 2010. *Datos del Censo Nacional de Población,* Hogares y Viviendas.Database. Available at: https://www.indec.gob.ar/indec/web/Nivel4-Tema-2-41-135, accessed November 30, 2021.

Jauri, Natalia. 2011. "Las villas de la ciudad de Buenos Aires: una historia de promesas incumplidas." *Question/Cuestión Vol. 1,* no. 29. Available at: https://perio.unlp.edu.ar/ojs/index.php/question/article/view/565, accessed November 30, 2021.

Macchia, Alejandro, Daniel Ferrante, Gabriel Battistella, Javier Mariani, and Fernán González Bernaldo de Quirós. 2021. "COVID-19 among the Inhabitants of the Dlums in the City of Buenos Aires: A Population-Based Study." *BMJ Open* 11 (1): e044592.

Motta, Martin and Florencia Almansi. 2017. "Gestión y planificación por proceso-proyecto para el mejoramiento de villas y asentamientos de gran escala. El caso de la Re-Urbanización de Villa 20 en la CABA". *Medio Ambiente y Urbanización* 86 (1): mayo, 145–68.

Observatory on Latin America (OLA). 2020. *Summary of the Final Report · Monitoring Processes and Outcomes in Slum Upgrading in Buenos Aires Villa 20.* New York, NY: The New School.

Peoples Dispatch. 2020. "Activist Who Denounced Lack of Water in Poor Neighborhoods in Buenos Aires Died of Coronavirus." *Peoples Dispatch,* May 19, 2020, https://peoplesdispatch.org/2020/05/19/activist-who-denounced-lack-of-water-in-poor-neighborhoods-in-buenos-aires-died-of-coronavirus/

Perlman, Janice E. 2010. *Favela: Four Decades of Living on the Edge in Rio de Janeiro.* New York: Oxford University Press.

UN-Habitat. 2011. *Building Urban Safety through Slum Upgrading.* New York, NY: United Nations Settlements Programme (UN-Habitat).

Vales, Laura. 2021. "La policía de CABA desalojó a mujeres y niños de la Villa 31." *Página 12,* October 1, 2021, https://www.pagina12.com.ar/371713-la-policia-de-caba-desalojo-a-mujeres-y-ninos-de-la-villa-31

9   What next? Seven short reflections on inequality in Latin American cities

As the world continues to urbanize, inequality in cities is likely to persist or may even widen. It is, however, not a rule of nature or necessary for economic stability. Incomes and assets and their distribution are all historical constructs and can be regulated to reduce rather than amplify inequality.

This book intends to illustrate trends and drivers of inequality in Latin American cities, focusing on Argentina, to inform policy decisions on how to create more just societies and economies. The overarching questions that motivated the book are: why are some cities more successful in reducing inequality? What national factors influence intra-urban disparities, and what is the role of city-level characteristics? And, how does income inequality relate to the spatial divide in cities?

In this concluding chapter, I take a step back and offer a broader perspective highlighting the intersecting themes and messages that emerged throughout the book. The chapter is part reminder of the book's main points, part prediction of the future, and part agenda for change. It is organized around seven questions concerning income distribution and urban fragmentation that will be important in the years to come.

1. What are the lessons from rising and falling inequality in Latin America?

In the 1980s, poverty and inequality increased in almost all cities in Latin America. This widening gap came during economic crises that pushed millions into unemployment and poverty, a time that scholars would later refer to as "the lost decade" (Minujin 1996; Cornia 2011). Governments responded with radical adjustment programs and far-reaching reforms, including privatization, financial liberalization, and the reduction of the state in the economy. Prominent Washington DC-based institutions like the International Monetary Fund (IMF), the World Bank, and the US Department of Treasury promoted these practices, which came to be called the Washington Consensus.

The first lesson is that neoliberal reforms caused further suffering and polarization instead of generating economic prosperity for all. Employment

DOI: 10.4324/9781003201908-12

became more precarious; millions of people experienced poverty and hunger and opted to live in slums as they couldn't afford to live elsewhere. A small share of the middle-class became richer, whereas the majority was pushed into poverty.

Argentina exemplifies these times like no other. Carlos Menem, who took office in 1989 amid a deep economic crisis, introduced sweeping market-based reforms to turn the country into an "internationally competitive" economy. His administration privatized over 20 services within just two years, more than the Thatcher administration did in ten years in the United Kingdom. Argentina became the "poster child" of the Washington Consensus (Cohen 2012). While the policies first had an expansionary effect, it did not last as it pushed the economy further into a vicious cycle of contractions, reducing tax collection, and deteriorating fiscal accounts (Cohen and Gutman 2002).

Up to 2001, the population living in informal settlements in Argentina's cities would grow daily (Prévôt-Schapira and Velut 2016). The years of extreme and rising inequality ended in the country's worst economic crisis when nearly 40 percent lived in poverty. It also affected Argentina's political stability; four presidents governed in a span of two weeks as widespread demonstrations and accounts of severe police violence left the country clamoring for solutions.

The second lesson is that Latin America achieved remarkable reductions in poverty and inequality by changing course in the early 2000s. Before the turn of the century, in 1999, nearly 15 percent of Latin Americans, about 72.5 million people, lived in extreme poverty on less than US$1.90 a day. By 2019, this share dropped to 3 percent.

The region's return to democracy and shift toward center-left governments introduced a new approach to social, fiscal, and economic policy-making. Cornia (2014) described the "redistribution with growth" paradigm as inspired by the European social-democratic model, leading to a policy approach that placed labor, social protection, and public services high on the agenda. Argentina saw social protection programs like universal child allowances enacted, public services were renationalized, and labor market institutions strengthened.

More recent lessons from the region are also mixed as countries like Venezuela, Peru, or Argentina are plagued by economic uncertainty, currency fluctuations, and deteriorations of living standards (Cárcamo-Díaz and Pineda Salazar 2014). Argentina who received one of the largest IMF bailout loans in 2018 (US$57bn) to bolster market confidence still awaits the intended results. Like a painful flashback to the 1990s, the loan conditions included strict reductions in public spending, a loosening of labor protections, and cuts in subsidies and retirement benefits, all of which increased poverty and inequality in cities across the country (Cohen 2019).

2. Why should we be concerned about the privatization of public services?

The privatization of public services was a common practice in Latin America during the neoliberal 1990s. It was heralded as a solution to the region's economic oscillations and the neglect of public services. The idea was that it would bring cash into empty government coffers and shift some of the state's responsibility to third actors, improving the quality of services for everyone.

But as the case of water in metropolitan Buenos Aires highlights (see Chapter 4), corporate control does not automatically increase access to public services. Without contractual stipulations to extend the service to low-income areas at affordable rates, private providers skipped these neighborhoods because of the higher incidence of non-payment. Water, sewers, and other trunk infrastructure were extended only to the wealthier parts, while low- and middle-income neighborhoods and municipalities were left high and dry. Access to water and sanitation turned into a commodity only enjoyable to those who could pay, reinforcing territorial inequality, with ripple effects on health outcomes.

Corporations extracted value from struggling systems by raising tariffs and connection rates and, in many cases, cutting corners to reduce their operating costs, negatively impacting service quality. And while millions of people awaited the benefits of water privatization, private investors raked off huge dividends and windfall profits. Instead of investing these profits in extending water infrastructure for those who couldn't afford new connection fees, they were shipped off to stockholders in Europe.

While much has changed since the 1990s and governments are now cognizant of the potential repercussions of privatizing public services, the COVID-19 pandemic may entice cash-strapped local governments to again involve the private sector in delivering public services like water or health care. However, upgrading and repairing needed physical infrastructure are ways that governments can achieve a more equitable economic recovery. These investments can create jobs and ensure that people and businesses in the future have the infrastructure needed to support a more equitable economy. Rather than privatizing public services or cut budgets, governments should thus invest in public services.

3. Why are some cities more unequal than others?

Findings presented in Chapters 6 and 7 suggest that there are at least six shared characteristics among cities with higher or lower inequality.

For one, inequality tends to be worse in low- and high-income cities and lower in middle-income cities. The relationship between income and inequality appears to be U-shaped, like an inversed Kuznets curve: inequality decreases as average incomes rise, yet only up to a certain point, after which inequality rises.

This relates to the next finding, that high-income and high inequality cities in Argentina tend to be small, with less than 200,000 people. Except for Buenos Aires, all high-income cities (Ushuaia, Rio Gallegos, Neuquén, Rawson-Trelew, and Rivadavia) rely on extractive industries, mainly oil and gas.

Third, economic growth rarely lifts all boats. After the 2002 crisis, formal sector wages recovered, while informal wages remained at subsistence levels. The informal sector in Argentina is extensive, with nearly half of the urban workforce engaged in informal activities, with vast variation across cities. In Ushuaia and Rio Gallegos, just 18 percent work in the informal economy, whereas 58 percent in Salta and Tucuman.

A fourth finding is that cities with high informality have higher income inequality. This may be due to the immense income differences of informal and formal jobs. Jobs with similar attributes and industries tend to pay just about half the wage for an informal worker compared to formally registered workers. Due to their low incomes, informal workers are more likely to live in poverty and reside in informal settlements. Inequality-reducing policies need to consider their impact on informality carefully. Future research may be necessary to understand better the linkages between informality and other demographic and labor market variables.

Another finding is that expanding social protection measures is one of the most effective tools to reduce poverty and inequality. But informal workers are often excluded from social protection owing to the challenges inherent in collecting contributions and determining subsequent entitlements to services. Ensuring assistance for all can best be achieved via universal benefits, delinked from formal employment status. The expansion of public pensions and the introduction of the Asignación Universal por Hijo (AUH) (Universal Child Allowance), which deepened the noncontributory nature of Argentina's social security system, did so very effectively.

In addition, a more progressive income tax system, alongside luxury taxes and a tax on inherited wealth, can help generate funds needed to sustain universal protection in the future. In most Latin America, tax systems are regressive, with heavy burdens on consumption taxes falling on people with low incomes (Hanni et al. 2015). Personal income and property taxation remain weak despite the tax burden increasing in the last 20 years.

Sixth, cities with higher primary and secondary school completion rates among girls have lower income inequality. Since 1996, schooling improved notably in urban Argentina, and today, almost all girls complete primary education. Significant differences, however, remain in secondary education. Women with lower education are more likely to have large families and work in the informal economy and, in turn, generate lower incomes or experience poverty. From a policy perspective, promoting female secondary education in cities with the lowest completion rates might positively affect the labor market and reduce economic and gender inequalities.

While education is crucial, it may not be sufficient to tackle the underlying structures of inequality. Improved prospects for low-income earners do not erase the duality of the labor market, where informal sector workers are significantly worse off. Despite the wage premium for those with higher education, the structure of a city's labor market remains the perhaps most decisive factor shaping inequality. Both the degree of informality and the sectoral specialization of the urban economy ought to be analyzed when drafting policies to tackle inequality.

4. What about spatial inequalities?

While income inequality declined in Argentinian cities in the early 2000s, territorial divides persist. Cities increasingly become the sum of fragments, gated communities, and privatized public spaces. Despite the achievements in reducing income inequality after 2002, the right to the city is still out of reach for many, as the cost of owning and renting housing has reached unprecedented heights.

The intense pressure for the supply of serviced land coupled with an absence of the state in cooling the market contribute to today's inflated land and housing values. Since the early 2000s, the cost of housing has increased at unprecedented scales, much faster than average incomes. In Argentina's largest cities, the cost of renting has multiplied by more than five between 2009 and 2018. In Rosario, where almost a quarter of the population rents their home, average rent in real terms has increased by 678 percent in this period, equivalent to an annual rent increase of about 25.6 percent. The hip Palermo neighborhood in Buenos Aires city recorded the highest increment, with more than 31-percent yearly increase.

As housing and land in the inner cities become unaffordable for low- and middle-income households, sprawling neighborhoods far from the center, with low-quality services and without infrastructure, are the only affordable alternative for people with low incomes. It is little surprise that informal housing has increased in tandem with rising rents. Although fewer people in Argentina live in informal settlements compared to other countries in Latin America, it is a long-standing problem and a delicate social conflict. With about 14 percent of Argentine households living in an irregular tenure situation, squatting and violent resettlements symbolize the tension between the market for land and housing (Goytia and Dorna 2016).

Policies to fight inequality should consider incomes together with access to housing, land, and quality public services. This means investing in neighborhood amenities and infrastructure to reduce segregation and unequal access to quality services. Their absence can create obstacles for growth and turn services into scarce and costly commodities that only the well-off can afford.

Increasing the housing supply is crucial to address the shortage of affordable homes. Still, it requires political will and regulations to ensure that adequate housing is accessible to all and doesn't exclusively cater to those with the most resources.

5. Can cities win the fight alone?

There are several ways for cities to make a difference. For one, they can overhaul the urban growth and land policies that reinforce inequality, where urbanization contributed to the emergence of a powerful landowning elite. Public investment in infrastructure and services helped fill their pockets by increasing land values. These linkages between public services and land prices allow ample room for speculation, clientelism, and other kinds of influence between public and private interests.

The practice of biased public investment has been well documented in Buenos Aires (see Cohen and Debowicz 2004). Public spending has favored the rich, with high-income neighborhoods receiving more than 30 times the per capita public investment than lower-income neighborhoods. This type of regressive urban practice requires change. We need the inverse: social and physical intervention in the parts of cities that have been long-neglected and are characterized by high marginality, segregation, and poverty. The spatial allocation of public investment thus represents an opportunity to redistribute and balance existing territorial inequities.

Medellin, Colombia, became the emblem of such progressive transformations referred to as social urbanism, combining education, culture, and entrepreneurship programs with a "face-lift" of the poorest neighborhoods. The city made significant investments in public libraries, parks, transport, housing, and complementary social protection programs (Chau 2017). While infrastructure alone cannot defeat inequality and poverty, its symbolic value can profoundly change a city.

Other cities have taken radical measures to combat the phenomenon of "gente sin casas y casas sin gente" (people without houses and houses without people).[1] In 2016, Barcelona expropriated empty houses that were vacant for at least two years. The units were then used for social purposes to protect people's right to housing. In Buenos Aires, the city's housing institute (IVC 2019) estimates that about 9.2 percent of apartments are empty – a number almost equivalent to the city's housing deficit (around 130,000 households, CEM 2019). Repurposing empty buildings, especially those owned by international corporations or banks, as was the case in Barcelona, is an intriguing way of creating cities where everyone has adequate and affordable housing.

In Argentina, several cities (e.g., Rosario, Córdoba, and Trenque Lauquen) use land-value capture to recover land-value increments generated by actions other than the landowner's direct investments, such as granting development rights or changing land use and density patterns (Smolka 2013). The idea behind this process is that the benefits provided by governments should not remain with the benefitting private entity but support the community. Cities can invest the collected funds in parks and services to previously neglected areas like informal settlements. Rosario has earned millions of dollars in this process, mainly from the Puerto Norte, a massive development project alongside the river (BID 2015). The city used the funds to invest in social housing, infrastructure, and public spaces. Yet, while land-value capture ensures that the public gets a slice of the increasingly large pie of landowners and generates much-needed local funds, it does not counter the process of rising housing costs and residential segregation.

But cities in Argentina face several obstacles in fighting inequality due to their limited financial, economic, and legislative weight. Their budgets are small, and their autonomy is restricted. Most cities are not responsible for delivering public services like water and sanitation. Legislative powers and the financial resources are concentrated at the federal and the provincial levels, leaving cities inept at responding to local needs (Prud'homme et al. 2004).[2]

A nationwide approach to reducing inequality requires more integration and collaboration across the multiple levels of government and higher capacities and responsibilities of cities. At the federal level, social assistance systems and educational programs need to consider local idiosyncrasies. Most importantly, considering city characteristics in national policies that aim to reduce inequality may yield more effective results.

For example, the relevance of social transfers in household incomes and the size of the informal sector vary significantly across cities. Although policies concerned with informality or social transfers are generally crafted at the federal level, they should consider local differences. Besides, strengthening the capacities and responsibilities of cities, expanding their tax base, and encouraging more cooperation provide the necessary support for intervention. A course for action would be to make municipal governments active participants in decentralization rather than standby spectators. Besides, new institutions at the metropolitan scale should be created to capture the social and economic complexity and the differences between the periphery and the urban core and support municipal endeavors.

6. Can urban intervention projects like slum upgrading make a difference?

Slum upgrading initiatives have great potential to reduce urban poverty, improve people's living standards, and even reduce intra-urban inequality. Yet, several stars have to align for these effects to materialize.

Chapter 8 critically examines the experiences of slum upgrading in Villa 20, a slum with nearly 30,000 residents in Buenos Aires' south. Until recently, upgrading initiatives have oscillated between insufficient, hostile, and nonexistent. In 2016, the city government launched a new campaign to integrate the slums into the urban fabric.

The team leading the upgrading initiative in Villa 20 has since achieved the unimaginable: bringing deeply conflicted local actors and residents together and collectively designing the upgrading process's components and steps. These experiences show that meaningful participation is possible. It has also underlined its importance for outcomes, as residents took ownership of the process and appropriated the upgraded houses and newly created public spaces.

However, the participatory process alone cannot guarantee the financial sustainability of the initiative. As part of the redevelopment, the city built 1,671 units on a lot adjacent to the settlement, an area now called Papa Francisco. The city offered these units to Villa 20 residents who had to give up their houses to make space for wider streets, public spaces, or other renovation projects. Residents could purchase them with special mortgage rates that residents were to pay back within 30 years (IVC 2018).

Just one year after moving into the new houses, most families reported difficulty paying the mortgage, and more than half (53 percent) said they were behind on their installments. Since the vast majority of the families live in poverty, many face great obstacles putting 20 percent of their low income aside for a mortgage, plus pay for expenses such as electricity, gas, and water (OLA 2020).

The notion that turning slum dwellers into mortgage holders would integrate them into the city seems to ignore the difficult life choices people in chronic poverty face. It follows a neoliberal market logic that emphasizes private homeownership and the extension of credit to groups who previously had little access.

Integrating slums into the rest of the city shouldn't mean exposing residents to the same market whims that contributed to their precarious living situations. Creating housing solutions for people in poverty requires thinking outside the box of market solutions. Via community land trust models, social housing projects, and financing patterns that truly redistribute – a different city is possible.

To have an inequality-reducing effect, slum upgrading projects cannot be divorced from housing, economic, and labor policy. Without a comprehensive and ambitious citywide affordable housing strategy, slums will always be part of urbanization and mark the deep divides in cities.

7. Will inequality in cities disappear, as they become richer and recover economically?

No. Unless there is political will and a national plan to tackle inequality in cities, the gains from economic growth will not be evenly distributed.

In many regards, Argentina is more equal today than it was in the 1990s. What's more, inequality has become unacceptable for many, and the voices for greater equality become louder in everyday conversations and political agendas. But the achievements will remain fragile unless we reconceptualize policymaking and the role of the state in urban land and housing markets, which will generate intense debates around societal values and economic goals. Piketty (2020) argues that to rewrite inequality, we need "participatory socialism," where people actively push back against the powers and narratives feeding into inequality. I would add that we need bold policymakers at all levels of government that innovate, because tinkering at the edges and relying on the market to fix societal ills is a recipe for a further divide.

Notes

1 This refers to the misdirected response by governments to the increasing affordable housing demand in cities. While thousands are homeless, housing units in the city center have turned into speculation objects and remain empty.

2 Argentina has 23 provinces and the city of Buenos Aires. Provinces pre-date the formation of the nation and thus receive a unique role in the country's constitution. Each province has its constitution and the right to organize its municipal regime by provincial law, defining the degree of autonomy for local governments. Provinces have the authority to create and control municipalities. For this reason, the number, status, and power of cities vary across provinces, and so do the taxes and responsibilities allocated to cities.

References

BID. 2015. *Gestión Urbana, Asociaciones Público-Privadas y Captación de Plusvalías:El caso de la recuperación del frente costero delrío Paraná en la Ciudad de*. Rosario: Argentina.

Cárcamo-Díaz, Rodrigo, and Ramón Pineda Salazar. 2014. "Economic Growth and Real Volatility: The Case of Latin America and the Caribbean." *Macroeconomics of Development Series 161*. Santiago de Chile: United Nations.

CEM. 2019. "XI Monitor del Clima Social." *CEM*. http://estudiosmetropolitanos.com.ar/2019/10/08/xi-monitor-del-clima-social/

Chau, Rebecca. 2017. "Social Urbanism: Transformational Policy in Medellin, Colombia." *GPEIG case study prize*. https://bit.ly/3ahuVQG

Cohen, Michael A. 2019. "Assessing the Macri Legacy." In *Public Seminar (Online Blog)*. September 17. Available at: https://publicseminar.org/essays/assessing-the-macri-legacy-2/, accessed November 30, 2021.

_____. 2012. *Argentina's Economic Growth and Recovery: The Economy in a Time of Default*. Oxfordshire: Routledge.

Cohen, Michael A., and Dario Debowicz. 2004. "The Five Cities of Buenos Aires: An Inquiry into Poverty and Inequality in Urban Argentina." In *The Encyclopedia of Sustainable Development, by Saskia Sassen*. Paris: UNESCO.

Cohen, Michael A., and Margarita Gutman. 2002. *Argentina in Collapse: The Americas Debate*. Buenos Aires: IIED-AL.

Cornia, Giovanni Andrea. 2011. "Economic Integration, Inequality and Growth: Latin America versus the European Economies in Transition." *DESA Working Paper No. 101*. New York: United Nations.

_____. 2014. *Falling Inequality in Latin America: Policy Changes and Lessons. WIDER Studies in Development Economics*. Oxford, New York, NY: Oxford University Press.

Goytia, Cynthia, and Guadalupe Dorna. 2016. *What Is the Role of Urban Growth on Inequality, and Segregation? The Case of Urban Argentina's Urban Agglomerations*. Working Paper N° 2016/12. Buenos Aires: CAF.

Hanni, Michael Stephen, Ricardo Martner Fanta, and Andrea Podesta. 2015. "The Redistributive Potential of Taxation in Latin America." *CEPAL Review*. Santiago de Chile: United Nations.

Instituto de la Vivienda de Buenos Aires (IVC). 2018. "Addressing Buenos Aires's Housing Challenge Housing Institute of the City of Buenos Aires". In *Presentación de Martín Motta, coordinador del proyecto de reurbanización de Villa 20 en.* New York, NY: The New School.

IVC. 2019. "Mesa de Estudio de Viviendas vacías." https://cdn.buenosaires.gob.ar/datosabiertos/datasets/informes-coyuntura-habitacional/informe_mesa_de_estudio_de_viviendas_vacias.pdf

Minujin, Alberto. 1996. *Desigualdad y Exclusion.* Buenos Aires: UNICEF.

Observatory on Latin America (OLA). 2020. *Summary of the Final Report · Monitoring Processes and Outcomes in Slum Upgrading in Buenos Aires Villa 20.* New York, NY: The New School.

Piketty, Thomas. 2020. *Capital and Ideology.* Cambridge, MA: Belknap Press of Harvard University Press.

Prévôt-Schapira, M., and Sébastien Velut. 2016. "El sistema urbano y la metropolización." *La sociedad argentina hoy,* G. Kessler (comp.). Buenos Aires: Siglo 21: 61–84.

Prud'homme, Rémy, Hervé Huntzinger, and Pierre Kopp. 2004. "Stronger municipalities for stronger cities in Argentina." *Paper for the Inter-American Development Bank.* Available at: https://publications.iadb.org/publications/english/document/Stronger-Municipalities-for-Stronger-Cities-in-Argentina.pdf, accessed November 28, 2021.

Smolka, Martim Oscar. 2013. *Implementing Value Capture in Latin America: Policies and Tools for Urban Development.* Cambridge, MA: Lincoln Institute of Land Policy.

Index

Note: Page numbers in *italics* refer to figures and those in **bold** refer to tables.

Printed in the United States
by Baker & Taylor Publisher Services